the travel

Kalyan Karmakar started his foo[d]
India's earliest food blogs and w[on?]
Association of India (FBAI) awards, in 2007. He has written
on food and culture for NDTV, *Femina* and *BBC Good Food
India* among others and has been a speaker at international
food summits like Host Milano, Casa Asia and Madrid Fusion.
He was rated 'top Indian food influencer on Twitter' by
@IndianCuisineRR in 2016. He currently lives in Mumbai, where
he conducts food walks and represents the city at Foodie Hub,
an international association of food and travel writers. He can
be found on Twitter at @Finelychopped.

Praise for the book

'Kalyan Karmakar takes his food seriously and it shows in his
writing. He has curiosity, enthusiasm and a spirit of adventure.
Add to that his knowledge and experience and you can see why he
is India's leading food blogger.' – Vir Sanghvi, journalist, food critic
and author of *Rude Food*

'As someone who has followed Kalyan's blog, his mother's food-
related memories of Iran, his wife's obsessive quest for the most
flavourful, lightest macarons that Paris has to offer and his
grandmum's reminiscences about a world that is fast fading from
public memory, I'm delighted that [Kalyan] has metamorphosed
from an anonymous blogger to a friend to an author.' – Marryam
H. Reshii, *Times of India* food critic and author

'[Kalyan has] extended his food interests outside actual blogging
to events like the food walks he conducted… Now he's brought all
this experience into a book…[and] Indian food writing remains the
richer for it.' – Vikram Doctor, food columnist at *Economic Times*

'I've always been a fan of Kalyan's writing, and this book is like having one long happy conversation on food with a man who knows no other passion.' – Kunal Vijaykar, food writer and television personality

'I have always believed that food-travels unlock our view of cultures and help us evolve as human beings. Kalyan's book is proof of that evolution. [His] writing brings out the best in food, people and places.' – Ranveer Brar, celebrity chef and television personality

'What keeps me returning to Kalyan's [writing] is his gift for placing the ingredients and foods he writes about within their larger cultural context; his informal voice...and his eagerness to give credit where credit is due, by throwing the spotlight on the street vendors, sweet-makers and restaurant cooks who work hard and long hours keeping customers like Kalyan well-fed.' – Robin Eckhardt, food blogger at *EatingAsia*

'I've enjoyed Kalyan's relaxed yet engaging narrative style whenever I dip into his blogs. This book is such a wonderfully natural extension of his stories.' – Mayur Sharma, television personality, host of *Highway on My Plate*

'[I]n this book, [Kalyan provides] wonderful insight into the history [of] places where the diversity of Indian cuisine can be sampled.' – Vineet Bhatia, Michelin-starred chef

'Kalyan's energy and passion for his subject shines through everything he writes. India is blessed to have such a wonderful ambassador for its incredible cuisine.' – Pamela Timms, food blogger, author of *Korma, Kheer and Kismet: Five Seasons in Old Delhi*

the travelling belly

EATING THROUGH INDIA'S BY-LANES

28/10/17

Jimmy Boy, Forty

Kalyan Karmakar

Dear Chrissie,

Here's to more
Parsi Food memories

Best wishes,

Kalyan

hachette
INDIA

First published in India in 2016 by Hachette India
(Registered name: Hachette Book Publishing India Pvt. Ltd)
An Hachette UK company
www.hachetteindia.com

1

On the cover, Pandiyan Konar, Sai Balaji Stall, Bandra East, Mumbai.

Parts of the section 'The Maharashtrian Soul of Mumbai' (p 277-299)
have been reproduced in *ScoopWhoop*, October 2016.

Parts of the section 'The Quest for Kulcha' (p 102-107) and
'The Essential Dal Baati Churma' (p 120-123) have been reproduced
in NDTV Food, February 2016 and November 2015 respectively

ISBN 978-93-5009-910-0

Hachette Book Publishing India Pvt. Ltd
4th & 5th Floors, Corporate Centre,
Plot No. 94, Sector 44, Gurgaon – 122003, India

Typeset in Chaparral Pro by SÜRYA, New Delhi
Printed and bound in India by Manipal Technologies Ltd, Manipal

To my father, whose memories inspired my writing;
my mother, whose writing genes I have inherited;
my wife Kainaz, whose support allowed me to pursue my
food-blogging career;
and
the readers of my blog,
whose love and affection keeps me going

CONTENTS

CONTENTS

FOREWORD

I first met (or should I say encountered?) Kalyan Karmakar online in 2006, when my blog *Dos Hermanos* was in its early stages of development. If I recall correctly, his comments on my posts came under the *nom de plume* of 'The Knife' and were noticeable not only for their supportive good humour, but also because he actually seemed to know what he was talking about, particularly when it came to the joys of Indian cuisine.

I was intrigued, and decided to find out more. My research (which in truth consisted of little more than clicking on his name) took me back to his own, then-nascent, blog *Finely Chopped*. Once there, I discovered that we had even more in common than just being food bloggers, including a Bengali heritage and parents in the medical profession. I also discovered a treasure trove of blog posts that showed a genuine pride in the cuisine of his homeland, a determination to investigate its myriad regional variations and a shared passion for the ability of food to bring friends and strangers together.

I was lucky enough to finally meet Kalyan face to face (or face to chest, as he was a lot taller than I had imagined) on one of my all-too-infrequent visits to my father's homeland in 2012. Inevitably, our meeting involved food, as he took my wife and I on a whirlwind eating tour of the Bohri Mohalla area of Mumbai, which included pan-fried brain curry, udder roasted to a beautiful char over an open flame and a custard apple ice cream whose flavour still provides me with one of my greatest taste memories. Such was his joy in sharing these culinary delights that it came as very little surprise to me that these food tours soon became a successful commercial enterprise, highly sought out by people all over the globe.

It is also unsurprising that Kalyan has now emerged from the blogosphere to become a noted food journalist and spokesperson for the delights of Indian cuisine. People recognize in him a rare level of intellectual curiosity that marks him out from those who see and write about food only in terms of volume or gluttony. For Kalyan, food is far more than just a way to fill one's stomach, it is a way to nourish the soul as well as the body, and a history lesson about who we are and how we got here.

And that is what *The Travelling Belly* is all about – one food-obsessed man's unapologetic love song to the most remarkable cuisine on earth. A love song that is imbued with wit, nostalgia, energy and passion, and one that is articulated both through an impeccable palate and a skilled writer's fingers. It's a winning combination that makes me even more determined to return 'home' soon to share more meals with 'The Knife'.

Simon Majumdar
Los Angeles

Simon Majumdar is a British-American chef, author and television personality. He is the author of bestselling books such as Eat My Globe *and* Eating for Britain, *and stars in American TV shows such as* Cutthroat Kitchen, Iron Chef America *and* Extreme Chef.

THE STORY OF THE TRAVELLING BELLY

A t the risk of sounding dramatic, I must say that writing this book changed my life.

It all began when I started my food blog, *Finely Chopped*, in 2007. To be honest, it was my wife's idea. She was tired of us going out to restaurants which ended with me coming home and telling her how the food could have been better. 'Why don't you write whatever you have to say about the food on this thing called a blog instead of bugging me incessantly?' was her argument then.

Blogging was still a fairly new phenomenon. My wife found out how to start a blog from a friend of her's at work. She then came home and started mine. She was also the one who named it *Finely Chopped*. Just as she was the one who named this book *The Travelling Belly*.

My wife's plan worked. I didn't burden her with my food-related rants any more. But a new problem emerged. I began to obsessively photograph what I ate. As my wife wryly says, she has forgotten the taste of hot food since then, thanks to my blogging.

I became addicted to blogging. I would spend hours keying away blog posts late into the night. I began to write not just about the restaurants I went to and the dishes I ate there, but also the people I met, the places I travelled to, the dishes I cooked. What had started out as a place to vent became a place for me to celebrate my love for food instead.

Fast forward six years.

The concept of this book began taking shape in 2013. I

had taken a break from work after fifteen years of being a full-time market-research professional. The idea was to go on a sabbatical. To stop and smell the flowers, as the saying goes.

By then, my years of blogging were starting to pay off. A couple of exciting blogging-related international trips came up. I wrote about the people I met on my travels, the dishes I ate, the discoveries I made. For a while, I was on a high: living the ultimate cubicle worker's dream of having no boss to answer to.

Then reality kicked in. I actually began to miss my daily routine: the task of waking up, getting ready and heading to work.

Turned out that blogging wasn't a substitute for filling time sheets, as strange as that might sound. That was because for me, blogging was a hobby, a passion, something I enjoyed doing. There are, of course, people for whom blogging is very task-oriented – they have schedules, goals, traffic targets, SEO keywords. I had never done my blogging like that. This meant that blogging didn't give me a structure to adhere to. For a middle-class, middle-aged Indian, that was a pretty scary thing. I would wake up in the morning and wonder what to do with the rest of my day. It sounds like fun when you are on the corporate treadmill. Not so much in real life.

That's when I got a mail saying that the book idea I had discussed recently with my publishers had come through. The contract couldn't have come at a better time. Suddenly I had a goal to work towards, something that would take me out of the spiralling sense of frustration and restlessness. I had a routine: Wake up, go to Candies (a neighbourhood café which we call our second home), have breakfast, write, come home, have lunch, go through the day's writing, nap and go for yoga. By the time I returned, my wife would be back from work. We would go for a walk by the sea or to the park, where I would discuss my day's ideas with her. Then we would come back, have dinner and end the day.

A lot of what has gone into the book actually reflects how my life changed after I began to blog. I have always loved food. A lot of my childhood memories were based around food. After I grew up and went to Mumbai, I got to travel quite a bit, thanks to my market-research career. In the early years, I would stay in fancy hotels and order room service. But after I started blogging, I became more curious about food. I began to go out and explore the cities I travelled to in search of the food stories. Stories that found their way into the blog, and eventually, this book. I called this process 'grunge eating'.

Miraculously, things began to fall into place by the time I finished writing the first draft of the book.

Social-media-based food writing and food consulting were fairly new in India even in 2014. To make a career here, I didn't have a track to follow, unlike in more established professions. But slowly, I began to get opportunities to write for online and offline publications. I got to work with brands on promotional activities. I began to conceptualize and edit a website dedicated to Indian food. I got a chance to meet leading food writers, editors, hoteliers and chefs. The lack of purpose that I had felt before I began writing the book was taken care of. My days were now filled with interesting assignments in the world of food, which gave me some financial stability and, more importantly, made me happy.

So now you know why I call this book my lucky charm.

What is this book about? Let me start by telling you what it is not.

This book is not a directory of the best places to eat across India. The word 'best' is almost always subjective: I prefer the term 'favourite' to 'best'. You won't find addresses or phone numbers of restaurants in this book, or geographical lists sorted by cuisine type. Or any lists, for that matter.

It doesn't have recipes. It is not a book on Indian culinary history. As I often point out, I am not a chef, not a restaurant critic, nor a food historian. Just a guy who loves food and loves to eat.

You might find some of the places in the book touristy, for want of a better term. I have still included them in the book. This is because I firmly believe they have become 'touristy' for a reason. These restaurants are easier for first-time visitors to access. And most importantly, I have realized over time that one should not stress too much about eating at 'better' and more 'authentic' places. Don't let visions of that perfect 'most authentic' meal mar your present plate of food.

So what *does* this book have? Stories. Stories of eating my way across India. Stories of the restaurants I went to, and the people who led me there; the things I have learned through conversations I had with people over a shared meal.

Most of the restaurants featured in the book are small, family-run restaurants offering traditional food. These are the type of places that I seek out while travelling. These are the places where my smile is the widest, and my palate the most satisfied. The greasier, the better.

I have started the book by writing about Kolkata. It is not the city I was born in. I was born in the UK; we then moved to Iran before we went to Kolkata. A lot of the influences on my formative years were not very Bengali, but Kolkata is where I first discovered my love for food. To me, Kolkata is all about nostalgia: for my childhood, for my family, for the food I grew up eating. Even today, whenever I go back 'home',

I try to visit my old haunts when I can, and that's what I have written about here.

Then there are the many cities that my work had taken me to. First as a market researcher. Later as a food writer. There are a few cities which I have visited multiple times, and each time I've come back with a different food experience, a new perspective, some of which I have tried to share with you.

The book ends with Mumbai, the city I have called home for close to two decades now. Mumbai is where my love for food grew from a hobby to a profession; and I hope that's reflected in my more detailed and nuanced writings on the food experiences in the city. The places that I have written about in this section are the ones I would strongly recommend that you visit, to see Mumbai the way I do and fall in love with the city the way I did.

How should you read the book? You can read it sequentially. Or dip into individual chapters. It is not a novel, after all.

If you live in India, I hope this book inspires you to explore your own city for its hidden culinary gems, and then seek out food experiences in the rest of India. If you don't live here, I hope this book makes you want to set out in search of the many culinary marvels of our wonderful country. Above all, I hope it leads you to many memorable meals.

This book is only a starting point; I've included food walks at the end of each chapter to point you in the right direction. But the rest is up to you.

Make your own notes, google addresses and travel tips, talk to locals for recommendations. Meet new people, try new dishes, have new experiences. Eat well.

Write your own stories.

SWEET HOME KOLKATA

I came to Kolkata (then still Calcutta) as a pampered, *bilet pherot* (foreign-returned) child, when I was about eight years old. My parents moved to the city in 1980 from Iran after the Revolution. They had spent just a year or so in Iran after moving there from Liverpool, UK, and before that, Canterbury, where I was born.

When we arrived, I was a spoilt kid who refused to eat Indian or Bengali food. The regular bhaat, dal and maachh – rice-lentils-fish curry – was not for me. I refused to eat what was on the table and gave my family a hard time at every meal. So my mother continued to cook the dishes that I had grown up on: burgers, spaghetti with meatballs, noodles, fish and chips, fried chicken and chips – international flavours that were more to my taste.

Things changed when my father passed away soon after. My mother, younger brother and I moved into my maternal grandparents' house in the suburbs. My mother eked out a living by teaching in a college in Howrah, a two-hour trip each way from our home, and my pampered existence came to an end. Now I had to eat whatever was put on the table, which was mainly Bengali fare: shuktos, chorchoris, jhols, dals and dalnas traditionally made in Bengali households. It would make for a wonderful turn in my food tale to say that I fell in love with Bengali cuisine overnight, but that wouldn't be the truth. It would be a long time before Bengali cuisine became my favourite.

Eating out after my father passed away was a rarity. When he was around, I was pampered and our meals together would be in five-star hotels, clubs and trendy Park Street restaurants. This lifestyle was not possible for my mother to sustain on her meagre teacher's salary. I would cherish the outings where my mom took my brother and me out for dosas or the rare Chinese treat. I couldn't get enough of the egg roll I would have every evening after school with the money my mother left for me everyday. Sometimes, I would save up and 'upgrade' my evening snack to the much-treasured mutton roll. There was a sense of adventure to it, as my mother didn't want me to eat mutton cooked outside. 'It's dog meat,' she would insist.

My food horizon began to expand when I started going to St James' School in Central Kolkata. My friends and I would sometimes go for movies and couple it with sharing a biryani in old Muslim-run restaurants like Nizam's and Aminia. Then, when I started going to Presidency College, I experienced a different level of freedom. I found I could explore the city more. But as a college student, I was on a tight budget. I studied Sociology, where there were 18 girls and three guys in class. We three would often get the girls to buy us cold drinks! I remember sharing chops and cutlets at Pramod-da's canteen in college, splitting them between four or five guys. There was a certain joy to those hand-to-mouth college days, which cannot be recreated. And everything tasted so good: from the 'infusion' (black coffee) and pakoras at the Indian Coffee House and the mishti doi (sweetened curd) at Putiram to the noodles at Tasty Restaurant and the vegetarian stew at the YMCA counter opposite the swimming pool at College Square.

Then, while pursuing my MBA, I was introduced to the world of dating and its expenses. What I remember most fondly of those college romances was saving up money and going for lunches at Kolkata's 'continental' places like Peter Cat for its chelo kebab (grilled meat served with grilled tomatoes, buttered rice and a fried egg), Mocambo for its Fish a la Diana and devilled crabs, Lazeez for its chicken tetrazzini, Floriana for its Baked Alaska and other restaurants like Moulin Rouge, The Princess and Kwality – and feeling very posh. But those were special-occasion meals; the more regular dates would end with budget Chinese at Chung Wah or occasionally the more expensive Jimmy's Kitchen in New Market, where you could share a ham fried rice, with no side dishes. With funds becoming tighter near the end of the month, movie afternoons would often culminate in shared aloo rolls at Karko, which were way cheaper than mutton or egg rolls.

Funnily enough, my most vivid memories of college, B-school, my friends and my dates centre on food, something I realized in retrospect.

Though I was not born here, Kolkata is where I grew up and this is the city where my love for food began. This is the city whose cuisine inspired my tastebuds and inspired me to write.

What I missed most when I moved to Mumbai from Kolkata after B-school was the food. My trips back to Kolkata were carefully planned around what I would eat. I would inform my mom about what I wanted to eat and what I would like for her to cook. Topping the list were aloo posto – potatoes cooked with khus khus or poppy seeds, and maachher muro diye dal – fish head cooked in lentils. Street food stars like rolls (we don't call them kathi rolls in Kolkata) and phuchkas became obsessions on these trips. Restaurants like Mocambo, Peter Cat, BarBQ and Zeeshan were must-visits for me. Over the years, my choices changed slightly. Some old favourites like Mocambo and BarBQ were abandoned. Old Kolkata classics such as Flurys, Jimmy's Kitchen, Nizam's, Shiraz and Dolly's The Tea Shop were rediscovered. Like most immigrants when they return home, my choices were driven largely by nostalgia. Even now, I rarely go to the new places that have opened up in Kolkata. When in the city, I want to relive my past. I want to reconnect with my roots. I want to revel in my Bengaliness.

SOME CHA TO BEGIN WITH

My wife is a Parsi and a Mumbai girl. I was apparently the first Bengali she had ever known. And she had never been to Kolkata till we went there when we got married.

Our marriage was a simple affair in Mumbai. It was attended by just our immediate families – so a total of nine guests. We had a registered marriage at the family court beside Mumbai's Asiatic Library. We then took a flight to Kolkata, where my mother had called our close relatives and a few neighbours over in the evening for tea and luchi aloor dom.

Luckily for me, my wife fell in love with Kolkata and its food on her very first trip to the city. My mom and grandmother would cook lots of fish, which she loved. Apart from home food, she began to fall in love with the restaurants and cafés I took her to. Her favourite eventually turned out to be Dolly's The Tea Shop, which she now makes a trip to every time she visits Kolkata.

We came across Dolly's The Tea Shop during our second trip after marriage. Looking for things to do one afternoon, we headed to the Dakshinapan Shopping Centre in Dhakuria in South Kolkata. This was my first visit there too. It was a rainy afternoon and we found shelter inside the shopping complex. The Dakshinapan complex consists largely of desultory government-run handloom shops and on this lazy, sleepy, cloudy afternoon, the staff at the shops were quite annoyed when we tried to buy something. It was time for their siesta! Still trying to escape the rain, we headed to Dolly's The Tea Shop, which we spotted on the ground floor, tucked away in a corner.

Dolly's The Tea Shop is a small place. It has a few chairs

and tables outdoors, surrounded by greenery, but since it was raining that afternoon, we sat inside on the tiny chairs by the tea boxes that double up as tables. The room was dark and damp because of the rain and it was dimly lit by lamps. The yellow bulbs gave the place a warm glow. The staff was a group of matronly Bengali ladies dressed in saris and wearing huge bindis. And sitting in a corner was Dolly herself.

Dolly Roy started her tea shop in 1988 as a tribute to her love for tea. She is India's first female tea taster and the world's first female tea auctioneer.

'What will you have, my dear?' she asked my wife in a husky and kind voice. It was the beginning of a beautiful friendship and my wife felt as if she had been adopted by Dolly. Dolly suggested some lovely iced teas, since we weren't fond of hot tea. These were very refreshing and so cheap compared to the iced teas in the cafés of Mumbai. We sat there and chatted with Dolly and told her about our lives in Mumbai while she listened indulgently. Soon the skies cleared and we stepped out, refreshed.

Since then we have returned to Dolly's every time we go to Kolkata. My wife will not have it any other way. Though of late we have not always seen Dolly there, the staff we met the first time are still around.

So what do we usually have at Dolly's?

Well, what we go for are the iced teas, which are made with crushes poured from wrinkled plastic squash bottles and water from a plastic jug. The drinks are as basic as they get – no plastic umbrellas on top or floating pieces of kiwi or mangosteen – reasonably priced and full of flavour and love.

When my mom joins us, she has a hot cup of Darjeeling tea there. They have a variety of Darjeeling teas – Dolly's favourite and my mom's too – and Assam teas as well.

It's also a good place to buy different varieties of tea to gift folks, though sometimes the staff push you to buy the more expensive ones. It's all part of the experience.

They serve grilled sandwiches at Dolly's, with the ham and cheese sandwich being quite popular. They are shut on Sundays and during Durga Puja. If you leave a tip, one of the *mashis* (as the staff is referred to here) will tell you to put it in the charity box instead.

It's apt that our Kolkata food *adda* (chat) started with tea. Kolkata lives on tea or cha. This is not the masala chai that is popular in Mumbai. In Kolkata, many, like my mother, prefer not to have anything come between them and their tea. Spices are rarely added, but on occasion, a bit of ginger is used for milk tea or a few drops of lime juice are added to black tea (lebu cha). The milk teas are made with just a dash of milk and are not too milky, unlike the ones that Mumbai seems to love.

Buying tea is an art in Kolkata. This is one market where loose teas still hold their ground over packaged ones. People will buy their own mixes from shops. Liquor and flavour, as my mother would say, referring to her mixes of Assam and Darjeeling teas.

 Tip: A pack of tea from Kolkata is always a good gift to take back home.

Tea is the preferred brew out of the house too. At its most humble, tea is sold across cities at roadside stalls. It was earlier served in *bhnaar*s or earthen cups and today in tiny disposable plastic cups. You normally get some thick unbranded biscuits to go along with the tea.

If not at busy street corners, such stalls are found at *paaras* (local neighbourhoods) where people gather for *adda* over tea. At their most regal, tea shops have taken the form of Flurys, the restored European tea room on Park Street.

LOVE ON THE STREETS OF KOLKATA

It's impossible to talk of tea and not discuss the street food of Kolkata. Kolkata's street food lies at the core of its eating-out culture. For people like me, street food is about nostalgic indulgence. However, for many, this street food is a basic necessity, since it's so cheap and so easily available.

One thing I have realized after moving to Mumbai, and meeting people from all parts of India, is that people swear by the street food they have grown up on. So when I say that the phuchkas of Kolkata – tiny deep-fried dough balls filled with a spicy stuffing and eaten with flavoured water – are better than the pani puris of Mumbai or the golgappas of Delhi, that jhalmuri is better than bhelpuri (both made by mixing puffed rice with spices and condiments) and that rolls are better than frankies, you can choose to take me at face value or with a pinch of salt.

What is for sure, though, is that Mumbai is full of migrant Kolkatans lamenting the unavailability of good (read Kolkatan) street food in the city.

The one thing that I miss most in Mumbai is the Kolkata phuchka. The mashed potatoes, the bits of chopped chilli, the sour tamarind juice that makes your hair stand on end – I love it all. My wife is as much, or more, of a phuchka addict as me, though she is a Mumbai girl. Whenever we go to Kolkata, we have our fill of phuchkas and, at times, have even stopped at phuchka stalls on the way home from the airport.

The verdict on the best phuchka place in Kolkata is divided, but the most famous are probably the ones at Vivekananda Park in South Kolkata. They have even won local awards and along with regular phuchkas, serve doi phuchkas, a special kind of phuchka where curd is added to the mix, similar in concept to the dahi puris of Mumbai.

As my trips to Kolkata are now shorter, I can't afford to be choosy and travel about looking for my favourite phuchka spots. So I jump off my car at any phuchka stall I spot on the road and pop in a few. It helps that every street corner of Kolkata has a phuchkawala.

I have had good phuchkas outside New Empire Cinema on Lindsay Street, opposite New Market and in the south, in front of the Spencer's outlet at Netaji Nagar and at the stalls outside South City Mall. If you have a weak tummy, then phuchkas could be a bit of an adventure, as you are not sure how reliable the water is. In all my years of phuchka eating, my tummy went for a toss only once, but I picked myself up and went for phuchkas again.

 Tip: Always go to a phuchka shop which has a crowd of people eating there. If this is your first time, say so to the phuchka-wallah, as regulars are expected to eat it really fast. If you can handle heat, ask for chopped green chillies to be added to the mix. To have the phuchkas I have grown up on, tell them not to add the mishti jol or sweet water.

The other Kolkata street food favourite is the roll. The original 'kathi' roll refers to the wooden skewers or *kathis* on which the kebabs were made in Mughlai restaurants.

I have grown up on an egg roll every evening after school, bought from the local roll shop outside my grandparents' house. In high school, when I began to move around the city, I discovered the rolls of the Mughlai restaurants of central Kolkata and realized that the ones served here are different from those in the Bengali-Hindu-owned roll shops of the suburbs.

In Muslim-run shops of Central Kolkata, the paratha is a work of art. It is thin and slightly crisp versus the chubby and slightly thicker-textured ones available in the suburbs of South Kolkata. Mutton and chicken are more popular here than egg rolls, as these places specialize in making kebabs. The meat is skewered and barbequed and then fried on a flat tava (griddle) before being served. In the suburbs, they often use kosha mangsho (mutton in a very thick onion-based gravy) instead of kebabs in rolls. Another key difference is that the Muslim roll shops just add a bit of lime juice, finely chopped green chillies, sliced onions and dry chaat masala-like spices to flavour the rolls, unlike the bright red and yellow sauces (allegedly tomato and chilli) along with sliced cucumber and carrots – and even beetroot at times – used in the suburban roll shops. There is a certain subtlety and finesse to the rolls of Central Kolkata versus the more over-the-top rolls of the suburbs. The latter are more spicy and tangy and possibly closer to the frankies of Mumbai than the 'original' Kolkata roll. Both have their loyalists. I have grown up on the suburban *paarar dokaner* (neighbourhood shop) roll but prefer the Central Kolkata rolls now. Tastes evolve over time, after all.

My favourite roll shop is Nizam's, which is a restaurant behind Kolkata's iconic (though not very new) New Market. There are two outlets close to each other. One sells beef dishes, the other doesn't. Nizam's is where rolls are claimed to have been invented. The story goes that the owner thought of putting kebabs in a paratha, wrapping it with paper and giving it to the sandwich-loving British sahibs who didn't want to get their hands dirty while eating. The restaurant claims that the idea then travelled across the city, giving employment to thousands who run roll shops across Kolkata now. So when you are at Nizam's, you get a bite of heritage with its rolls.

What I love about the rolls at Nizam's is that the paratha is thin and delicate, allowing the kebabs to be tasted in their full glory. The beef roll is particularly recommended. They have chicken, mutton, khiri (udder) and egg variations too, which are also delicious.

Some of my other favourite roll places are Badshah Bar & Restaurant in New Market for mutton rolls and Hot Kati Rolls and Kusum Rolls on Park Street for egg chicken rolls. In my college days I used to love the massive egg rolls at Peep Inn at Rabindra Sarobar. The rolls of Campari are pretty famous too, but I am yet to try them.

 Tip: Always ask them to fry the onions in the roll. The sweet caramelized taste of the onions adds to the taste.

You can also try the cutlets, chops and patties at the parar dokaner roll shops in the residential areas of Kolkata. I am particularly fond of the rather unique 'patties' here. This is a dish where minced meat is enveloped in a layer of flour and deep fried, not baked. The contrasting textures and flavours of the minced meat and the crunchy flour casing are symphonic and I can never resist having them whenever I go to get a roll in my neighbourhood.

 Tip: Pair chops and cutlets with kasundi, the local spicy (though somewhat watery) mustard sauce.

Another iconic street-food dish of Kolkata is jhalmuri, which is puffed rice infused with mustard oil, a mix of spices and, depending on your tastes, potatoes, slices of fresh coconut, chopped cucumber and onion. There are other add-on ingredients to it too. The dish is available in many parts of Bengal and even in trains where hawkers get up on at train stations to make jhalmuri for hungry passengers. It's a popular post-work snack and is more pungent than the bhelpuri of Mumbai.

The most popular khau gulley or eat street in Kolkata is Dacres Lane, which is primarily an office area. Apart from the ubiquitous rolls and jhalmuri, you will get deem paruti, which is a savoury French toast where fat chunks of bread are doused in an egg-and-chilli mix, and deep fried. Then there is haldi (turmeric) and garam masala-doused chowmein, a very Bengali take on Chinese food. Tele bhaja, which are Bengali fritters – usually gramflour batter-fried potatoes, aubergines or onions – are also sold at small stalls on Kolkata's streets. Chittoda's stall is very famous for its stews. The jury is out on the quality of the food on offer here but it sure does sustain the babus of Kolkata's vintage office *para* (central business district).

My friend Kanishka Chakraborty, whose taste buds I trust, swears by the prawn cutlets at a place called Allen Kitchen at Shobha Bazaar. Another place popular for cutlets and kobiraji (a lacy egg-batter-coated cutlet) is the rather ancient but historic Dilkhusha Cabin at College Street. I went there a couple of times while studying at Presidency but we found it a bit expensive and preferred to hang out at Pramod-da's canteen in college instead. The vegetable chops that he made, sandwiched between thick slabs of white bread, would make for a cheap but filling meal.

 Tip: *You can also try spotting a Benfish van run by the Bengal fishery department. If you do, try the fish batter fry.*

JOL KHABAR FOR THE SOUL

Every Bengali has grown up on the concept of *jol khabar*. While it literally translates to 'water and food', it usually refers to snacks eaten between meals, particularly sweets available in *mishtir dokan*s, Bengali for sweet shops. For some, this could be breakfast too. Nothing like a sweet start to the day, after all.

Bengali sweets are renowned across the country but not everyone knows that you get a plethora of savouries in *mishtir dokan*s too. There is the shingara, of course, which is the Bengali version of samosas. Here, the potatoes inside are usually cubed and not mashed. In winter, when all the vegetables in India are at their tastiest, cauliflowers are added to the mix. The *mishtir dokan*s also have khasta kochuri (which is how we pronounce kachori in Bengali) and koraishootir kochuri (puris stuffed with peas), which owe their origin to the folks from Varanasi in Uttar Pradesh who opened shop in Bengal; and the Bengali version of these, dal puri, which is puri stuffed with mashed lentils.

Bengali sweets, which are mostly cottage-cheese-based, are considered to be the lightest amongst Indian desserts. Sweet shops dot every neighbourhood of Kolkata and some suburbs have close to ten of them. Sweets are sold by piece and are fairly cheap compared to sweets sold in cities such as Delhi and Mumbai, which is why very few Bengalis end up making sweets at home. In the good old days, the sweets would be covered with flies. But now, quite a few shops are air-conditioned and have even introduced variations such as baked roshogolla, dark chocolate shondesh (which is the correct way to pronounce 'sandesh') and the occasional alcohol-infused liquor shondesh variants too. Sweet shops in Kolkata offered 'diabetic shondesh' well before sugar-free desserts became a fad in India.

Traditionally, the north of the city is more famous for its sweet shops than the south. Now, the south is picking up with places like Banchharam, but still no shop has the legendary status of sweet shops like Nokur, Bhim Chandra Nag or K.C. Das of the north, whose legacy has been built over years of consistent quality. Some are famous for specific items, like Nokur for shondesh, Bhim Chandra Nag for mishti doi and K.C. Das for roshogolla. The most famous of this lot would possibly be K.C. Das, whose founder claimed to have invented roshogollas, although, more recently, Odisha is claiming inventor rights, leading to angst-filled articles in Kolkata newspapers.

During my student days at Presidency College, I used to frequent Putiram on College Street for its rare white mishti doi (normally mishti doi is a pale beige colour) and dal puri. The doi looked and tasted fresher, with more subtle flavours. The texture was lighter too. Bhim Chandra Nag in Bowbazar was another place I was introduced to in my college days and I loved the mishti doi there. I am yet to go to the famous Nokur of the north, as I am a South Kolkata boy and the north is rather far.

In the south, one of my favourite places for *jol khabar* is Jugal's at Park Circus. This is a branch; the original shop is at Sealdah and was opened in the early 1970s by the late Jugal Ghosh. When I went to the Park Circus branch, there was a very kind elderly gentleman manning the counter. I had stepped in after eating biryani next door at Arsalan. The gentleman at Jugal's was most tickled to see me take out my DSLR and start taking pictures.

Another South Kolkata favourite is Ganguram & Sons in Golpark. Ganguram & Sons is a 100-year-old shop, which was opened by a gentleman of the same name who came to Kolkata from Varanasi. The 'newer' outlet in Golpark was opened in the 1940s. I went there on one of my recent visits to Kolkata, chasing memories of visiting the place with my father when we had moved to Kolkata in the 1980s. I had some lovely khasta kochuri, dal puri and mishti doi there. Biting into the kochuris made me forget that I had just entered my forties and I felt like a chubby eight-year-old whose father would spoil him, once again. Food memories are indeed precious.

Close to Golpark, and near Deshapriya Park, is Maharani, once a tea stall on the road, which is now a hole-in-the-wall shop. You get some crisp, freshly fried kochuri with an aloo curry there. The owner of this shop, Ram Chandra Gupta, came to Kolkata from Varanasi too, sometime in the 1970s. He is a fairly reticent man, but is a pretty hands-on owner and cooks everything himself. The kochuris here are maida puris stuffed with spices and dal and then deep fried, which make them different from the more simple luchis of Bengal, which are plain puris but made from maida, and not stuffed. The aloo curry at Maharani is thicker than what you usually get in Bengali houses. Coupled with tea served in an earthen cup, the Maharani fare makes for one of my favourite breakfasts in Kolkata.

Located close to Maharani is Maharaja, a shop which sells the same dishes. It is newer, a tad larger, and the folks there are more market-savvy and become very proactive if they see you take out a camera!

 Tip: The best time to go to a sweet shop for savouries is in the evening, when they are freshly made.

THE LEGEND OF THE KOLKATA BIRYANI

Few things divide India as much as the topic of one's favourite biryani, and in Kolkata we can get pretty passionate about our biryani. We are a pretty cheerful and tolerant lot, but try telling us that our biryani is a pulao and not a biryani and we will call a Bangla Bandh.

The story of biryani, documented by quite a few food historians and journalists, is an interesting one. The most prevalent view is that biryani owes its origins to the pulaos of Persia and is named after the Persian word *birian*, which in Farsi means 'fried before cooking'.

According to this theory, the Mughals brought their favourite dish, pulao, with them when they invaded and settled in India. India has always had this intrinsic way of sneaking up and captivating its invaders. It took the pulao and transformed it into something very local that the Mughals loved too.

The Persian pulao was essentially a meat-and-rice dish with very few spices in it. However, Indian rice dishes at that time were quite spicy. Slowly, as Indian cooks started working in Mughal kitchens, the pulao started getting an Indian twist and biryani began to take shape. The pulao became spicier and spicier, even more so as it went further away from the courts of the Mughals, who were based in Delhi. You can see a marked difference in the biryanis of South India today. Lizzie Collingham's excellent book, *Curry: A Tale of Cooks and Conquerors*, is a good read on the subject.

So the Lucknowi biryani, which originated in Awadh, close to Delhi, depends more on the flavours of the meat than on spices to pull it through. However, as you go down south to the courts of the Nizams of Hyderabad, the biryani begins to have more masala.

The origin of the Kolkata biryani is said to lie in the former courts of Lukcnow. The story, they say, began when Nawab Wajid Ali Shah was displaced by the British and exiled to Kolkata. The Nawab was a man who loved to eat and to feed others. When he shifted to Kolkata, his entourage included his cooks too. Biryani, of course, had to feature on the table even when he was in exile. However, the reality was that money was scarce. The spices were toned down and the biryani of Kolkata became more subtle than that of Lucknow and had a lower meat-to-rice ratio. Then the cooks had a stroke of brilliance. Meat was expensive, so they decided to add potatoes instead, to give contrast to the rice. But of course, the thing with Indian food history is that a lot of it is conjecture-based, as not much has been recorded. There are descendants of the nawab who say that the aloo was added in Kolkata as it was an exotic vegetable at that time, and not because of fiscal restraints.

What is not beyond dispute, though, is that the potato in the biryani, or the aloo, is what makes all Kolkatans go weak in the knees today, and is even more sought-after than the meat at times!

Some places add a boiled egg too, though, this is often reserved for what is labelled as 'special' biryani on the menus of Kolkata's Mughlai restaurants. 'Special' usually means the same amount of rice, but with an extra piece of meat and an egg added in.

 Tip: If there are two of you at a Mughlai restaurant in Kolkata, and you're not very hungry, ask for a special biryani with extra aloo instead of asking for two biryanis.

Opinions on the best place to have biryani in Kolkata are severely divided, but what is widely accepted is that the

Muslim-run restaurants of Central Kolkata make it best. Some of these establishments are close to a 100 years old. Most look like they are frozen in time. These are eating houses at their most basic – they are packed during lunchtime; you have to share tables at times, eat and move on. The trick is to not look down at the floor, for you might spot the odd chewed chicken bone there. Yet, given the heavy turnover, the food is never stale. These are no-frills places – wooden chairs and tables and no air-conditioning.

My favourite biryani joint is Shiraz Golden Restaurant in Mullick Bazar. It offers the most subtle, delicately flavoured and non-greasy of the Kolkata biryanis that I have come across. If brilliance in taste is what you are looking for, Shiraz is where you should go. A couple of accompaniments that you can try, in case you find the biryani too dry for your taste, are the mutton rezala and the chicken chaap. The rezala of Kolkata is a dish that has a ghee- and curd-redolent silken sauce with a slightly sweetish taste. The chaap is a slow-cooked crushed-poppy-seed- and cashew-paste-based dish. Both pair very well with tandoori rotis.

 Tip: When it comes to chicken, always ask for the 'leg piece' (chicken drumstick) and hope for the best. The chicken breast in biryani joints is often overcooked.

Shiraz is fairly crowded and you might have to queue up at meal times and share a table with strangers. They also have a franchise under the brand name Lazeez, which has outlets across Kolkata and even in Bangalore.

Another favourite of mine for biryani is sleepy old Nizam's in New Market. The biryani here is very good, although the ambience is a lot grimier than Shiraz. The first time I took my wife there, she steadfastly looked at the wall to avoid looking at the dirt on the floor while she chomped on her egg roll, which she really enjoyed. I end up going there on most of my visits to Kolkata and both the roll and the biryani quality are surprisingly consistent.

Another place I used to be pretty fond of was Zeeshan near Ice Skating Rink. My first job after B-School was at an office next door and I would often go to Zeeshan for biryani. Later, after I had shifted cities, I would often stop at Zeeshan to pack biryanis and rolls to bring back to Mumbai.

Arsalan in Park Circus, which came up after I left Kolkata, is one of the new favourite biryani places in the city, especially with the young folks. I find the biryani here a bit too greasy for my liking. Closer home in South Calcutta, I like Aminia at Golpark.

What I find amazing is that a dish that originated in Persia, was perfected in Lucknow by its Muslim ruler, and then migrated to Kolkata, and has now metamorphosed into a dish that all Bengalis, irrespective of caste and faith, consider their own. That, to me, is the beauty of Indian food – its ability to absorb influences from all over and give it its own unique take.

KOLKATA CONTINENTAL

The city of Kolkata has a huge British hangover. Calcutta, as it was once called, was the first capital of the British empire of India, after all. (So much so that when the Metro started in Kolkata, there were enough folks who would refer to it as the 'Tube' as it was earlier called in England!)

Park Street is the place to go to for what is called continental cuisine or 'conti', which is the Indian interpretation of dishes cooked in British kitchens and clubs. In the 1950s and '60s, Park Street restaurants were famous for the cabaret acts, live bands and ever-flowing alcohol. Today, it is quieter, and popular restaurants like Peter Cat, Moulin Rouge and Mocambo, are more intent on holding on to the remnants of the past than on recreating the vibrancy of the earlier decades. But you can go to Trinca's and catch some live 1960s music even today, I'm told.

I used to be quite fond of the continental fare at Park Street but having been introduced to modern European food in Mumbai, and through my travels round the world, the béchamel-sauce-heavy, frozen-in-time food of Park Street no longer excites me. However, if history on your plate is what you seek, do make a trip to Park Street and be wooed by its romance.

One vintage place that I still do enjoy going to on Park Street is Flurys. After my father passed away, Flurys largely belonged to a world we could no longer afford. I remember going there once in college when Biswaranjan Jethu, our neighbour in Kolkata, had given me ₹100 when I had done well in my final-year exams. He told me to go to Flurys with the 'girl who calls up for you at our place' (this was an era when not every home had telephones and one would give the phone number of neighbours who had phones, to others, for receiving calls.)

Years later, Flurys was taken over by the Park Hotel group who did a brilliant job of restoring it into a European-styled tea room. Since then, the place has become a favourite of my wife and I.

Locals often don't understand my love for the bitter coffee, the somewhat dry 'classic sandwiches', the simple baked beans on toast, with finely chopped green chillies and onions, from the heritage menu, and the old-school strawberry pastry. Many Kolkatans tell me that they find the food at Flurys ordinary and overpriced.

What they don't understand is that sitting down by the big windows of Flurys, reading a book, watching people walking down Park Street, symbolizes a life in Kolkata that was snatched away from me after my father passed away, a life that I so aspired to while growing up. And the coffee *has* improved over the years.

THE BENGALI *RANNAGHAR*

And now we come to Bengali food itself. By 'Bengali' food, I am referring to the diet of the Hindu community of the state and Kolkata in particular, though many of these dishes feature on the plates of people of other communities too and even in kitchens of Odisha, Assam and Bihar. The Bengali menu is nuanced and there are variations depending on whether you hail from East Bengal, or modern-day Bangladesh, or West Bengal. You will get a mix of both in contemporary Bengali restaurants.

The phenomenon of the 'Bengali restaurant' is also relatively new. There were hardly any Bengali restaurants when I left Kolkata for Mumbai in the late 1990s. The Bengali kitchen, or the *rannaghar*, was still lorded over by the matriarch of the family, who always felt that going to a restaurant was a 'waste of money'. So while continental, Chinese and Mughlai fare were favoured options for eating out, going to a restaurant to eat Bengali food was unthinkable.

Things have changed quite a lot in the last decade or so. The movement started with places such as Suruchi, Kewpie's and the more expensive Aaheli opening up in Kolkata. This was followed by Bhojohori Manna, 6 Ballygunge Place and the Mumbai-based Oh! Calcutta. Now even five-star hotels such as ITC Sonar, The Oberoi Grand and others offer pretty good Bengali food for their guests. These are great for visitors to the city who want to try out local food and for new-age Bengali families who don't have the time or inclination to cook traditional recipes in their kitchens.

I am yet to come across a Bengali restaurant that hasn't faced its share of flack from Bengalis who feel that the food served is not 'authentic'. But the whole definition of 'authentic' Bengali cooking is, in my opinion, a tad shaky, because chances are, if you taste maachher jhol (fish curry) in five different houses, you will find variations in each. The same goes for Bengali restaurants.

One of the first Bengali restaurants in Kolkata that I tried, just before leaving for Mumbai, was Suruchi on Eliott Road. I remember it being a fairly basic place where the focus was on food, which was served in a very homely, non-restaurant-like manner. I have never had the opportunity to go back there, but I have been told that this has now become one of the most popular Bengali restaurants in town. It also gives opportunities to women from less-privileged homes to work there and earn a living.

My first full-blown Bengali restaurant meal in Kolkata after I moved to Mumbai was at Kewpie's, when my wife and I took my family there for lunch. I have been there a few times after that too. Kewpie's is located near Forum Mall and Netaji Bhavan on Elgin Road. It's a single-storeyed house that has been converted into a restaurant. Each room has been converted into a section that is a throwback to rooms in old Bengali upper-class houses.

Kewpie's has à la carte dishes, but it also has a *thala* – a set meal comprising multiple dishes, showcasing Bengali fare in all its glory. This is what I would recommend for a great introduction to Bengali food. You get most classic Bengali dishes at one go in the *thala*. There are different *thala*s that you can get. In the vegetarian ones, you can choose from Bengali vegetarian classics such as shukto, chorchori, mocchar ghonto, chhanar dalna and bhaja. There are *thala*s with mutton curries, chicken curries and fish curries which feature different sorts of fresh-water fish such as rohu, pabda, parshe and, when in season, ilish and chingri (prawns).

There is a quaint, warm homelike feel to the place. Even my grandmom felt very much at ease here and approved of the food when we took her. This is my mother's favourite restaurant in Kolkata, as she finds the food to be homely and not too oily. The service can be haphazard at times and the odd dish could be served lukewarm. But then, as TV food show anchor Aneesha Baig once told me, 'When is food ever served hot in Bengali houses?'

Back home in Mumbai, I got to meet Pia Promina Dasgupta Barve, who set up Kewpie's with her father and her sister Rakhi Purnima. Kewpie's was set up in 1989 in memory of Rakhi and Pia's mother, the late Minakshie Dasgupta, who had written popular cookbooks such as *Bangali Ranna* and *The Calcutta Cookbook*. Pia lives in Mumbai and is a food entrepreneur and consultant. She occasionally hosts pop up and catering events where she offers dishes from the Kewpie's menu to Mumbaikars. Rakhi Purnima is based in Kolkata and you might occasionally bump into her at the restaurant.

Another place that offers a *thala*, along with à la carte dishes, is Aaheli – located in The Peerless Inn at New Market. Aaheli had opened when I was a student and had caused quite a few ripples as it positioned itself as a one-of-a-kind Bengali fine-dining restaurant when there were none in the 1990s.

I finally went to Aaheli when I went to Kolkata on a work trip and used the opportunity to introduce a Malayali colleague, who was travelling with me, to Bengali food. The course-by-course meal accompanied by the expensive boneless ilish or hilsa that I had specially ordered wowed us. Aaheli is a lot more expensive and plush than Kewpie's and is the place to go if you want to impress someone with the many wonders of Bengali cuisine.

Bhojohori Manna, my favourite Bengali restaurant in Mumbai, originally started in Kolkata and has many branches there. It was started by a group of five food lovers who belonged to diverse fields and included film directors, actors, corporate folks and businessmen. Their first outlet was a garage-like place in South Kolkata's Ekdalia Park, which was opened in 2003. It was initially meant to be a place which offered simple and reasonably priced maachher jhol and bhaat. Their model was that of the 'pice hotels' that dotted Kolkata: humble eateries where there is a daily menu that is served till stocks last.

Bhojohori Manna has expanded since then, has multiple branches in Kolkata, and has moved beyond the city. Siddhartha Bose and Rajeev Neogi, who are active partners and manage the operation and food of the chain, have become dear friends of mine.

We once ate at their new flagship branch at Ekdalia, which looks fairly posh compared to the outlet at Mumbai's Oshiwara that we are used to. The meal was delicious, right from the plump begun bhaja – or fried brinjal; to the aloo posto – potatoes cooked in poppy seeds; chingri malai curry – prawn in coconut milk gravy; and the brilliant boneless ilish – fish prepared in a mustard sauce.

 Tip: Bhojohori Manna gets very crowded during lunch hours, so be prepared to wait.

So what should one order at a Bengali restaurant?

Well, a true-blue Bengali meal has many courses and we eat our meals course by course. Myths that Bengalis eat only fish, or do not eat vegetarian food, are completely unfounded. There is no ultimate rendition of a Bengali dish because each house has its unique take, as I've said earlier.

Bengali dishes can be broadly divided into two categories: Ghoti and Bangal.

The Ghotis are natives of what was West Bengal or the Indian side of Bengal. The Bangals are from erstwhile East Bengal, or what is today Bangladesh. At the risk of making a broad generalization, you can say that the general rule of thumb is that Ghoti dishes are a bit sweet, while Bangal dishes are spicy, have a strong chilli element and are savoury. When it comes to fish, Ghotis love prawns, while Bangals love ilish. When it comes to football (yes, Indians play football despite what our FIFA ranking indicates), Ghotis support the Mohun Bagan Athletic Club, while Bangals support East Bengal. (It is said that when these two clubs play against each other, the price of ilish or prawns go up depending on who won the game!) The Ghotis are also known for their use of the posto or poppy seeds in their dishes.

Like most things in evolving cultures, these differences are slowly disappearing as Bengalis like us have begun to travel, move out of the house and marry folks from other communities. This is why I am not too pedantic about this differentiation. Technically, I am a Bangal, as my parents were born in what is now Bangladesh. But living in Mumbai, and being married to a Parsi, has taught me to enjoy a touch of sweetness in my food that would most likely scandalize my Bangal ancestors.

When it comes to restaurants, you will get a bit of both

cuisines served there, though in my experience, Ghoti food dominates Kolkata-based Bengali restaurants. Kolkata is the capital of the Ghoti part of Bengal, after all.

Coming back to my guide to the classic Bengali meal, rice is the base of the meal, though nowadays families have whole-wheat rotis too. The cooking oil of choice is the pungent mustard oil, but many Bengali families use the neutral-tasting refined oil today.

You could start off your meal with the bitter stuff – the bitter-gourd-based mixed vegetable stew shukto or some fried neem leaves. This is supposed to aid digestion and increase one's appetite. Then vegetarian dishes follow. This is usually a dal with bhajas (literally 'fried') on the side. The popular bhajas are begun – brinjal – or aloo ones. Begun or aloo are dipped in gram flour or poppy-seed batter and fried, or fried just with a smearing of turmeric, salt and chilli powder. Sometimes the dal can be cooked with fish head – to make my favourite maachher muro diye dal. Another popular fish-head-based dish is mudi ghonto. You will find both in restaurants such as Bhojohori Manna. In Bengali houses, the fish head could also be added to mixed vegetable dishes.

 Tip: If eating a fish-head dal and not used to it, stick to the kaatla or rohu head, as it has fewer bones. The ilish head is too bony for novices. The joy is in chewing the head!

The more elaborate vegetarian dishes come after this. Some of the most popular and famous, especially among Bengali expats, are aloo posto and mochar ghonto, a banana blossom-based dish. Aloo posto is pretty easy to make but mochar ghonto is a lot tougher, as chopping the mocha, or banana blossom, itself take ages. Which is why cooking mocha is an art which was lost after our grandmother's generation. The chorchori, a mix of vegetables, is also quite popular in Bengali homes, as are cauliflower- and cabbage-based dishes. Then there is the chyachra, where mixed vegetables are cooked with fish head.

Then you move on to the more exciting part of the meal. Fish, to start with. Bengalis are fond of river-water-based fish, which tend to be a bit bony. The fish of favour can broadly be divided into kaata maachh (large fish cut into pieces) like rohu, kaatla and bhetki, and chhoto maachh (small fish) such as parshe, tangra and pabda, which are eaten whole and on the bone. The darling of the Bengali fish portfolio is the ilish and, to an extent, chital. Prawns and crabs are also much sought-after. Some of the popular fish preparations are shorshe bhapa (steamed in mustard), patla maachher jhol (thin curry), paturi (steamed in banana leaves), bhaja, doi maachh (cooked in yogurt) and kaalia (an onion-based thick sauce).

 Tip: Never drink a cola while having a mustard-based curry as it might make your tongue sore.

Fish is followed by the *piéce de résistance* of the meal, meat.

Mutton is more favoured and the most popular restaurant preparation is the slow-cooked kosha mangsho, which is best enjoyed with luchi or a sweet mishti pulao. The Sunday mangshor jhol, a thin mutton curry, still features in most Bengali homes.

Tip: Be prepared to get meat of uneven consistency in restaurants. Meat from multiple goats is used while cooking the dish in restaurants. The meat from older goats takes longer to cook and might end up being tougher.

Chicken has become increasingly popular, thanks to the anti-red meat brigade. It was not a part of the original Bengali diet, though. Beef and pork usually do not find a place in the classic Hindu Bengali dining table, though many of us enjoy eating them.

The serving of meat signals the end of the main course and then you move on to desserts. A sweet-and-sour dish, chutney, along with papad, acts as a palate cleanser and you then move on to the mishti dois, roshogollas and shondeshes. Phew!

This is, of course, a festive menu. On a regular basis, people usually have have two or three courses – dal, vegetables and a fish dish. Meat used to be more a Sunday phenomenon in middle-class homes in the 1980s and 1990s when I grew up in Kolkata, but is now eaten more often, I am told.

At a Bengali restaurant, you should ideally try to follow this sequence of dishes. This is difficult if you are eating alone and in a restaurant that offers only an à la carte menu. One cardinal rule of Bengali food is: *Don't* pile up all the food at one go on your plate. This gives Bengalis intense pain. We really like our food in courses.

If you are not a Bengali, and happen to find yourself in a Bengali restaurant in Kolkata, don't hesitate to ask your server, or even folks at the neighbouring tables, for recommendations and guidance. We Bengalis love people who show an interest in our food and are very happy to take them under our wing.

Tip: Be wary of waiters pushing golda chingri (king prawns), as these are the most expensive thing on the menu and often tend to be overcooked. Go for regular-sized prawns if you can. They are tastier.

Restaurants like Oh! Calcutta, Suruchi, Bhojohori Manna, 6 Ballygunge Place (which is pretty good too) and Kewpie's in Kolkata tend to largely serve the classical Bengali Hindu menu. There are a couple of Bengali restaurants that do not stick to this formula, though.

One is Kasturi. The original, two-decade-old branch is located near what used to be Jamuna Cinema Hall in Free School Street. It's a tiny two-storeyed restaurant. The ground floor showcases various cooked dishes displayed in a sweet-shop style. You pick and choose your dishes and then go up to the cramped first floor to eat. The dishes are available in small servings, making it possible for you to try quite a few even if you're alone. I saw similar displays in Bangladeshi restaurants in Brick Lane, London.

Kasturi, I am told, was opened to meet the dietary needs of relatives of Bangladeshi patients who came to Kolkata for medical treatment. They would miss home food and the idea behind the restaurant was to serve Bangladeshi food to them. That is why you will get a lot of bhortas (dishes with ground vegetables), mustard-based dishes and, most importantly, some very spicy dishes here. According to my grandmother, who was born in pre-Partition Dhaka, bhorta was a preparation made by the poorer Muslim sections of society. They would grind together all the parts of the vegetable, including the skin and the stalks, to serve more people.

Kasturi now has a posher outlet near 6 Ballygunge Place in South Kolkata. I have not been there, but I loved the atmosphere of the tiny place near Jamuna. It's very easy on the pocket too.

I must state a caveat though. Kanishka Chakraborty, a fellow food blogger and friend based in Dhaka, has a strong point of view on Kasturi. He ate there and said the food is anything but Bangladeshi! Ah, well. Like most 'authentic' cuisine, this too is subjective.

What I can assure you of, though, is that the food at Kasturi is brilliant and different from what is served in other Bengali restaurants in Kolkata.

 Tip: If eating at a Bangladeshi joint like Kasturi, and if you can't handle spices too well, take very little of the curries and use a lot of rice to counterbalance the heat.

So there you have it: The classic Bengali meal, from both sides of the border.

Kolkata is a city of people who worship food and live to eat. The term *bhojon bilashi* (lover of food) existed long before the English term 'foodie' became trendy. If you love food, you should plan a trip to Kolkata just to eat. I am probably biased, but I strongly believe that Kolkata is one of the nicest cities in India to eat in. I am sure you will agree once you go there.

FOOD WALK

👣 *The Park Street walk, ending at New Market*

Start with a breakfast at Flurys. Have coffee with baked beans and toast followed by a strawberry cube. Cross over and have a mutton roll at Kusum Rolls. Walk past Mocambo and step into Kasturi near the old Jamuna Cinema Hall for some bharta and rice for some Bangladeshi flavours. Look out for Kalman Cold Storage and pick up some bacon and cured sausages to take home.

👣 *The New Market walk*

Go to Nahoum and Sons, the old Jewish bakery, and try some of the pastries and puffs there, or pack some biscuits to take home. Walk through the narrow lanes of New Market and then go to New Empire Cinema and have some phuchkas near the theatre. Step into Nizam's. Have a mutton biryani with mutton rezala and chicken chaap and wash it down with a Thums Up. Get some shopping done at Lindsay Street – the hawkers on the streets have some interesting wares. When you have worked up enough of an appetite, head to K.C. Das at Esplanade and have roshogollas and mishti doi for a sweet end to the walk.

 There is quite a lot of food in this walk. So it's best to try it in groups of two or more. This works best as brunch.

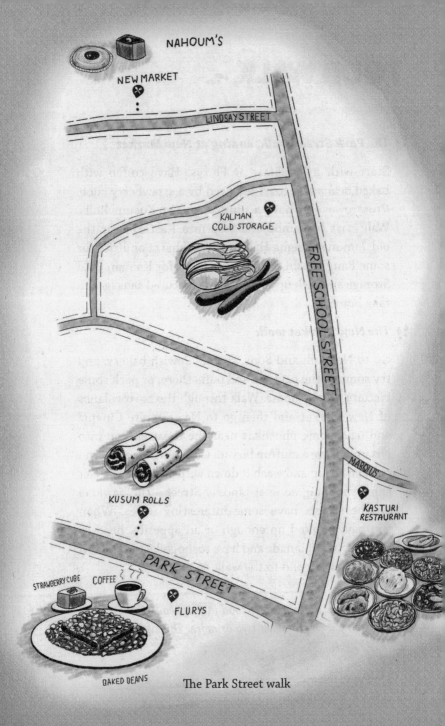

NAHOUM'S

NEW MARKET

LINDSAY STREET

KALMAN
COLD STORAGE

FREE SCHOOL STREET

MARQUIS

KUSUM ROLLS

KASTURI
RESTAURANT

PARK STREET

STRAWBERRY CUBE   COFFEE

FLURYS

BAKED BEANS

The Park Street walk

👣 *The South Kolkata walk*

This, too, works best as a brunch walk, though you could try it in the evening if you like. You will need transport such as local cabs or buses.

Start at Maharani near Gol Park. Have hot tea in *bhnaars* and kochuri with aloo dum. Then walk down Gol Park to reach Ganguram & Sons. Have your pick of mishti here and savoury khasta kochuri. Hop onto a bus and cross Dhakuria Bridge. Or walk it. Get off opposite Dakshinapan Shopping Centre, then stop for phuchkas at the couple of shops outside the complex. Then go inside and have some tea (hot or iced) at Dolly's The Tea Shop and indulge in some *adda*. Have some ham toasties there if you're still hungry.

THE LEGENDS OF LUCKNOW

My initial trips to Lucknow were at the start of my career as a market researcher. This was in the late 1990s. I used to go there to conduct focus groups and would stay at a hotel called Clarks Avadh. That's where I tried my first galouti kebabs, on the recommendation of the person taking the room service orders. I didn't step out of the hotel to try local restaurants in those days but the galouti kebabs that I had at the hotel were a life-changing experience for me. I had never had kebabs so soft in my life. I took a bite and let the smoky, meaty goodness engulf me. It felt as if I had been destined to visit Lucknow just to discover this culinary marvel.

I returned to Lucknow almost a decade later. I had gone there to conduct focus groups once again, but this time with a clear agenda to eat at the city's iconic restaurants. The city turned out to be everything I expected it to be...and a whole lot more.

Lucknow had me in its spell within two hours of my landing in the city. Over the last decade, it had undergone some changes, and the first thing I noticed were the massive roads leading from the airport to the city centre. My cab drove past the serene Bodhi Park, the old Cantonment area and then into the city's hub, Hazratganj, or 'Ganj' as the locals call it. The buildings there look like vestiges of the colonial rule of India. All the signboards there are in a uniform white-and-black colour, reminding me of Istiklal Caddesi in Istanbul – a classy commercial area where all the signboards are a uniform brass colour. My hotel was a fairly new one and gave out a bright and young vibe, though it was surrounded by history. Lucknow was looking promising already.

Before I had left for Lucknow, I had tweeted about my plans to explore the local food scene. In response, veteran journalist Kanchan Gupta sourced me a list of places to eat at from his field contacts. My brief to him was that I wanted a mix of Muslim and Hindu eateries and he delivered exactly that – his list was my Bible during my stay in the city.

First on my list was chaats or any other savoury snacks.

The place I was headed to was Dixit Chaat House in the Chowk area, one of the older parts of the city. When I reached there in the evening, I felt as though I were on the sets of the film *Mughal-e-Azam*. There were grand old buildings which were visibly past their glory days and yet looked so beautiful. There were loose electric wires hanging all over the area, connected to yellow bulbs that glowed all along the streets.

As I made my way through the Chowk, I met a group of people who were standing by a cart that sold peanuts and other assorted snacks. I asked them for directions to Dixit, which they pointed out to me before asking me where I was from. Once I told them that I had come from Mumbai to discover the food of their city, they insisted that I have a cup of tea with them. We chatted for a while and they told me to come back in winter, which is the season of weddings. The best food in Lucknow was found in the wedding feasts, according to my new friends. They even offered to take me to some weddings as their guests – such is the hospitality and warmth of the Lucknow folks! Shortly after, I left my companions for Dixit Chaat House.

It's a semi-structured shop and can best be described as something between a street-food cart and a proper shop. As its name suggests, it serves only chaats. Chaats are street-food dishes typical of the Indian subcontinent. They are said to have originated in North India and some say they sprung up from the cuisine of Uttar Pradesh, of which Lucknow is the capital today. Another theory, shared with me by Chef Manjit Gill of the ITC Hotel Group, is that the Mughal rulers of Delhi wanted a dish that people could have during the monsoon months and chaats were invented as a solution to that.

Whatever be their origin, chaats have spread across the country and each city claims that their chaats are the best. A large number of chaat sellers in cities such as Mumbai, Kolkata and others hail from Uttar Pradesh, which makes one believe that there may be some validity to the claim that the state is the wellspring of this cuisine. Chaats are dishes that are savoury in essence but bring in contrasting tastes of sweet and sour too. There are textural contrasts as well, ranging from extreme crunch to soft chunks and silken sauces. Which is why a chaat reduced to a sphere of foam, as it is often done in modern Indian restaurants, just does not work for me.

Dixit Chaat House is about 40 years old. It is run by a gentleman named Gaurav Dixit, who is the grandson of the founder of the shop and who is keeping the family tradition alive to date. The steady flow of customers shows how popular it is among the citizens of Lucknow.

The way it works here is that you place your order and then wait for Gaurav to assemble your chaat of choice. Once you get your order, you can sit on the flat wooden benches kept outside the shop and enjoy your chaat. Most of the food is fried in front of you, sanitizing it from the assault of the streets. The ingredients are fried in pure desi ghee, as the signboard at the shop proudly proclaims. The chutneys are something one has to be wary of when eating on the streets, as they are water-based and use ingredients which may not be washed properly. Going to a shop with heavy traffic and turnover is an assuring sign in such cases.

I asked Gaurav what the most popular chaats were and then ordered a small portion of the ones that he recommended – dahi aloo tikki and matar chaat.

Both were splendid. The dahi aloo tikki was a beautiful medley of tangy curd, sweet tamarind chutney and a wonderful fried aloo tikki, or what Western cuisine would view as a flat potato croquette. It was a synthesis of diverse flavours in a dish, which, in India, is possibly best exemplified in chaats.

The matar chaat is a Lucknow specialty, I was told. It consists of boiled gram pulses, cooked and mashed in spices and then drenched in lime juice. The sharp taste of the lime cuts the robust and solid taste of the legumes and the indulgent ghee, and somehow complements it perfectly. It is served with crushed flakes of the deep-fried crust of the khasta kachori.

If I were forced to choose between the two, I would go for the tikki simply because I am a slave to the sinful, starchy bite of potato. The tikki was incredible, with its beautiful airy crunchiness, and I prefer it to the more dense potato-based ragda pattice of Mumbai.

It would be a tough choice though because the matar chaat is such a unique experience.

I got up to pay, but Gaurav waived it off, saying I was a guest. A Lucknow thing, he assured me. It took a bit of convincing before he agreed to take the payment of ₹30 for the two chaats.

I had another aloo tikki experience at a more swanky-looking sweet shop named Chhappan Bhog at Sadar Bazaar, which my local colleague had strongly recommended. The tikki was again served straight off a flat tava, where it was fried fresh for the customer. It was richer, fuller, more expensive and even more intoxicating, with its curd, chutney and potato-straw mix, than what I ate at Dixit Chaat House.

I liked the matar there too and the shop looked a lot posher than Dixit's. Later Zamir Boi, who works with the Massive Restaurant group and has grown up in Lucknow, told me that Chhappan Bhog started as a tiny stall in Lucknow. The business has grown over the years and today Chhappan Bhog is even an exporter of sweets and snacks. An inspiring story indeed.

I later tweeted to Shirin Mehrotra, a Mumbai-based food blogger and writer who grew up in Lucknow, asking her about her favourite chaat haunts. Her go-to places for chaat in Lucknow are Shree Kalika Chaat House in Aminabad, Tiwari in Ganpati Ganj, Jain Chaat at Lalbaug Chowk and Pandit Chaat Corner at Naka Charbagh.

She did not mention Dixit. It just goes to show how each person has their own favourite when it comes to street food places in India.

While on the subject of chaat, you should try what the locals here call 'pani ke batashe'. This is Lucknow's version of Kolkata's phuchka, Delhi's golgappa and Mumbai's panipuri.

I first tried one at Kailashnath Shau's stall opposite Chhappan Bhog at Sadar Bazaar. He told me that he has been practising his art for more than three decades – and the food showed that he has mastered it.

The stuffing of the pani ke batashe is different from phuchka as they put boiled chickpeas in it, unlike the masala, green chilli and tamarind-juice-soaked mashed potatoes in the phuchkas of Kolkata. But apart from the filling, its light crispy shell and sour tamarind water accompaniment come closest to the phuchkas of Kolkata as compared to the panipuri of Mumbai and the golgappe of Delhi.

A couple of days later, I got to try out another version of

this Lucknow specialty. This was at a street stall at Hazratganj, where they serve their pani ke batashe with a variety of chutney and masala water mixes of differing tastes and consistencies. They take great pride in the fact that none of the mixes taste the same and that they serve each puri or batasha filled with a different mix. I tried out a range of chutneys with my batasha at the stall. This was culinary wizardry of the highest order, served in the humblest of surroundings.

The gentleman making the pani ke batashe earnestly added some slices of boiled potato when I asked him if they serve pani ke batashe with potatoes, like it is done with phuchkas. I didn't have the heart to tell him that the potato should be mashed and mixed with chaat masala, chilli powder, chopped green chillies, tamarind water and coriander leaves to satiate a Bengali phuchka epicure.

His good intentions and warm heart won me over.

THE BLISS OF KACHORIS AND KHASTE

The standout vegetarian experience for me on the streets of Lucknow was at Vajpayee Kachori Bhandar at Hazratganj. Forget the 'vegetarian' bit. It was a brilliant food experience. Period.

I went to the shop one sunny and very hot afternoon. Despite the blazing sun, people had queued up outside the shop as they inched patiently towards their goal of piping hot kachoris served straight out of the wok. The kachori is a deep-fried flat puri that is usually stuffed with a spice mix. Variations of this dish are found across South Asia, but the one I was in line for today was the flat one served with a helping of chhole (a chickpea curry). The kachoris were cooked by a man in a singlet and lungi who was frying them in the heat with zen-like composure.

Seeing me standing in the queue, and looking out of place, a man from the shop called out to me and gestured that I could move up to the front. It turned out that the gentleman was Manish, the owner of the shop, who had taken over the family business, which had been opened by his late grandfather. Manish introduced himself to me and spoke fondly of his grandfather, Balkrishna Vajpayee, who was apparently related to the former prime minister of India, Atal Bihari Vajpayee.

You need to stand in a queue at Vajpayee's to get your goodies. Given how long the queue was, I felt grateful to have got my food out of turn. The kachoris were served on a plate of dried sal leaves and there were rickety wooden tables kept to the side of the stall where you could gorge on your food. Carefully carrying my plate of kachoris to a table, I took photographs of these sizzling treasures with my huge DSLR. I use my iPhone for photos these days, but the DSLR ensures that you can jump the queue. Tourists are warmly welcomed in Lucknow. Photography done, I gingerly broke a piece of the kachori. It was straight out of the kadhai and rather hot to touch. When it reached a palatable temperature, I finally took a bite without the chhole.

The first bite transported me to the garden of Eden. Everything was perfect. Right from the consistency of the crust, the seasoning, the wholesomeness. This is the sort of dish that can rejuvenate the weariest of souls on the hottest of afternoons. I then mopped up a bit of the chhole with the kachori. The moment I combined the kachori along with the spicy and tangy chickpea curry, I knew that I had come across one of the defining culinary moments of my Lucknow trip.

Just imagine how good a vegetarian dish must be to have muscled its way into my list of favourites, despite the meaty delights that Lucknow has on offer!

I liked the kachori so much that I felt that it was a good idea to go back to Manish and try out the other dish in the shop. This is the khasta, or khasta kachori, also served with chhole on the side. Khasta kachori is round in shape – its shell is made with refined flour and it is stuffed with spices, then deep fried in oil till the outer crust is crisp and flaky. The stuffing of kachoris can differ from city to city. In this case there was a dal-based filling, which reminded me of the flavours of the matar of Dixit Chaat House.

I was awestruck by the gourmet brilliance of the food served out of this grimy shop in the middle of a sun-soaked street. This was a taste of royalty and Manish made me feel special by first letting me cut the queue and then by absolutely refusing to let me pay, despite my insistence. 'You are a guest,' he told me, as did so many in Lucknow.

If you were to ask Shirin Mehrotra, her recommendation for khasta would be a place called Durga. I didn't go to Durga, but I think that Vajpayee Kachori Bhandar will always be my favourite.

THE MOTHERLAND OF THE KOLKATA BIRYANI

As I mentioned in my Kolkata chapter, it is said that biryani was brought to Kolkata when the last nawab of Oudh, Wajid Ali Shah, was exiled by the British after the 1857 War of Independence.

Well, one can keep dwelling on history but what I wanted to know was how the biryani of Lucknow tasted today and how it compared with what I used to eat in Kolkata.

There are people such as the former host of TV show *The Foodie*, Kunal Vijayakar, food historian Kurush Dalal and food critic Vir Sanghvi, who have told me since then that the biryani of Lucknow is actually a pulao. Vir Sanghvi mentioned some of the vintage cooks of Lucknow, whom he had met on his visits to the city, who had told him this. These were cooks who still remembered the royal kitchens and traditions of Lucknow.

I put this pulao versus biryani question to Lucknow girl Shirin Mehrotra. She explained that the biryanis of Lucknow are like classic pulaos. However, they are called 'biryanis' now because people associate pulao with vegetarian food.

I then met Dr Izzat Hussain, who is working on bringing back recipes from the royal kitchens of Lucknow for today's diners. He told me that the biryani you get on the streets of Lucknow today is pretty different from what one used to get in the royal courts, where the ingredients used were of superior quality. When I posed to him the question of whether the biryani of Lucknow is actually a biryani, Dr Hussain quipped, 'Biryanis are like one's mother...one should not say that one is better than another.'

The argument that Hyderabadi biryani is a biryani while the Lucknowi or the Kolkata ones are not is like saying that clay-court tennis is tennis but grass-court tennis is not – in my opinion. One should respect food history, of course, but one must also acknowledge that cooking traditions and tastes evolve over time and so could the definition of biryani.

There are so many strains of biryani – Moplah of Kerala, Irani of Mumbai, the hot and spicy Andhra ones, the Tamil Ambur and Dindigul ones, the Punjabi frying-pan biryanis which often have tomatoes and onions in them, the spicy Maharashtrian ones that you get in Malvani restaurants... the greasy Mumbai stuff of Jaffer Bhai. The definition of what constitutes an 'authentic biryani' today is an amorphous one and the answer to this question should come with qualifiers.

I'll go a step further and say that India is a federal country, which is both united and divided by its choice of biryani. The sooner we learn to accept the differences, the better. The phrase 'Indian biryani' is as much of a misnomer as 'Indian curry'. If anyone tells you that they know where you get the best biryani in India then they are suffering from extreme hubris. There is no such thing as the 'best biryani' in India – just personal favourites.

IN SEARCH OF THE BIRYANIS OF LUCKNOW

My first biryani in Lucknow was at Wahid Biryani. I spotted the shop when I was on my way to the Tunday Kababi outlet at Aminabad and decided to stop there instead, as it was on top of my list for biryani, along with a place called Idris. Unfortunately, I could not make it to the latter restaurant.

Wahid Biryani is a small restaurant. I shared my table with two young boys who had come to Lucknow to take some exam and chatted with them till my biryani arrived. They had a half-plate option, which made sense if you were eating alone. My biryani arrived soon after I placed my order. It was heaped with mutton and looked delicious.

The biryani in Lucknow is all about the meat. The rice and everything else exists alongside just to celebrate the meat. I had chosen mutton, which is the meat traditionally eaten in biryani. The chunks of goat meat in the biryani were sizeable – larger than what I had seen in a small biryani place earlier in Lucknow's Tulsi Gully.

I took a bite of the mutton first. It was juicy, full of flavour and so tasty that it almost made you drool like a child. Rarely had I tasted meat so succulent. So sensuous. So full-bodied and bursting with flavour.

The rice was seasoned perfectly and was a perfect foil for the glory of good honest meat. It also had a nice light raita to go with it.

The key differences that I observed in the Lucknow biryani from its descendants in Kolkata are:

1. There's no potato in the Lucknow biryani.
2. The meat is a lot more glorious in the Lucknow biryani than what I have found in Kolkata restaurants.
3. The rice is richer in Lucknow biryanis and slightly more greasy than what you get in Kolkata.
4. There were more specks of colour – green, orange, red and yellow – in the Lucknow biryani rice as compared to that in Kolkata. I think I read in Lizzie Collingham's book that at the royal feasts in the olden days, these specks of colours were supposed to represent jewels.

My hypothesis is that these differences exist because the DNA of the Lucknowi biryani lies in the more glorious times of the Oudh kingdom while the Kolkata biryanis are the children of exile. From a royal dish in Lucknow, the biryani became a dish of the masses in Kolkata.

On the way out, I met octogenarians, Wahid saab and his brother Wazid, who had founded this restaurant and still run it.

'Have a cup of tea before leaving, beta,' said Wahid saab to me.

I am not a tea drinker but could not refuse his kind offer and sat down to sip some chai. I asked him about when he had opened his shop.

'In 1950,' he replied and with full humility, added, 'Since then, we have been trying to make our biryani perfect.'

I told them that the hard work they had put in showed in the great taste of the biryani. The two brothers smiled.

I felt perfectly at home.

My second stop for biryani was Lallaji's shop at Chaupatiya Chauraha. It had been recommended by a Twitter friend of mine, Aashim Tyagi.

I first went there one afternoon in between work. When I got there, I saw a gentleman adding meat, cooked separately, to a big vessel of rice. In the Lucknow and Kolkata biryanis, the meat is cooked separately and then layered into the rice with spices, which are then cooked together. This is called 'pakki' or cooked meat biryani versus the 'kachchi' gosht biryani that you find in Mumbai and Hyderabad, where the meat is cooked raw, along with the rice.

The gentleman mixing the meat into the rice was Lallaji himself. Lallaji explained that he was preparing biryani for the night, as he opens only for dinner.

I returned in the evening and sat at one of the benches outside the little garage-like biryani shop. They do have an option for you to pack your biryani and take it home, but I preferred to sit there and eat.

Once again, the biryani was all about the meat. This was the mutton that I saw Lallaji lovingly layer into the vessel earlier in the afternoon.

And what exquisitely cooked mutton it was! The meat was so juicy that it made me forget my weariness at the end of a long day. What was served on my humble stainless steel plate was a sheer work of art.

The rice here was a bit more colourful than what I had had at Wahid earlier. This was a biryani that was filled with extra cheer. The deal with the biryani at Lallaji is that it comes with his big smile and blessings. He is a very warm and affable person and that changes the way you experience the food. I could easily understand Aashim's affection for him. The kind gentleman patted my cheek and gave me a warm smile when I told him that I had loved his biryani.

As Aashim tweeted to me, Lallaji is possibly the only Hindu running a successful biryani shop in Lucknow. Biryani is traditionally a Muslim dish, after all. When I asked Lallaji about the origin of his business, he told me he got the idea of setting up a biryani shop more than three decades ago. He got a Muslim friend of his to teach him how to make biryani and has been making biryani since. It's rare that you hear such a wonderful story of communal gastronomic integration but I am sure Lallaji has done his friend proud.

What I realized after trying out various biryanis in Lucknow is that the wizards of this city have got it right. Biryani perfection to them is all about the quality and taste of the meat, accompanied by some rich – and yet not overly spiced – rice. They kept it simple and uncluttered here. There are no excesses in this school of biryani. It's all about letting the core ingredients, rice and meat, speak out clearly.

Just the way food should be.

Unlike Aminabad, Chowk or Hazratganj, there are no other food places of note near Lallaji's Biryani at Chaupatiya Chauraha barring the odd kulcha, kulfi and lassi shops. Yet, I would strongly recommend a trip to Lallaji's just to experience this wonder of Lucknow. As a gentleman at Wahid Biryani told me when I mentioned that I would be going to Lallaji's – 'Sirf khaane ke shaukeen ko unke baare main maloom hain.' Only true gourmands know of Lallaji's!

You get some shammi kebabs there too, which you can have with the biryani.

TAKING STOCK AT TUNDAY

The first thing people will tell you on hearing that you are going to Lucknow is 'go to Tunday for kebabs'. Then there are others who will tell you 'Don't go to Tunday, it's a tourist trap and it's overrated.'

Conflicting views can get confusing no doubt, but I did want to check out this legendary place for myself and did go there eventually. For whatever it was worth, Tunday featured right on top of the list Kanchan Gupta had sourced for me.

I had two meals at two different Tunday outlets. One was at what I was told is their original outlet at Chowk and the other at their second outlet at Aminabad. The first one is run by the late Tunday Kababi's son, while the second is managed by Tunday Kababi's grandson. 'Tunday Kababi' was the name that the late Haji Murad Ali was better known by and both the outlets have continued business in his name. On both occasions I stuck to the basic bade – buffalo meat – kebabs. I had these with parathas one time and with a roti called shirmal the second time.

To cut a long story short, I found both experiences phenomenal and loved the kebabs. I don't have the perspective of the locals so I can't say if things were better before, but I hope things have not gone downhill since. Sometimes, it is best to listen to your own instincts on these matters.

THE CENTURY-OLD TUNDAY KABABI AT CHOWK

I first went to the Tunday at Chowk the evening I landed in Lucknow.

I headed to Tunday down a long deserted alley. It was around 9 p.m. and I stopped to ask for directions at shops that were still open.

'Walk on,' urged the voices in the dark night. '*Bas thoda hi aage hain.*'

Convinced that I would soon reach my destination, I walked for quite a while, expecting the restaurant to be around the corner. The build up to my first Tunday experience was as cinematic as it gets. There was a cold breeze around me and my driver called me on my mobile, warning me that there could be an *aandhi*, a dust storm. I walked on, trying to shield my eyes from the dust, shrugging off the eeriness of the empty streets.

And then there it was – after a ten-minute walk through the dust clouds – the Tunday Kababi shop.

The first sign of the restaurant was not a signboard or shop display but the throng of people standing outside it. They surrounded a huge tava, behind which sat a gentleman in a singlet and a lungi. He rhythmically took a handful of meat from the tray of minced meat placed in front of him. He rolled it into a ball. Then flattened it. Then tossed it expertly into the hot tava. The kebab sizzled as it hit the hot oil. Its maker reverently patted it into shape, then turned it over after a short time and then took it out of the tava.

Behind the kebab maker was a stark cavernous hall. This was the 'restaurant' – a hole in the wall, if there ever was one, albeit a big one. This was not a place for the faint-hearted. The eatery was dusty, lit in dim neon, and its tables were spread haphazardly across the hall. I could see men sitting down and eating with serious intent. There were hardly any women around.

Service was chaotic. I looked around and feebly asked a couple of folks, who *seemed* like waiters but were not wearing uniforms, on what to do and how to place my order. They walked on, looking hassled, without answering me.

Then I spotted an empty chair at a table occupied by two gentlemen and asked if I could join them. They gave me permission to do so and I sat down.

My table mates seemed to be regulars and confidently called for the waiter. I took advantage of this opportunity and placed my order for kebabs and parathas when the waiter arrived.

Then my neighbours and I got talking. They explained that they were of Nepali descent but were born in Lucknow and that they came to Tunday's once a fortnight when they felt like having kebabs. 'You can't eat this every day. Your body will give up. But we love the kebabs here. My wife has a government job. I don't work. Once in a while she gives me money and we come here for kebabs,' said the more talkative of the two.

'We get "special" kebabs and parathas here. Different from what other customers get,' he told me proudly.

'Are these "beef" kebabs?' I asked, using the English word.

'Beef?' he asked.

'*Gai ka*,' I explained, wanting to know if they really used cow meat.

'*Nahin. Bhaains*,' he replied, confirming my suspicion that the restaurant uses buffalo meat after all.

The bigger-built of the two, whose name was Ashok, did all the talking while his friend kept smiling. It seemed like that they had decided to take me under their wing.

'Wait, I will tell them to get our special kebabs and parathas for you too. The ones we get,' offered my new friend. I smiled happily and then we chatted while our order was prepared. We spoke about my job as a market researcher and they asked me about job satisfaction in my field. Our conversation was cut short by the arrival of our kebabs and parathas.

The paratha was thin and muslin-like. It was made in the manner in which rumali rotis are made – by placing the flattened dough on an upturned wok placed on a fire, which is why it is called ulta tawa ka paratha.

I broke a bit of the kebab with a bit of the paratha and popped the combination into my mouth. The first bite brought a smile to my face.

The sheer delicacy of the soft minced meat, formed into

thin kebabs, near pâté-like in consistency, with its slightly chargrilled and smoked edges, wowed me. This must have been the 'special touch' that Ashok promised. The spices of the kebab mixed with the residual heat of chillies was tantalizing and yet not overwhelming. The kebab held me in its spell.

It was just the sort of simplicity in taste that I am willing to travel the world for.

I was in a happy place, as were my dinner mates when they saw the expression of bliss on my face. They were so happy to see my enjoyment that they refused to let me pay. My dinner was on them, they told me.

This was, in fact, a story which was repeated a few more times in the big-hearted city of Lucknow. I had to struggle, often unsuccessfully, to get people to take money from me. It was as if all the honest and humble eateries of Lucknow, and the people there, had decided to adopt me.

After dinner my new friends introduced me to the elderly gentleman at the counter, Haji Raheez Ahmed. His father was known as Tunday Kababi, I was told, who had set up this restaurant almost a century ago.

They had hit on a winning formula here with the kebabs and parathas and had stuck to it – neither expanding their menu nor spreading themselves thin. These are simple principles which made so much sense. This is how legends are made.

I said goodbye to my new friends and traced my way back through the long alley in the dark. The promised dust storm was flaring up and added to my sense of adventure as I headed back for the night.

 Tip: This alley is not accessible by car, so be prepared to walk a bit.

TUNDAY AGAIN IN THE MEAT MARKETS OF AMINABAD

My Tunday tales didn't end that night at Chowk. A couple of days later I landed in Aminabad and went out in search of lunch.

I was told by folks on Twitter that I *had* to go to Aminabad if I was looking for the meaty marvels of Lucknow. There was of course the big daddy of them all, Tunday Kababi, located there. Some even say that this is the original outlet and not the Chowk one. In fact, more people knew of this outlet than of the one at Chowk.

You can't miss Tunday Kababi when you enter Aminabad.

Unlike the original one, which is hidden away in the depths of time at Chowk, the 'newer' Tunday outlet stands bang in the middle of Aminabad and dominates the lane. In front of the restaurant is a big tava with kebabs being made on it by the minute. A man sits in a corner, making parathas, while a table fan kept by his side cools him. The saffron-coloured shirmals, local breads whose dough has milk and saffron mixed into it, are made in another corner. They also dole out a technicoloured biryani for customers.

I walked into the restaurant. This was different from the basic hall outlet at Chowk. Even though the Aminabad outlet was also very spartan in ambiance, it was air-conditioned and divided into sections. The overall look was grey and dour and yet the atmosphere seemed lively. Here, the crowd was mainly families and tourists.

The decor consisted of pictures of film stars. Among them was Shah Rukh Khan with his 1990s haircut and jacket with the sleeves rolled up, Anil Kapoor in his pre-Oscar and MI4 days, in a bathrobe of the sort that heroines of the '80s would wear, and some other modern faces from Bollywood. I realized that this was the Tunday hall of fame – these were celebrities who had eaten there.

I spoke to the gentleman at the counter while I was there. His name is Muhammed Usman. He told me that he is the grandson of Tunday Kababi. Mr Usman confirmed that the 100-year-old shop at Chowk, which his father manages, is the original Tunday outlet. The shop at Aminabad, where he sits, is about thirty years old. Most of the other 'Tunday' restaurants, according to him, are owned by folks who have used the Tunday name but have nothing to do with the family. Mr Usman just shrugged when he said this. Copyright infringement didn't seem to keep him up at night. In fact, you will now see Tunday outlets all over the country, in Gurgaon, Mumbai and other locations.

I placed my order with the waiter who came to me. The service here was not as chaotic as in the Chowk outlet. My order was a plate of bade galoutis, which is what the grand old man Tunday had started his empire with, and shirmal – a sweet, orange-coloured bread.

For the first time I had a table to myself in Lucknow. I didn't know what to do with the sudden solitude of an empty table! Luckily, the food came soon. I tore a bit of the shirmal and scooped up a bit of the kebab and popped it into my mouth.

With the very first bite I smiled broadly just as I had smiled the other night at the other Tunday's. My smile broadened as the warmth and finesse of the delicately spiced kebab and the hot, soft and crisp-at-the-edges shirmal embraced me. It was a burst of meat-and-carbs goodness, which filled me with abundant happiness.

With each bite I marvelled at the sheer culinary artistry that had gone into what I was eating. I took each bite with increasing anticipation and subsequent ecstasy.

So to return to those pressing questions – Is Tunday's overrated? Are its best days over? Is it a tourist trap?

Well, all I can tell you is that the hot bites of the bade galouti and shirmal that I had at both Tunday outlets were the standout experiences of my trip to the city of many gastronomic delights, Lucknow.

A SWEET ENDING

To satiate my sweet tooth on one of the nights, I went to Moti Mahal, the sweet shop just outside my hotel at Hazratganj. I had earlier seen a group of people eating kulfis at this shop and there were some who were eating imartis and rabdi too. The imartis looked like fat and chunky versions of jalebis, similar to what is called amritti in Kolkata. These are deep-fried whorls which are soaked in sugar syrup and then served. A mix of gram and rice flours go into the batter and some mix crushed dal too.

The imarti at Moti Mahal was piping hot, having been freshly fried and dunked into sugar syrup, then served with cold rabdi. It remains to this day, one of the most amazing mithais I have ever had. The combination of the searing hot, juicy and crunchy imartis with the cool milky rabdi was divine, and its taste lingered on long after the rest of my trip to Lucknow became a distant memory.

I had hot gulab jamuns there the next night on a Twitter recommendation. They were sweet, chubby and very comforting. I preferred the imarti though.

What struck me as most interesting was that even though it was close to midnight, there was so much life on the streets of Hazratganj. There were families eating sweets at Moti Mahal, children dragging their parents along to ice-cream carts and groups of people standing at paan shops, chatting away. A happy place.

To me, Lucknow is all about great food and hospitality. It's

a city whose people will go to great lengths to make you feel at home and comfortable. It's also an impressive blend of old-world romance, like you find at Chowk, and a modern Indian feel, which you find at its heart at Hazratganj.

It is indeed a city where all are welcome and where every meal is momentous and memorable.

FOOD WALK

👣 *The brunch walk*

Go to Vajpayee Kachori Bhandar and have piping hot kachoris with chhole. Then head to Aminabad. Pop into Tunday's there for kebabs with sweet shirmal flatbreads. Then go to Wahid Biryani next door for some delicious mutton biryani. Finish your lunch with a paan at the local paan shop.

👣 *The dinner walk*

Start this trail at about 6.30 p.m. Go to Ganj and have pani ke batashe at one of the many stalls. Then drive down to Chaupatiya Chauraha to try some biryani at Lallaji's food stall. He should open by 7.30 p.m. Then go to Chowk. First try some tikki and matar chaat at Dixit's. Then walk down the narrow lanes to the Tunday's at Chowk for freshly made mutton kebabs and parathas. Head back to Ganj and end your night with imartis and gulab jamuns straight from the wok at Moti Mahal sweet shop.

 Tip: Hiring a car/cab would help you for both trails. Try to do these walks in winter if you can, as the food is pretty heavy.

THE DELIGHTS OF DELHI

Over the years I have noticed a bit of a Mumbai–Delhi rivalry between those who live in these cities. This rivalry between the cities extends itself to food as well. Despite being a Mumbaikar, I must admire Delhi-ites for their unabashed love for food. They have the advantage of history when it comes to food as well, since Mumbai, in its modern form, is a comparatively younger city.

Delhi is special to me, as it is where my mother grew up after she was born in Dhaka. My late grandfather used to work in the city and consequently it was the first city I had visited in India as a kid. So I have a lot of fond memories of the place. As an adult, work took me to Delhi often, as a lot of market research focus groups happened there and I had clients based in Delhi too. Then my brother and sister-in-law moved to Gurgaon, which is part of Haryana but near Delhi, and I would try to visit them whenever I could. Now that they have a daughter, all my trips to Delhi will be at the disposal of this little princess.

Over the years I have eaten out a fair bit in Delhi, and in Gurgaon, but there are a few localities that fascinate me more than its glitzy new-age restaurants. To name a few – Connaught Place, the core of Delhi, where my grandparents used to take me when I was a child; Chittaranjan Park, the Bengali hub; and, of course, Old Delhi, which is supposed to be the Mecca of Delhi food.

The thing about Old Delhi is that people will tell you that many of its iconic eateries are overrated tourist traps. So what does an outsider do? If you are lucky, you will have good-natured souls to guide you, and that's what happened when I finally made it to Old Delhi. It's a lot more accessible now with the Metro and in my case I had blogger friends who offered to pick me up and show me around.

I have Anurag Mehrotra to thank for taking me to Old Delhi for the first time. He is a foodie who believes that there is more to Old Delhi than Karim's. When I asked him about Old Delhi eats, he offered to take me on a food safari, something I had wanted to do for years.

EXPERIENCING THE JOY OF SLOW-COOKED FOOD

Our first stop was a tiny shop called Kallu Nihari, which had tons of people thronging it. This shop doles out nihari from 5.30 p.m. and its stocks get over before 6.30 p.m. Nihari is a classic meat-based dish from the Muslim community of India and is most famous in cities like Lucknow and Delhi.

Anurag introduced me to the owners of the shop as a food writer who had come to eat at their establishment all the way from Mumbai. A few smiles appeared in the crowd on hearing this and I was able to part the proverbial Red Sea and go inside the shop.

The heat from the open ovens hits you the moment you enter the small shop. Workers were putting the nihari together. They took out the shank meat, marrow-filled bones and animal fat from three different steaming pots and assembled them, serving the final dish on a plate. There were a couple of men sitting on the edges of a tandoor oven (yes!) and putting rotis inside to bake them. I tried to click photographs inside the kitchen but the heat seared me, fogged the camera lenses and the spices made my eyes smart.

Now imagine sitting inside and cooking there day in and day out!

There were evidently a few food lovers around who couldn't wait to eat, who sat in the heat inside and pounced on the nihari the moment it was served to them. For my part I found the heat difficult to bear and stepped out. We met Kallu Miya, the owner of the shop, and his son. Kallu Miya had been running this place for about 20 years after moving from his earlier location.

'*Main Kallu ke naam se mashoor hoon* (I am well-known as Kallu),' he introduced himself to me, a big grin lighting up his face.

'*Mera naam Kalyan hain* (My name is Kalyan),' I replied. '*Aur school mein main bhi Kallu ke naam se mashoor tha* (And in school, I was famous as Kallu as well).'

My Hindi sounded like French to him, I am sure, but we chatted away like old friends.

It was our lucky day. Unlike many others who made long journeys to Kallu only to find that the elusive nihari was over, we managed to get plates of nihari and soft, plump, freshly baked tandoori rotis to eat them with.

I hurriedly dipped my finger into the nihari and my finger almost got scalded. Then I took a piece of roti and began mopping up the curry. The meat, which was cooked over six hours, gave in lovingly to the gentle pressure of the roti. It was so soft and tender.

I took a bite. I was immediately overwhelmed by the intense heat of chillies and the robust, meaty flavours of the mutton which, combined with the soft roti, created one memorable mouthful.

I asked Kallu Miya if nihari referred to just the cut of meat or if it was a way of preparation. He said that it is the use of the marrowbone, with the meat around it, that characterizes this rich gravy-based dish. Hours of cooking softens the meat and is the secret behind its charm. He uses water buffalo, that is, bade ka gosht in his shop. You can also get mutton nihari at places such as Karim's, but I'm glad that Kallu's buffalo nihari was the first one I tried.

Some people have told me that the word 'nihari' comes from the word 'nahari' and refers to a morning repast. Evening worked better for me, though, as I am not a morning person.

The warmth of Kallu Miya's welcome, and the grandeur of the food served in his humble yet very popular shack was the perfect start to my introduction to Old Delhi.

I was really sad to hear that Kallu Miya passed away a few months later due to ill health. He was a true star of Delhi's food landscape and Old Delhi will never be the same for the devotees of his nihari without him. I count myself lucky to have been able to taste his fabulous food.

 Tip: Nihari makes for a great breakfast dish too and it is perfect on a Delhi winter morning if you can wake up early enough for it.

THE GASTRONOMIC KULFI STOP

Meat fest done, we headed for our next stop, to cool down the passions raised by the nihari and prime us for the rest of the trip.

We crossed the Turkman Gate, which is one of the many gates in Old Delhi, past carts selling what looked like the tiniest potatoes in the world and others selling grapefruits, past a hardware shop with a goat frolicking in front of it, past buildings and gates with intricate architecture, while the setting sun shrouded the grime of our surroundings.

This was the Delhi of the Mughals.

It had begun to drizzle but we forged on undeterred.

We reached a kulfi shop named Lala Duli Chand Naresh Gupta at Sita Ram Bazaar. It was a quiet shop and the owner was sitting in the corner. He was a gentleman of few words but he did tell us that this shop was more than 40 years old.

The first on the plate was the mango kulfi.

I was expecting a flat disc of kulfi like the ones we get in Mumbai but I was in for a surprise. One of the attendants at the shop opened the fridge and took out a mango. A whole mango. A frozen mango.

He meticulously peeled the mango, put it on a plate and sliced it. There it lay on the plate, looking like the Sydney Opera House, with a filling of kulfi inside!

They apparently use a machine to take out the seed of the mango, then pump the kulfi mix inside the mango and freeze it. Meet the Heston Blumenthals of Delhi. Mind you, this was a simple 40-year-old shop and not a modern Indian high-end restaurant.

You are given a spoon to eat this with but the slicing of the kulfi makes it easier to eat, as the texture is hard and icy, not creamy. The initial bites of the kulfi sent shivers through my gums as the mango was too cold. I couldn't taste anything as my tastebuds were numbed by the chill of the dish.

The magic began once the mango began to thaw a bit. The sheer genius of combining chilled raw mango with the creamy filling of kulfi was as cutting-edge as gastronomy could get – and yet it was an old technique here.

Next up was the phalsa kulfi.

I was wondering how this local berry would be served in kulfi form and when the attendant took the kulfi out of the mould, I saw that it was nothing like the milk-based kulfis that I was used to. This fruit-based kulfi is crushed and served as a sorbet. One bite of the kulfi and I was taken back to a dessert I had had in the Italian restaurant of The Trident Hotel, a five-star in Mumbai's Bandra-Kurla Complex. It was very similar to their cassis sorbet and I told the owner about my observation. I don't know what he understood from my 'Bengali Hindi', but he replied saying that his was the original!

 Tip: Try the fruit-based kulfis or the mango kulfis first here as the milk-based ones are more easily available at the other places too.

After the meaty nihari, the kulfi break was just the palate cleanser we needed. Refreshed, I now wanted to try some of the famous Delhi chaats. There is a theory, after all, that says that chaats were an Old Delhi innovation. I couldn't come to the home of chaats and not have chaat, could I?

CHAATS AT EVERY CORNER

After a short walk we reached what looked like a huge spaceship-like orb which was covered with grime. This was the Chawri Bazaar Metro Station.

Beside that was a shop called Ashok Chaat Corner.

It is a tiny shop, which reminded me of the chaat shops near Vile Parle Station at Mumbai. Like Kallu Nihari, Ashok too was surrounded by a large crowd of hungry people waiting to place their orders. There were four men sitting inside the shop, mechanically churning out the dishes on offer with practised precision.

I ordered a dahi papdi chaat. I took a couple of bites of the chaat and was immediately wowed by the mélange of tastes and flavours in it. Cold, crunch, sour, salt – they were contrasting flavours and textures and yet in harmony. All the ingredients of the dish balanced each other out. It's surpising how fulfilling the simple ingredients of curd, masala, chutney, boiled potatoes and crisp papdi can be. I did find the salt a tad in excess, however, which seems to be typical of Delhi chaats.

The thing with street food such as chaats in India is that everyone has their own favourites. While Ashok looked pretty crowded that evening, some Delhi-ites have told me that there are 'better' chaats available at other places. I admit that I don't have the seasoned chaat palate of a Delhi-ite but this tasted pretty good to me.

When I had finished eating my chaat, Anurag said, 'You know, the real thing is at Hiralal down the road. They make an aloo chaat which is my favourite and they are famous for a chaat where they scoop holes in the aloo and add fruits into it.'

'I don't want to overeat. I need some space for kebabs. I can't lose followers by tweeting about so many vegetarian things,' I replied wryly.

But Anurag convinced me to try it out, since I had the opportunity to be in Old Delhi. I couldn't find fault with his logic and we headed towards Hiralal for more chaats. It was just 200 metres away and we reached quickly. It was a much quieter shop than Ashok's. The sons and grandson of the founder are still manning the shop and wielding their magic on their flat-iron tava, maintaining a tradition of 120 years.

I ordered a plate of aloo chaat. Cubed boiled potatoes were first put into hot oil till perfectly fried, then tossed in a spicy chaat masala and placed on our plates with some toothpicks to pick them up with.

The potatoes were crisp on the outside and soft and delicious inside. Once again a tad salty. I was once told that the reason for the comparatively high level of salt in the food in Delhi was that it was believed that the salt helped people perspire and keep them cool. But if you leave the saltiness aside, this was another truly royal dish.

We set off from Hiralal's down dark, crowded lanes. Dusk had set in but Old Delhi was full of life and colour.

 Tips: Do read up on the best chaat shops if you like but be warned, opinions can vary quite a bit on this. My advice is to look for a shop with a fair bit of crowd around it.

FINDING THE MILK OF HUMAN KINDNESS

We then headed to Bade Miya ki Kheer, a place that is so popular that the kheer often gets over early, I was told.

We walked down the quiet lanes under a persistent drizzle. On the way we stopped to take photographs of some little children with toothy grins who requested us to click their snaps.

At last we saw the Bade Miya ki Kheer signboard at the end of the road. The shop was brightly lit with neon lights. There were a few spartan tables and chairs inside, making it look like an inn for weary travellers. It seemed to speak of a time long gone by.

'Bade Miya' himself greeted us with a smile and a twinkle in his eyes. Thanks to his long white beard, he looked as if he might have been at the shop since Sher Shah's time. When I asked him about how long he had been in business, he told us that he had been making this kheer for decades.

The kheer, a kind of a milk-and-rice pudding, is layered out over a huge flat pan, in which it had been cooked for more than six hours, and then set and chilled. On top is a thick layer of malai, beneath which lies the soft, sweet, and yet not overtly so, kheer. You specify the amount that you want and they then weigh out the kheer and serve it on simple plates. There are benches at the shop where you can sit and have the kheer.

I took a bite of the kheer and basked in the warmth and glow of Bade Miya's labour of love. It was as though the dish was filled with his goodwill; 'the milk of human kindness', as Shakespeare would have said.

The kheer was richer and thicker than the Bengali version of the same dish, called chaler payesh, and I counted myself lucky to have had a chance to taste this delicious version. It is difficult to find, especially in the holy month of Ramzan when stock gets over pretty soon.

 Tip: You can pack the kheer from here to take home. Keep it refrigerated and consume within a day or two.

MOINUDDIN QURESHI'S LEGENDARY SEEKH KEBABS

It was still raining intermittently as we walked towards our last stop – one that was going to be a fitting finale for a great evening: Moinuddin's kebabs.

On the way, we stopped at a mithaiwala where I bought sweets for folks at work. Of course every place in Delhi has a story and this nameless shop's story goes back four generations. The proprietors of the shop saw that my camera was getting wet and considerately gave me a plastic bag for it before we left.

We stopped at another kebab stall to take refuge from the rain. The young man making the kebabs asked me where I was from.

'Mumbai,' I replied.

'Mumbai!' he said with some excitement. 'I would love to go there. I am a big fan of Salman bhai. I hope to see him some day.'

He was thrilled to hear that I lived in the same suburb as his hero did, and that I had seen the actor a few times in the neighbourhood. We left the stall shortly after, with me hoping that the young kebab maker would get to fulfil his dream of meeting his idol someday.

We finally reached Moinuddin's rather elusive kebab shop. The rain and the walk had built up my anticipation of the food. I had been warned that the cook and owner of the stall, Ustad Moinuddin, was a moody person and that he didn't always set up his shop. It turned out to be my lucky evening because Ustad Moinuddin and his son, Imran Qureshi, were both there, working their magic on the skewers of meat.

I ordered seekh kebabs and found that they were well worth the effort it had taken to get there. The kebabs were juicy, flavourful and tasted better than what I have had at the iconic Mumbai kebab joints such as Bade Miya and Do Tanki. I savoured each delicious bite as we stood there with the rain threatening to start once more. You don't need any roti or carb to go with this. It's a plate of pure protein-packed pleasure.

Like Kallu Nihari and Bade Miya ki Kheer, Moinuddin's too is a one-dish shop and, boy, do they excel at making it! I sat hunched on the pavement watching the ustad at work, the night flowing into the flaming embers of his open grill. The aromas of the meat and the damp earth made the experience mystical. My stomach was full and I was happy.

The kebabs at Moinuddin were the fitting finale to my first Dilli 6 odyssey.

 Tip: Nizamuddin, close to Old Delhi, is another great place for kebabs. The mosque also has Sufi song recitals on Thursdays.

BACK TO THE CHARM OF OLD DELHI

I was back in Old Delhi a few years later. It was winter this time. I was completely immersed in food blogging and writing by then and was gradually moving away from my market research job. I was invited by a number of kind chefs, stalwarts in Delhi, to eat in their restaurants during this trip and was kept busy the whole time. The food I sampled in their upscale restaurants seemed to push the envelope in modern Indian food. Yet I longed to get back to the streets of Old Delhi. So I reached out to my friend, Mohit Balachandran. I am a regular reader of his blog, Chowder Singh, where he chronicles his hunt for Indian food.

Mohit is a chef by training and a restaurateur by vocation. He was working on a project close to his heart at that time – the setting up of the SodaBottleOpenerWala chain of modern Irani-café-themed restaurants, championed by restaurateur A.D. Singh. Despite his busy schedule, Mohit made time to accompany me to Old Delhi. He is obsessed with Indian street food, so I really wanted to experience Old Delhi through his eyes and palate!

Mohit picked me up after work and we drove down the deserted wintry streets of New Delhi till the many chicken fry shops of Daryaganj signalled that we were entering Old Delhi. Soon, we were near Jama Masjid and Mohit found a parking lot manned by local youngsters.

We got down and walked past Gate No. 1 of Jama Masjid. I immediately felt like I had been transported into a world that was very different from the New Delhi we had just come from.

We were in a lane full of little food stops – some selling kebabs, some selling fish fry, some offering what I was told was dubious Kashmiri culinary fare. The street was lit up by the bright lights of the shops. There were loads of people around, even women – some of whom were by themselves. As an outsider, I was under the impression that women do not venture out alone at night in Delhi for safety reasons. That was not the case in Old Delhi evidently. There was so much life around.

Our first and possibly the best stop of the night was at Anmol Chicken Corner in Urdu Bazaar. You get 'butter cream chicken' here, which has nothing to do with the iconic Delhi dish, butter chicken. Mohit placed our order: 'Boneless, original-recipe chicken'. I was a bit wary of his order as I normally find boneless chicken too chewy because most eateries use the breast cut but I trusted Mohit. The man at the counter got our chicken ready on an open grill, melted a pot of butter and then applied it onto the chicken. The grill reminded me of the grill used at Beera's in Amritsar.

While we waited, Mohit told me the story behind the Anmol Chicken Corner stall. The apocryphal story goes that the owner's grandfather once used to sell beef kebabs on the streets of Old Delhi. The gentleman then packed up his business and moved on. Then his grandson returned and now sells chicken, rather than beef, to tap into a larger market.

There is another butter cream chicken shop which is famous here called Aslam Chicken, which I didn't get to try. But from what I understood, Anmol and Aslam are the most popular joints here. Apart from these two eateries, there are many chicken fry shops scattered down the street, a trend that has spread rapidly here, according to Mohit.

Our plate of butter cream chicken arrived soon, and we hungrily dug into it. I was held under the dish's spell from the first bite. The meat was amazingly juicy and the hit of butter complemented it beautifully. It reminded me of the Amritsari butter-baked fish that Mohit and I had eaten at the much-celebrated modern Indian restaurant, Indian Accent, the previous night. The little stall named Anmol was, of course, light years away from this fine dining restaurant in terms of ambience, panache, sophistication and acclaim. Yet, the chicken we had at Anmol could match up to the best of what Delhi has to offer in terms of intricacy of taste and texture. I basked in the warm, buttery glow of that brilliant chicken on that cold wintry night.

Once we had wiped our plates clean, Mohit and I walked down the small, crowded lanes past the many food vendors selling their wares. Mohit took me to where the legendary Pehelwan sits. Pehelwan means wrestler, and is the name of a big-built, white-bearded gent with twinkling eyes, who is famous for the biryani that he dishes out on the streets of Old Delhi. He didn't seem to have a shop – just a vessel kept on the street, from which he sells biryani. The biryani that he served us from his cauldron-like pot was of the Lucknowi street food variety. I thought it was a decent biryani for something that was being sold straight from the vessel, though not earth-shatteringly good.

We then went to the Matia Mahal precinct and stopped at a 50-year-old bakery for biscuits, and I bought some to take home too. The name of the bakery is Diamond Pappe. Pappe is the local name for rusks, explains Mohit. The taste of the biscuits were truly memorable and folks back home really liked it. We then traced our way back towards Urdu Bazaar, wondering what to do for 'dinner'. I had Karim's on my mind. Though there are branches of Karim's across New Delhi now, I wanted to go to the 100-year-old branch of the original Karim's here. I was a bit hesitant to ask Mohit, as most Delhi food nerds I know tend to look down on Karim's. 'At least go to Al Jawahar next door,' they say. Apparently, Karim's is no longer 'the way it used to be'. Mohit's verdict was that the food at Karim's was 'good but not memorable', but he agreed that I should try it out at least once.

'Good but not memorable' did sum up our experience at Karim's that night. We had the mutton bade kebab, which was well-spiced and tender, though it didn't hold a candle to the Anmol butter cream chicken in terms of brilliance.

I had recently read Pamela Timms's ode to the food of Old Delhi, *Korma, Kheer and Kismet*, so I decided to order a mutton korma at Karim's as a tribute to her lovely book and to her love for Old Delhi. The mutton pieces were fairly nondescript but the oil-redolent gravy was quite sinfully tasty.

Our last order was for mutton seekhs, which didn't really match up in terms of the juiciness and flavour that I remembered of the kebabs that I had had from Ustad Moinudeen's stall the last time I was in Old Delhi.

The dinner at Karim's was indeed not spectacular but I was still happy that we tried it, as seemed everyone else there.

The seating at the restaurant is distributed into a number of rooms, which were pretty packed, even though it was close to midnight. There was no air-conditioning, but given the cold outside, it was the perfect setting for an oily red meat binge. Service was a bit patchy, possibly because of the crowds but like everyone else in Old Delhi, the folks here were pretty warm.

I noticed that both Karim's and the quieter Al Jawahar had 'no beef' signs displayed like the many biryani shops of Kolkata.

'That's how they can draw in larger crowds and can cater to the tastes of people from all communities,' explained Mohit.

With dinner done, it was time for dessert. Mohit insisted that we go to a vendor who had set up stall opposite Al Jawahar. He was selling freshly cooked shahi tukda – fried bread dipped in cream and served with an extra helping of ice cream – and was surrounded by a crowd of hungry eaters standing in the open, who didn't seem to mind the chill.

One bite of the decadent, crunch-meets-cream, sugary hot shahi tukda and I knew why. This was elixir on a plate. I couldn't imagine handling its richness in the Delhi heat, but it was just what the doctor ordered that cold night.

Satiated, we left Old Delhi, driving past the phantom walls of the Red Fort and down the deserted streets of New Delhi.

SHUBHO SENGUPTA'S ZAKIR NAGAR

Old Delhi is probably the most iconic spot for Mughlai food in Delhi, but I did get to try some more Mughlai food in a part of Delhi that is rarely spoken about in the food media. This was thanks to a Kolkata Bengali who has made Delhi his home, named Shubho Sengupta. He is a former network agency adman and now an independent digital media consultant. He often says that he is not much of an eater, but his offer to take me around one of the most interesting places to eat in Delhi did make me curious. I had seen Shubho upload pictures of everything from Nepali restaurants, Chittaranjan Park pujo stalls to hole-in-the walls eateries online, and I knew that his definition of 'interesting' would be mine too.

So we met one day after we were both done with work. This was at about 5 p.m. on a rainy evening at Greater Kailash-2. I had not eaten since breakfast and I had brought quite an appetite with me.

We got into the car and Shubho began juggling work calls, his cigarette and giving directions to the driver. He was trying to figure out where he wanted to go that evening and he called up a friend to confirm some details. I felt a bit nervous when I heard Shubho talk to his friend. I am used to going out to eat with food-obsessed folks – people who would not set off on a food safari without knowing where they were going to eat and what they were going to eat. This man seemed a bit lost. I had eaten breakfast at 10 a.m. and it was now 5.30 p.m. Was I wise to have left my lunch in his hands?

The roads around us began to change as the car drove on. From the grand manicured asphalt trails of Lutyens' Delhi, we had shifted to a dirt track – the sort of road which would be very acceptable in Mumbai but not in Delhi. We passed what Shubho told me was a university area, commenting wryly that 'some call this the Harvard of Delhi'. He was talking of none other than the famous Jamia Milia Islamia University, and we zipped by its campus to reach our destination.

We finally got out of the car and began to walk through the drizzle. It was a crowded lane with vendors selling utensils, fruits, fish – including rohu, which we Bengalis love – clothes, glass bangles and other miscellaneous items. Some operated from handheld carts and others from makeshift shops. The lane was packed with people, making it near impossible to walk there.

'This is Zakir Nagar. It's nowhere near as famous as Old Delhi or Dilli 6 when it comes to food options. No one comes here to eat,' said Shubho, 'except those who live here. This gives it a sense of peace and quiet, which I love.

'Have you noticed that no one talks loudly here or shouts here and there's none of the "Delhi attitude"? There is a certain no-nonsense touch to this place that I like. I come here once in a while, usually by myself, to eat...' said Shubho, leading me down the winding lanes towards our first stop. It was for nihari – and my excitement for lunch had just begun.

DISCOVERING NIHARI ONCE AGAIN

We had come to a restaurant on the mezzanine area of a building. Well 'mezzanine' and 'restaurant' both seem to be very grand words in the context of the place, but it's enough to say that it was the most 'aromatic' eatery around and the smell of the food made me really hungry.

'This is Javed's and you get excellent nihari here,' said Shubho.

We walked in and it was evident that Shubho was a known face here. The place was packed at 6 p.m. but we eventually got ourselves a bench and a table to share with another diner. Shubho placed our order and we sat down.

Soon, a plump gentleman with a big moustache and a bigger smile got two bowls of nihari and fluffy white rotis to our table. We both fell on the food with gusto. I dipped the soft roti into the curry, which was searing hot, and then broke a piece of the very soft meat from the marrow bone or nalli.

My first taste of the dish told me that I was in good hands with Shubho. I revelled in the robust flavours of the curry and the soft, delicate texture of the meat. Clearly, the art of slow cooking had been perfected here over the two decades that the shop had been in operation. The meat had been cooked for over six hours, I was told. The rotis, served fresh from the tandoor, were hot, soft and delicious. They take their rotis as seriously in Delhi as the French do their breads, it seemed.

More rotis came our way, more of that luscious meat and then the smiling gentleman added some ghee too. '*Taakat aayega*,' he grinned. The ghee added a slight tinge of dairy to the taste of the dish and Shubho and I felt that the nihari was better balanced without it.

Javed's was as good an opening ceremony as one could ask for.

My stomach was happy and I was excited to sample more of Zakir Nagar's delicacies. So we set out in search of kebabs and biryani.

 Tip: Try the nihari without the extra ghee.

DELHI'S VERY OWN MORADABADI BIRYANI

We walked down a few more shops and stopped for some very cheap but delicious kebabs at a stall with no name. I was enthused by the fact that these were so readily available as street food and so appetizing as well. Dusk had set in when we arrived at our last food stop.

This was a shop where a gentleman was selling what they called Moradabadi pulao. We went in and sat down, ordering the chicken pulao, as the buffalo meat version was sold out.

The pulao at this stall was lighter and less greasy than the biryanis I had eaten in Lucknow. The spicing was more delicate, the meat more tender. It was a great end to our food journey for the day.

The pulao and the stall, or anything at Zakir Nagar for that matter, would never qualify as 'fine dining'. The truth, however, is that this is the sort of food that is born from lots of soul and passion. It is food that makes itself truly available to those who love it back.

As we left Zakir Nagar, I said to Shubho, 'I thought you are not into food.'

'I am not,' he replied, 'but when I like something, I eat a lot of it.'

To make his point, Shubho stopped at a corner by a wall where we had shahi tukda for dessert. The dishes packed in a lot of flavour and taste. On hearing the two of us talk in

Bengali, the shopkeeper joined in and said that he had come to Delhi from Bengal.

We left soon after and, on the way past C.R. Park, Shubho pointed out a phuchka cart and said 'next time'.

THE BENGALIS OF DELHI

I did go to C.R. Park a few years later and had the phuchkas too, though not with Shubho but with my brother and sister-in-law.

C.R. Park or Chittaranjan Park or 'Chitto Park', as it is often affectionately called, is possibly the only dedicated Bengali settlement outside of Bengal. From what I gather, it was set up just after India's independence when the Indian government had set aside a piece of land in the national capital for families displaced from what was then East Pakistan and now Bangladesh. Over the years, C.R. Park has developed into a unique Bengali microcosm – almost the equivalent of the Chinatowns that you see across the world.

My brother found a spot to park near Market No. 1 at C.R. Park. We got off and walked into the market complex. The first thing that struck me was the plethora of hoardings and signages in Bengali, then the loud buzz of people speaking the language. As I looked around, the familiar facial features and the many women wearing saris tied in the traditional Bengali style suddenly took me back to Bansdroni Market close to our house in Kolkata. Then I spotted phuchkas and was excited to taste them in the hope that they would taste like the authentic ones from Kolkata.

'Wait,' said my brother with an air of confidence. 'The phuchkas will remain. The ghugni gets over early. Let's find that first.'

I meekly followed him down the alley till we came across a sign which said 'Ghugni and Momos'. We were in luck. The ghugniwala was still there. We ordered two mutton ghugnis and one vegetarian ghugni for the lady.

Ghugni is a Bengali brunch dish, which is often served with luchis as breakfast or with kachoris in roadside tea stalls and humble sweetshops. It is a curry made with Bengal gram, which are called motor in Bengali. These are round and smaller than the chickpeas used in the Punjabi channa or Mediterranean hummus. The curry is made with onion, turmeric, garam masala and chillies. Condiments are often added to it once it's been cooked and at Subrata's stall in C.R. Park, each serving is topped with lime juice, chaat masala and finely chopped red onions. At times, mutton keema (minced meat) is added in ghugnis in Kolkata. Subrata explained that he added whole mutton pieces, as customers need to see the meat to feel satisfied that it is mutton, which might not work if its minced. That would ensure customers got their twenty-rupees' worth!

I took a couple of bites of my ghugni and gave Subrata a big smile. This was delicious stuff. It had beautiful, uncomplicated, pure flavours which warmed the cockles of my Bengali heart. Snuggled within the ghugni were bites of luscious mutton.

'The ghugni is very good,' I said.

'I know. People who leave C.R. Park and go back to Kolkata call me and tell me that they miss our ghugni in Kolkata. My mother makes this ghugni, it's her own recipe,' replied Subrata.

'Please tell her it's very good!'

'She knows,' replied Subroto with quiet pride and self-assurance.

Well, the ghugni was so good that I went back for seconds. So were the phuchkas for that matter, but the phuchka shop closed before the ghugni stall did that day.

Tip: Do have the ghugni with mutton, unless you are vegetarian.

The phuchka stall, my next stop, was called Raju's Phuchkas.

It was 'manned' by a tiny boy called Karan who said that he was twelve years old. The phuchkas that he served (four pieces for ₹10) were at par with the best in Kolkata. Soft, delicate maida phuchkas and not the hard rava puris of Mumbai. Phuchka purists would be happy to know that there were no motors or chholas in the potato mix. There was a separate sweet water which I've seen vendors in Kolkata serving as well, but I wouldn't touch it. For me it has to be *tok jol* – sour water – when it comes to phuchkas.

I had two plates at Raju's, tanking myself up like a camel at an oasis, because I knew I had to head back to the phuchka-less Mumbai.

We were not done with Market No. 1 yet. I wanted to check out the fish markets here – shopping for fish is one of my favourite activities.

We walked into the covered fish market and I just gaped at the sight of the huge cut pieces of katla, gleaming ilish and loads of freshwater prawns. It was one of those rare moments when I envied Delhi. The fish market at C.R. Park's Market No. 1 was almost like a Kolkata art installation in the middle of Delhi. It offered the smells, sights and sounds that can charge the heart of any red-blooded Bengali. We bought our fish and decided to head off to Market No. 2.

We were in search of Dadu's Cutlet Shop, a small eatery whose cutlets are a bit of an urban legend in C.R. Park. Unfortunately it was past 10 p.m. and Dadu (grandpa in

Bengali) had probably gone off to sleep and shut the shop. Disappointed, we went to the Annapurna Sweets shop next door instead. I remembered the name of the shop as the sweets for my aunt's wedding in Delhi, which had taken place in the early 1990s, had come from there. I had a fantastic mishti doi and a lovely dorbesh – which is the Bengali version of the laddoo, but softer and juicier – and packed some sweets for some friends I was to visit the next day. The shop was a lot less glamorous and cheaper in comparison to Sweet Bengal, the main Bengali sweet shop in Mumbai.

 Tip: Cutlets are an evening snack and not a dinner item. Which explains why Dadu shuts early, so don't leave your cutlet-stop till the end.

We stopped for some Kolkata-style egg rolls at a stall before the night came to an end. The rolls were similar to what you get in the suburbs of Kolkata, though they had different sauces added to them. These are different from the rolls that you get in the Mughlai shops of Central Kolkata where the parathas are flakier and where they are served without sauces.

To sum up, the evening consisted of three hours of being surrounded by Bengalis. Three hours of speaking Bengali. Three hours of listening to Bengali. Three hours of shopping for all things Bengali. Three hours of eating Bengali food. Three hours of being Bengali. All in the middle of New Delhi!

So is C.R. Park a slice of Kolkata? Well, to me there were flashes of Kolkata in it, but at the same time, this was different, this was unique. C.R. Park is an entity in itself, it has the soul of Kolkata, but is an independent Bengali settlement in its own right.

I admit that being a Bengali I am biased toward Bengali

food, but I strongly feel that no eating experience in Delhi is complete without a trip to Chitto Park.

CHHOLE BHATURE AND A TASTE OF DELHI'S PUNJABI SIDE

To many, the heart of Delhi's food is the Punjabi fare that you will get there. For outsiders like me, this would often be summed up by two iconic dishes – chhole-bhature and butter chicken. There's a lot more to Punjabi food of course, but these are the first dishes most travellers would like to get their hands on when they come to Delhi.

I always try to have a chhole-bhature breakfast in the sweet shops of Delhi when I am in town. My first such experience was at a sweet shop called Nathu's. It was located close to my hotel on Barakhamba Road, having been suggested to me by some folks on Twitter when I asked for chhole-bhature options close to my hotel. Others said it was too 'commercial' and that I should go to Sitaram Diwan Chand Chana Bhatura, which was open till 5 p.m.

However, practicality won. I didn't have the time to travel to Sitaram. Moreover, I was meeting Pamela Timms for breakfast and Nathu's worked for both of us. I was lucky to have met her that day, as she and her family left Delhi sometime later, when work took her husband back to the United Kingdom. She was a Scottish expat in Delhi, who lovingly chronicled the food of Delhi in her blog, *Eat and Dust*. When I met her, she was in the middle of writing her book.

Pamela greeted me with a cheerful smile. We were meeting for the first time but it seemed like we knew each other for ages. The shop had a clean, near-sterile feel to it. It was air-conditioned. There was a counter for sweets and a seating area with rather functional chairs and tables.

We started our breakfast with lassis instead of my usual choice of double-shot cappuccinos.

We both frowned at the colourful paper cups in which the lassis were served. Where were the *kulhads* – the earthen cups – or at least the standard dhaba lassi glasses? In subsequent visits to other sweet shops in Delhi, I realized that these paper glasses are the norm now. No one seemed to serve lassi the way they used to. Still, the taste isn't compromised and that morning's lassi was sweet, made with full cream and flavoured with a touch of saffron.

Pamela chose an uthappam, the South Indian breakfast favourite. South Indian in Delhi? This was apparently not as strange as I thought it was. A few years later, I went to a similar sweet shop called Evergreen at Green Park with some colleagues from Mumbai to eat chhole-bhature. It turned out that we were the only ones having chhole-bhatures that morning while all the locals were polishing off dosas.

As Delhi-based veteran food writer Sourish Bhattacharya once told me, 'We take our South Indian food very seriously in Delhi.'

Coming back to our morning at Nathu's, I ordered chhole-bhature. I was intrigued to see that they had given black gram channa with the chhole-bhature and not the chickpea-based chhole that I was used to. I often find the chhole served with bhatures in Mumbai to be a tad oily. The chhole at Nathu's was not that oily, though, and had a near home-cooked feel to it.

Bhature are Punjabi breads which are made with maida and deep-fried. They are different from the other Punjabi refined flour-based bread, kulcha, as the latter is baked in a tandoor oven and not fried. The bhature at Nathu's that day had an interesting texture. It was crunchy outside and slightly soft and doughy inside.

When I put up the picture of the Nathu's bhature on Facebook, some locals said that the bhature should have been a fried a bit less. Well, perhaps I hadn't gone to the most iconic place for chhole-bhature that morning. Maybe I had not eaten the perfect rendition of chhole-bhature. Yet, I will never forget the wonderful breakfast I had at Nathu's that morning with Pamela.

 Tip: If you are a visitor to the city, definitely try a chhole-bhature breakfast at least once.

COMING BACK HOME TO CONNAUGHT PLACE

If Calcutta has New Market, and Mumbai has Colaba, then New Delhi has Connaught Place. This is the old city centre which everyone once flocked to. Things have changed everywhere in India now, with cities expanding and multiple downtowns coming up. Yet, for an entire generation of people who have grown up in these cities, these erstwhile city centres are special.

I have memories of being taken to Connaught Place by my late grandfather when I had first come to Delhi as a kid. My aunt, who used to work in Delhi, took me to Nirula's there to have their massive sundaes when I came to visit her later during my college vacations. I would spend a lot of time at Connaught Place when I used to travel to Delhi at the start of my working career as well.

I did not visit Connaught Place much in later years as I tended to spend more time in South Delhi or in Gurgaon. I did go there by myself one evening just before the Commonwealth Games were held in Delhi. The roads had been dug up because of the preparations for the Games. I remember loving the warm vibe of the place and feeling very welcome and at home.

I recently returned to Connaught Place when I was working on the final stages of this book. I was staying at the ITC Maurya Hotel then, and set out into the city one sunny afternoon with Manisha Bhasin, their senior executive chef. I asked Manisha how it felt to be a female executive chef in an Indian hotel kitchen. She said that she had never looked at herself as a woman in the kitchen, just as a chef when she came to work and 'that's all', over the last 28 years that she has worked as a chef with the ITC Hotels Group.

Manisha had offered to take me to Connaught Place to some of her old haunts. Her father used to take her there when she was in school and she used to go there in her college days as well. Now she visits Connaught Place with her husband and children.

Our first stop was Wenger's, the 80-year-old confectionery at Connaught Place, which was originally started by a Swiss family, just like Flurys in Calcutta. Whenever I have been to Wenger's, I have always felt as though I were entering B. Merwans Cake Stop – an Irani bakery famous for its chicken patties – in Mumbai's Andheri. You see the same sponge cakes, packed sandwiches, patties and bakes at Wenger's that you see at Merwans. You see the same smiles on the faces of all inside and smell the same aroma of baking.

My brother loves the sandwiches at Wenger's, but the first thing I picked up on this visit was the shammi kebab, on Manisha's recommendation. It is more like a fried croquette than a traditional shammi kebab. It is spicy and moist inside, and probably the best thing I had that afternoon. Manisha had her favourite chocolate éclair. She didn't mind the cream that burst out of the éclair that made her face look like that of a messy four-year-old.

That's the thing about Wenger's. It's the sort of place that brings out the child in you. Almost everyone I know who has grown up in Delhi has tales of going there with their parents. My aunt's late father-in-law told her that Wenger's was once a sit-down restaurant. Now it is a just a bakery with no seating at all. You can stand in a corner of the shop and munch on what you bought in air-conditioned comfort before you head out.

 Tip: The shammi kebab is a must-try at Wenger's.

We then walked to Keventers – a Delhi institution just like Wenger's, popular with families and college kids for their affordable prices, as Manisha told me. Keventers is most famous for their bottled milkshakes, though they also sell some sandwiches and snacks. It is more like a counter by the wall and not a big shop. There is no seating there and people take their drinks and then have them on the benches close by.

I remembered the owner telling me that they were having legal issues with the name the last time I went there. This time I didn't see any sign which said Keventers. I asked the people queuing up what the name of the place was and everyone said 'Keventers!' But the Keventers at Connaught Place is now called Shake Square.

I had learned, the last time I was here, that this 60-year-old milkshake shop was set up by a family that ran a dairy in Delhi. The Keventers in Delhi has nothing to do with Keventers, the popular restaurant of the same name, in Darjeeling. The light, sweet, cold strawberry milkshake at the Delhi Keventers is quite refreshing, albeit synthetic.

I understand that Keventers has recently rebranded itself and now retails in Delhi's malls.

For our lunch we walked into United Coffee House. This too, like Keventers, is a 60-year-old place. It is a pretty awe-inspiring restaurant and has recently been renovated. With its high ceilings, grey-and-blue tapestry and grand chandelier, it looks straight out of a period film. It is privately owned and has nothing to with the Coffee Board-run Indian Coffee House in Calcutta and other cities. It's a popular stop for locals to take visitors from outside Delhi, though quite a few Delhi-ites go there too, as my brother does whenever he has meeting in CP.

The fare on offer is eclectic – Mughlai, Old Delhi, British club food. We chose keema roti, an Old-Delhi-style aloo dum, Lahori gosht and good old butter chicken.

I couldn't come to Delhi and miss the butter chicken, of course. Each restaurant I have been to here has a different one and I can't choose a favourite because the taste really varies from place to place. I have eaten one at Moti Mahal, whose founders are rumoured to have invented the dish. The butter chicken at United Coffee House seemed spicier than the one at Moti Mahal.

The dish of the afternoon at United Coffee House was the Lahori gosht, which was goat meat cooked in whole channa dal. The light and frothy lassis (a lot lighter than the ones in Mumbai) were great too.

There are several modern restaurants and eateries in Connaught Place now, which have been popping up over the last few years. Food writer Vir Sanghvi writes that the food scene at Connaught Place is seeing a resurgence now.

However, you will still find that the old establishments are as popular today as they once were, perhaps because every generation has been brought here to make new memories.

The love and affection shown to me by the countless kind souls in Delhi sum up the city for me. This is, after all, the city my mother grew up in. That's probably that's why it always feels like home when I come here.

So will this Mumbaikar admit that Delhi is the food capital of India?

The unrestrained love for food that the people of Delhi display makes a strong case for it. Some of the top writers of the food industry are based here and I must make special mention of my dear friend and veteran food critic, Marryam H. Reshii, who always makes it a point to take me to a new interesting place to eat at when in Delhi. The food that I have eaten in the iconic restaurants of Delhi has been memorable. As it has been in the small places tucked in its by-lanes. This is also the city where some of the most exciting new restaurant launches are happening these days. While you get great North Indian food here, Delhi offers a variety of Indian regional cuisines and diverse international fare too.

So, to sum it up, if you love food, then Delhi will surely love you back.

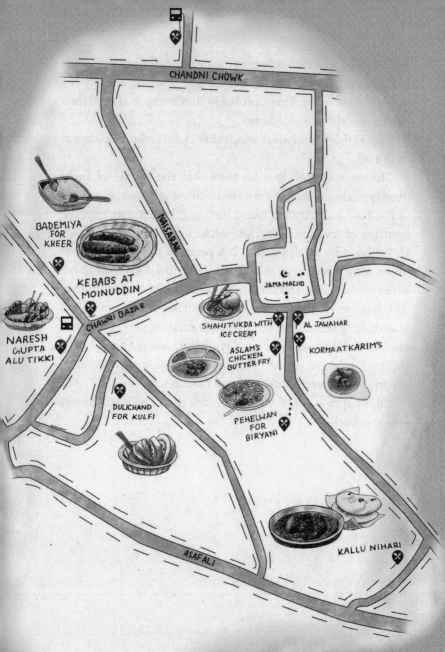

The Old Delhi walk

FOOD WALK

👣 The Old Delhi walk 1

Start at 6 p.m. Begin with nihari at Kallu Nihari, then head to Dulichand for kulfi. Next, go for a plate of aloo tikki at Naresh Gupta. Take a sweet stop at Bade Miya ki Kheer for kheer and end with kebabs at Moinuddin Qureshi's kebab stall.

👣 The Old Delhi walk 2

Start with butter cream chicken at Anmol Chicken Corner. Next, go to Pehelwan for biryani. Walk down the roads and soak in the sights of the flea market, then duck into bakeries such as Diamond Pappe for some locally made cookies. Finish your night with korma at Karim's and then shahi tukda and ice cream at the stall opposite Al Jawahar.

👣 The Connaught Place walk

Go to Wenger's and have the shammi kebab and eclairs. Pop into Shake Square, formerly known as Keventers, for milkshakes. Then head to United Coffee House for Lahori gosht or Kake da Dhaba for butter chicken. Finish your trail with ice creams in Nirula's.

👣 The C.R. Park walk

Go to Market No. 1. Have mutton ghugni at Subrata's. Look for Raju's and have phuchkas. Go to the local grocery stores and buy Bengali spices and condiments. Then head to Market No. 2. Have cutlets at Dadu Cutlet Shop. Finish with sweets at Annapurna Sweets.

THE DELICIOUS AND THE DIVINE IN AMRITSAR

I had visited Punjab at the beginning of my career as a market researcher. At that time I was staying as a paying guest (PG) with a Punjabi family in Bandra, Mumbai.

I was new to Mumbai and this was the first time I was staying away from home. This was also the first time in my life that I was sharing a room with a stranger and I found the experience unnerving. Though, to be fair, my roomie was quite easy to live with.

Then came the biggest shock. The family hosting me was vegetarian. Which meant no non-vegetarian food allowed at home and all the meals served in the house were vegetarian. Ironically, I had had visions of eating tandoori chicken every night when I was first told that the family running the PG was Punjabi. As a Kolkata boy, my clichéd understanding then was that all Punjabis were chicken-loving people. Moving out of home is part of growing up and broadening one's understanding of people from cultures different than one's own and that's what happened to me too in the PG. The Agarwal family, who ran the PG, were Punjabi Hindus and vegetarian. I didn't know how I would survive living in a vegetarian household. I had, after all, grown-up on a non-vegetarian diet. Back home in Kolkata, there was fish for every meal. If there was no fish on a given day at home, there would be eggs 'for protein'. Sunday would be all about murgir jhol or chicken curry.

As it turned out, I stayed with the Agarwals for three years.

Over time I moved from a shared room in the PG to a little cubicle in the hall, made with a wooden partition, which I had all to myself. I was one of the first PG-ites that they had hosted. Soon there were more people at home as PGs and at one point, there were twelve of us in the house, including the family and house help – sharing two toilets. It sounds rather bizarre, but that's Mumbai for many.

Life in the PG wasn't that bad, though. I think I survived the initial years in Mumbai because I stayed in a PG rather than renting a flat with other bachelors. The lady of the house, Mrs Agarwal, whom we called aunty, was a plump Punjabi matron who looked after me like she would look after her own son. She was very fond of me and would tidy my room when I went to work, make my favourite aloo parathas and pakoras on weekends and hand over the TV remote to me whenever I went to the hall. Though our worlds were far removed, she would listen patiently to my frustrations at work or even discuss my affairs of the heart. I moved out just before I got married and she bid me a tearful farewell; we have stayed in touch over the years.

That was my first brush with the large-heartedness of the Punjabis.

When I first went to Punjab for work, I preferred dining at my hotel. My company used to foot the bill for my stay in the four- or five-star hotels when I was travelling for work and in those early days, I was excited to eat the hotel food. Plus, staying in a hotel was a break from my spartan life in the PG. This meant that I would end up having toast and eggs in the hotel coffee shop for breakfast instead of going out and looking for dhabas dishing out fresh kulchas when in Punjab. Consequently I didn't discover much of Punjab's local food scene.

My trips to Ludhiana, Jalandhar and Amritsar came to an end after my initial years as a market researcher. I started blogging about food a few years after that. One of the things that I realized soon after, is how much of what is perceived as 'Indian' cuisine abroad, and even in India, is inspired by Punjabi cuisine. The Punjabi and Mughlai North Indian menu has dominated the Indian restaurant industry for such a long time that in most parts of India, you will still find restaurants that claim to serve 'Indian' food serving what is essentially a token Punjabi menu. Till a few years ago, you would hardly find food from other regions. When it comes to restaurants serving Indian food outside of India, the Punjabi menu still dominates.

The Punjabi community has played a big role in the spread of Indian restaurants across the world. Many of them set up humble dhabas which dot the highways of India. Most of the internationally fêted chefs of India such as Vikas Khanna, Vivek Singh, Atul Kochhar, Vineet Bhatia, Hemant Oberoi and Manjit Gill are Punjabi. As are India's popular TV chefs, such as Sanjeev Kapoor and more recently, Ranveer Brar and Kunal Kapoor. The owners of Delhi's Moti Mahal, started by people who had come to India from Pakistan, are credited for having invented the butter chicken. Dishes such as tandoori chicken, dal makhni, butter chicken and tandoori rotis defined the Indian restaurant experience for many of us for the last decade or so. These are the star dishes that sum up both Indian and Punjabi cuisine for many people, and ten years ago, you would have been hard-pressed to find a restaurant in India that did not have these items on the menu.

I had eaten Punjabi fare in restaurants such as Kwality and Dhaba (which has shut recently) in Kolkata. I eat Punjabi food in Mumbai pretty often too. Crystal at Mumbai's Girgaon

Chowpatty, with its economically priced vegetarian Punjabi food, was a favourite of mine during my early days in Mumbai. Khane Khaas in Bandra, with its homely Punjabi food, has been our go-to place to order in for years.

 Tip: When at a Punjabi restaurant, try the array of Indian breads on offer: Tandoori roti, kulcha, paratha, bhature, rumali roti, missi roti. Punjab is called the breadbasket of India and they do great stuff with wheat.

However, when I started blogging, I was keen to know how Punjabi food actually tasted in Punjab. I wanted to know if there was more to Punjabi food than tandoori chicken and dal makhni. For this, I had to go back to Punjab and try out the local fare.

The universe listened to me. Two food-writing trips to Punjab came up in the same year and I was lucky enough to make it to both of them. The first trip was with Vikas Khanna, who is the chef behind New York's Michelin-star Indian restaurant Junoon, a popular face on Indian food television, a prolific cookbook author and a former Amritsar boy. The trip was organized around the launch of his book on Amritsar in collaboration with Punjab Tourism. In our group was a mix of food writers, journalists and bloggers from across the country.

The second trip was led by Kunal Kapoor, a Punjabi from Delhi, who has worked in leading international hotel chains in India and is now a popular chef on Indian television. Incidentally, both Vikas and Kunal are judges on the Indian edition of Masterchef.

Kunal Kapoor was leading a dhaba trail organized by a media house where a group of food enthusiasts from across the country got together in Delhi and drove down in a bus across Punjab, trying out the dhaba food on the way.

Coincidentally, both my visits to Punjab were centred on the city of Amritsar, home to the Gurdwara Harmandir Sahib or the Golden Temple. The trips, made within a span of four months, were similar and yet very different. The food stops were pretty much the same but because the chefs leading us were different, the experiences varied too. To begin with, both of them brought in two very diverse perspectives to the trips. While Vikas Khanna's Amristar narrative was full of love and passion for its food and was high on nostalgia, Kunal Kapoor's seemed to be more analytical, as it was more of an outsider's perspective. Another factor that contributed to the difference between the trips was that the first visit was in September when it was hot and muggy and the second was during Christmas when it was very cold and much nicer from an eating point of view.

When I met Vikas Khanna on my first trip, it was evident that he loved his hometown. He had spent the first 30 years of his life in the city. Once we began our journey through the streets of Amritsar, he reminded me of an impatient child who wants to show you his favourite toys. He almost dragged us to the restaurants and sweet shops whose food he had grown up eating, while stopping in between to be hugged by his aunts, uncles, cousins, nephews and nieces from the city.

I always look forward to seeing a place through the eyes of its locals; they are the ones who really take pride in the place. Vikas Khanna turned out to be a great guide for our food safari, not just because he has his roots in the city but because of his endless enthusiasm.

The second trip with Kunal Kapoor was just as educational. Though Punjabi, he is a Delhi boy and had made recce trips before the visit. It was clear that he had done his research on the places where we went to eat and we were easily able to understand the food and the experience through his perspective.

I consider myself really lucky to have had the opportunity to experience Amritsari food with such accomplished chefs. I will try to share some of what I got to see there.

FEELING BLESSED AT THE GOLDEN TEMPLE

I had made it a point to go to the Golden Temple during my first visit to Amritsar in the late 1990s. This is the most revered temple of the Sikh community and its origins date back to the sixteenth century. What I remember from my first visit was the deep sense of peace and serenity that engulfed me the moment I stepped in. I remember sitting by the holy lake for almost half-an-hour, feeling very calm and at ease before I headed back to the hotel that evening.

A visit to the Golden Temple was at the core of both my Amritsar food trips a decade later.

The first visit was early in the morning. I hate early starts and cringed when I heard that we had to wake up at 3.30 a.m. so that we could reach the Golden Temple by 4.30 a.m. The aim, we were told, was to see the Palki Sahib ceremony, where they bring the holy book of the Sikhs to the sanctum sanctorum.

Once you reach the Temple, you leave your shoes outside, put your feet into the stream of water at the gate to cleanse them and then walk in. I saw devotees wash their faces with the water in which others had washed their feet. Sikhism teaches humility and the lessons start at the gate, it seemed. When we went there in winter, I noticed that the water was heated. How thoughtful!

It was surreal to see the Temple in the early hours of dawn and I felt a deep sense of calm. We watched the procession of people bringing out the holy book, the Palki Sahib, and I had to admit that there was something poetic in the rhythmic movement of the procession. Seeing the devotion of those around was indeed worth waking up early for.

Part of the ritual of visiting a gurdwara is buying kadaprasad – a sacred food offering. There are counters inside a hall in the Golden Temple where you can buy packets of different denominations starting with ₹10, which is what I picked up.

The aroma of the kadaprasad (made with water, sugar, ghee and whole-wheat flour, according to the recipe in Vikas Khanna's book on Amritsar) was warm and welcoming. I was a tad sleepy at that point and found the heat of the leafy envelope in which the prasad was served very comforting. I went to a corner by the holy lake and wolfed down the hot, ghee-laden, nourishing goodness of the prasad and felt sated and happy.

Then I joined the queue to the sanctum sanctorum in the middle of the lake. I looked around and noticed that people were taking the kadaprasad packets to a counter where volunteers used long swords to push the prasad into a deep container.

Mr Hardeep Chadha, co-owner of Khane Khaas in Mumbai, later told me that this is the sword which is also used in Sikh baptism ceremonies. The name 'kada' comes from the Sikh name for bangles. The *kada* (bangle) and *kirpan* (sword) are part of the 'Five Ks' that the Sikh spiritual leader, Guru Gobind Singh, had made part of Sikhism.

The folks at the counter then put the prasad that they had collected into a deep vessel and gave a small portion of the prasad back to the donor. On the way out, after paying our respects to the holy book kept inside, we were served kadaprasad from the prasad that had been earlier collected at the counters.

That was when the penny dropped. You are not supposed to eat the prasad straightaway, like what I did, after buying it. You first offer it as prasad at the counter and then consume what's left, or take it back for friends and family! A kind Sikh gentleman from Punjab Tourism who was guiding us and to whom I confessed my faux pas reassured me that there was nothing wrong if I ate it. '*Aapne kha bhi liya toh koi dhikkat nahin. Punya phir bhi milega* (Don't worry if you've eaten it; you will still be blessed).'

Still, I went and bought another pack of the prasad to give as an offering.

If you want to have breakfast at the temple, you can go to the langar or the community kitchen, where those who come to the temple are fed free of cost. Vikas Khanna explained that all Sikh gurudwaras have community kitchens. Not all are as grand as that at the Golden Temple but the spirit is the same. He went on to say that the langar of the Golden Temple is the central kitchen not just of the temple, but of the whole city. The food offered here is made from money and ingredients given by devotees. The cooking of it is voluntary too. People across gender, age and social classes come here and help in the cooking. The food is served by devotees too. There are Sikh organizations such as Khalsa Aid who provide food for people in disaster areas across the world and not just in the confines of the temples.

Mr Chadha of Khane Khas in Mumbai had told me that he often goes and volunteers as a cook at the langar of his local gurudwara on holy days, when lots of devotees come in. He has worked as a chef for 25 years, starting with five-star hotel kitchens and then in his own restaurant. Yet, he says, he finds the joy of cooking in the langar an experience that is hard to match.

In large temples such as the Golden Temple, you can expect to be fed round the clock. That morning, for example, they were serving tea and rusk biscuits at the langar hall, while volunteers sat outside and prepped for the afternoon meals.

I had the opportunity to have lunch at the langar when I returned to the Golden Temple a few months later. As I entered the gates of the temple that afternoon, I realized that I was truly fortunate. There are people across the world who pray all their life and work hard to be able to make it to this holy shrine. And here I was, back for my second visit in four months. It was almost as if the gods had taken me under their wing!

This time we got an opportunity to see the cooking process at the langar. There were huge vessels in which the vegetables and dals were cooked. Then there were people sitting in the courtyard and peeling green peas, cleaning spinach, skinning potatoes. To their left were folks washing the used vessels and lunch plates. We then went to the section where rotis were being made. There were people of all ages sitting on the floor and kneading the dough. The dough was then put into a machine, out of which rotis, which were baked and ready to eat, popped out into a conveyor belt. Once the rotis came out, they were placed in baskets. There were people assigned to add generous dollops of ghee onto the rotis. They did this as the rotis would be served a bit later and they didn't want them to become hard. Such is the nature of care and compassion of the *sevaks*.

As I walked past the people who were preparing the food, the one thing that struck me was the look of happiness on their faces. The sense of joy at being able to take part in preparing the food was visible and their bliss was infectious. After a while, I saw the people from my group, including Kunal Kapoor, ditch their cameras and bags and join those who were mixing the dough for the rotis and those peeling the vegetables, wanting to take part in the noble activity of helping to feed others. It didn't matter which religion one was from or which community one belonged to. Humanity was being celebrated here and the experience was truly humbling and inspiring for all of us.

 Tip: If at the Golden Temple, keep some time aside to help in the kitchen. All are welcome to join and it's a very humbling and happy experience.

We then went into the dining hall and sat down on floor-mats to have lunch. First a gentleman drove by in a small motorized cart. Drinking water was pumped out of this vehicle into the steel glasses kept for each diner. We were then served a very simple black dal and some kheer by volunteers, who individually put portions of the food on our plates. Then we were given rotis. Interestingly, the rotis are not put on the plate by the volunteers as with the rest of the food. You raise your hand instead, and receive them in your hands from the person serving the rotis. Chitrita Banerjee, in her book *Eating India*, says that this is a gesture that symbolizes gratitude. The rotis are pretty thick and heavy, so my advice is to start by taking one – you will be given more on request. When you have eaten your meal, you walk downstairs in single file and give your plate to the volunteers who clean them. Meanwhile there are others who mop the floors of the dining hall and clean it for those eating next.

How was the food? A deeply spiritual friend of mine, Talha

Nazim, had once told me, 'I heard that that you are a food critic. My request to you is – please love food, don't judge it. Food should be a source of joy, not an object of criticism.'

His words came back to me while I had the langar. This was food that had been prepared with much devotion and sincerity, then served with so much love. I almost felt as if my soul had been cleansed and my heart purified as I sat in the hall and received the food. This is food that nourishes you and mends your soul. It does taste good, but this is not when you dissect food on the basis of its texture, seasoning, spice levels, on the quality of ingredients used or on cheffing acumen. This is food that transports you into a world where there are no barriers, no preconceived notions, no complaints or churlishness. It's food for the soul.

 Tip: The food at the langar is heavy and nutritious. Start with small servings so that you don't waste any food.

THE QUEST FOR KULCHA

The dish that Amritsar is most associated with is the kulcha, to be specific, the eponymous Amritsari kulcha. I took the opportunity of my Punjab trips to learn more about kulchas and their distinguishing features and also tapped into the knowledge of local foodies.

It all started with Vikas Khanna taking us to his favourite kulcha joint on a hot September September morning, some time after our visit to the Golden Temple.

We were tired. We had earlier gone to Kanha Sweets and had had a lavish Amritsari breakfast of puris and a very interesting sweet and tangy potato curry washed down with

lassi, followed by gulab jamuns at Sharma's (which I will talk about later). We had walked down the lanes of Amritsar in the sultry heat to the Jallianwala Bagh, as a part of a heritage walk run by Punjab Tourism. In between, we had stopped to eat fresh jalebis at Gurdas Ram Jalebi at Jalebiwala Chowk. They were some of the best jalebis I have ever tasted.

It had slowly gotten hotter as the day progressed. All I wanted to do was get back to the hotel and have a shower and rest for a bit, so that we were fresh for the evening. We groaned at the prospect of getting down from our bus and at the thought of more food, for we had been eating all morning. But then this entreaty was from celebrity chef Vikas Khanna himself.

'You will really love the kulcha here. Please believe me. I know you are tired and want to get back to the hotel. Let us stop the bus for just five minutes. I will go down and get you the kulchas. You sit in the AC. Trust me.'

His enthusiasm convinced us to give it a try. So we got down from the air-conditioned cocoon of the bus and joined the chef at the Maqbool Road kulcha shop. It is an open shop with a thatched roof. There are a few plastic chairs where families sit and eat kulchas. Vikas Khanna ran to the oven in which kulchas were being made and said, 'This is where I learned to make kulchas. When I first came here, I was shorter than the oven. They used to use this as a measure for my height.'

We tried the freshly made kulchas and they were indeed way better than the ones we had eaten at a shop near the Golden Temple earlier that morning. Seeing no signboard, I asked Vikas Khanna the name of the shop and he said, 'Just ask anyone for the kulcha shop at Maqbool Road.' I must not have looked convinced at his answer, because he added good-naturedly, 'Does the Taj Mahal need an address?'

I figured out that this shop is also known as the All India

Famous Kulcha. I had first read about it in Pamela Timms's book, *Korma, Kheer & Kismet*.

My next kulcha experience was at a place called Kulcha Land just outside the Holiday Inn Hotel where we were put up. I went there before heading off to the airport.

Kulcha Land has just two dishes on the menu – aloo kulchas and paneer kulchas. You can have a lassi with your kulcha. It is more 'grand' than the Maqbool Road kulcha place, as it has a room where people can sit at plastic tables and chairs. I decided to sit at the tables kept outside by the road, closer to the kulcha ovens, and see life passing by while I had my kulchas. I shared my table with someone named Sukhvinderji, an elderly Sikh gentleman, who is a gram panchayat sarpanch. He told me that he has been coming to Kulcha Land for years. According to him, the owners of Kulcha Land had set up the restaurant 70 years ago near the Golden Temple or *sheher*, as the city centre is called. Thirty-five years ago, they moved to the current location, which is known as New Amritsar. Some local foodies contest this story. Whatever the story may be, I found the kulchas here delicious.

If you are near the Golden Temple you could also try out the 50-year-old shop, Bhai Kulwant Singh Kulchan Wale, for kulchas.

I was a bit intrigued by the kulchas that I ate on my trip. They seemed a lot like the parathas that we had eaten at a place called Murthal, near Delhi. The parathas at Murthal were baked in a tandoor oven. They were not fried on a tava, which is a common practice too. Both the kulchas and the Murthal parathas were stuffed. I went into the kitchen at Kulcha Land and asked the cooks about the difference between the two. They explained to me that kulchas are made with maida or refined flour while parathas are made with whole-wheat flour or atta. The traditional filling of Amritsari kulchas is either spiced mashed potatoes or crumbled paneer. Kulchas are always served with chhole, the spicy chickpea curry. A generous dollop of white butter is added on top of the kulcha when it is served. A good kulcha is crisp outside while the stuffing is soft, moist and flavour-packed, leading to a multi-textural and multi-sensorial culinary experience.

During my trip I found some Delhi-ites saying that the kulchas at Amritsar were different from those in Delhi. I brought up this issue with Jaideep Riar, who lives in Amritsar and who prides himself on going off the beaten track when it comes to food. Jaideep has lived in Delhi too and explained that the Delhi kulchas are stuffed tandoori rotis while in Amritsar they are layered like in a puff pastry. The Amritsar version uses yeast-risen dough, he said. I wanted to know from Jaideep what his recommended place for kulchas in Amritsar would be. He confessed that kulcha choices are very subjective, as the spices and chutneys and stuffing differ from shop to shop, as do people's preferences. His family is divided between the Maqbool Road Famous Kulcha and Monu Kulcha Hut at Loharka Road near Ranjit Avenue. Some of the other kulcha places they go to are Ashok Kumar Kulche Wala at Ranjit Avenue and Harbans Kulcha at Green Avenue. Jaideep has been to some of the smaller kulcha places in the Walled City too, but he feels that when it comes to kulchas in Amritsar, the 'big boys' do it better.

 Tip: Be careful when served a kulcha fresh from the tandoor. It will be very hot. Let it cool a bit or you might singe your mouth.

Amritsaris have an interesting take on why their food tastes different. 'It's the water,' explained Devenderji of Punjab Tourism when he took us on a heritage walk in Amritsar. While describing the food of Amritsar, he kept coming back to the water and how it makes everything taste special here.

The story of Amritsar's water followed me back all the way to Mumbai.

I met a young gentleman named Avinash Gupta while having lunch in Mumbai's Fort district. Avinash told me that he and his brother, Pankaj, run a few restaurants and cafés in Mumbai, including a Punjabi vegetarian restaurant chain called Oye Kake.

The brothers had apparently spent more than half a year in Amritsar researching recipes before opening Oye Kake in 2010–11. Avinash's favourite kulcha places in Amritsar are dhabas such as Sanjha Chulha and Kesar da Dhaba. He liked the kulchas in Kesar da Dhaba in Amritsar so much that he even got a cook who had worked at Kesar for 30 years to be the tandoor chef at Oye Kake.

This tandoor chef insisted that the brothers transport 40 litres of water from Amritsar to Mumbai by train every month to mix in the kulcha dough at Oye Kake. According to the chef, only that would do if one wanted to recreate the magic of Amritsari kulchas elsewhere!

GOING VEGETARIAN IN AMRITSAR

There is much more to Punjabi restaurant food than butter chicken and tandoori chicken, and Amritsar is a good place to discover that. For instance, try the puris at a place called Kanha or Kanhaiya Sweets in Amritsar. We went there for breakfast during the trip charted out by Vikas Khanna. A few months later I went there once again for breakfast in the trip led by Kunal Kapoor. Jaideep Riar recommends it too.

Kanha is most famous for its puris. The puris are fried at the front of the shop in large kadhais or woks and then brought into the large dining hall where the guests are seated. The puris here are like huge round balloons and look more like bhature than the comparatively smaller puris one is used to in other parts of the country. They are not very crisp, though, and are stuffed with a thin layer of spices. The puris are served with channa and a very interesting aloo sabzi. You would expect such curries to be savoury but this has a distinct sweet and tangy flavour to it. The idea is to have the puris with alternating bites of the savoury chhole and the sweet aloo sabzi, I am told.

The suji halwa is also quite famous at Kanha. It is dark red and is a popular breakfast dish, which is had with a milky tea. I would recommend that you try the lassi here as well. Kanha's lassi is a lot lighter, frothier and less sweet than what I was used to in Mumbai and has a layer of malai on top. It's the perfect foil to the deep-fried puris.

Located close to Kanha Sweets is a shack by the wall of a building, which Vikas Khanna insisted we go to after our breakfast at Kanha Sweets. The shop is called Sharma's. You get only one dish here – gulab jamuns. The gulab jamuns are fried in front of you and then dipped in sugar syrup. Gulab jamuns are normally spherical but the ones at Sharma's are flat and slightly disc-like in shape. Vikas Khanna told us that these are the only flat gulab jamuns in Amritsar. Khanna explained that the core of the gulab jamuns are intentionally left slightly undercooked, giving it a textural contrast like no other. Needless to say, the gulab jamuns were really delicious and lived up to the chef's enthusiasm for them.

When we were at Sharma's, I understood the depth of Vikas Khanna's relationship with the establishment. Before he left for New York, he had been a caterer in Amritsar and this was the joint from where he would order his gulab jamuns, he told us. While we ate our gulab jamuns, Vikas Khanna took out a copy of his book, *Amritsar*, which features the gulab jamuns at Sharma's, gave it to the owner of the shop and told him, 'This is for teaching me how to make gulab jamuns.' We left the shop impressed and happy.

Another place that you might want to check out near Kanha is Lubhaya Ram's stall, which Kunal Kapoor took us to. An elderly gentleman with a big smile, named Lubhaya Ram, made us aampapad, a kind of dried mango dish. You can buy packs of aampapad and take it home. People often like to season it with some lime juice or chaat masala.

There are other shops close by, as well as, near the Golden Temple where you can buy other Amritsar food specialities – papads and wadiyas. Wadiyas are dried dumplings made with ground lentils and spices. You can make curries with them.

A mithai that you should try at Amritsar, apart from the gulab jamuns at Sharma's, is the jalebi at a place called Gurdas Ram Jalebi, which dates back to the mid-1950s. It falls in the stretch called Katra Ahluwalia leading to the Jallianwala Bagh. Many locals often refer to the area as 'Jalebiwala Chowk', the square of jalebis. We came across this shop while walking to the Jallianwala Bagh. I wanted to try one of the jalebis displayed on the counter but the gentleman manning the shop insisted on making them fresh for us. Their jalebis were pale yellow in colour, unlike the orange ones one often finds in Mumbai, and I assume this is because they don't add any food colouring. The fresh jalebis were dunked in sugar syrup and then served to us. They were crunchy on the outside with a soft centre. The sugar balance was just right. They were undeniably the best jalebis I have had in my life. To this day, I am so glad that we waited while they made us fresh jalebis at the shop.

Tip: When it comes to jalebis, always, always try to have them fresh off the kadai.

While on the topic of jalebis and gulab jamuns, I must tell you about another sweet item which folks in Amritsar are fond of called fruit cream. Head to a place called Lohgar where there are a few small shops selling fruit creams and bottles of masala milk. They serve you chopped fruits on a bed of fresh cream in little bowls or plastic cups. It makes for a delectable and cooling end to a night of heavy eating. There are no bananas in the cup, though, as they turn black when cut and kept in the open. Heading out after dinner to have fruit cream at Lohgar is quite an Amritsari tradition, I am told.

What about the dhabas? A couple of the more popular dhabas in Amritsar are Kesar da Dhaba and Brothers. Both serve vegetarian food. There is also a Crystal dhaba owned by a branch the family that runs the restaurant Crystal in Mumbai.

We went to the 100-year-old Kesar da Dhaba during my second trip to Amritsar. The dhaba is located in what is referred to as 'old Amritsar'. You walk down tiny, garbage-strewn lanes, which is a sad contrast to the very clean Golden Temple complex close by. Interestingly, non-vegetarian food can't be served in the area around the Golden Temple. Nor can tobacco or alcohol be sold here, in deference to the sentiments of the pilgrims.

The interior of Kesar da Dhaba is very clean, unlike its surroundings. They have an open kitchen area where you can go in and see the food being cooked. The cooks are happy to pose for photographs. The centrepiece of the kitchen is the huge *deg* in which the kaali dal is cooked. They say that the dal is constantly kept bubbling in the pot and that it is cooked for at least six hours before being served. When we got there, it was the end of December and pretty cold outside, so the heat from the bubbling cauldron was very comforting, even at a distance.

We then sat down to eat and were floored by the quality of the food. The magic of slow cooking showed in the delectably flavoured dal; it was served with ghee-soaked rotis which were delicious. The gulab jamuns that we ate that night were some of the best gulab jamuns that I have ever had. I think the cold weather enhanced our experience of the food, which was comforting and filling – winter is the best time to eat the rich food dished out here.

BEYOND TANDOORI CHICKEN IN AMRITSAR

What about tandoori chicken, you ask? Truth be told, I have not eaten tandoori chicken during any of my trips to Amritsar. Nor have I had butter chicken!

What I did have, and loved, is something called bhatti chicken. I had this at a place called Beera Chicken House on Majitha Road. It's a restaurant that Vikas Khanna was very keen that we try out. The food we ate there showed why.

Beera Chicken House is a fairly simple place with an open kitchen outside and a cavernous, non-air-conditioned dining hall. The place looks very nondescript.

Vikas Khanna's order for our group was a dish called Beera's chicken. Incidentally, there was no tandoori chicken on the extensive menu of chicken dishes at the restaurant.

I am not a big fan of ordering chicken dishes in restaurants. We have chicken so often at home that I prefer to go for other meats and fish in restaurants. Plus, restaurants often use breast pieces in Mumbai and they are served tasteless with the texture of cardboard. The chicken at Beera held me in its spell, though. We were served the whole chicken. It had been grilled on a flat open grill (the bhatti) outside the shop and spiced minimally. The chicken was cut into pieces at the table and served with mint chutney. The meat, including the breast pieces, was very tender and juicy. The colour of the chicken was not the usual red which one associates with tandoori chicken but a pale creamish colour instead. The meat combined beautifully with the mint chutney, it was not oily at all, was beautifully seasoned and the spicing was restrained, which enhanced the taste of the great-quality meat. The meat was truly the star of the dish.

We also had some of the fried fish at Beera. The fish of choice in Amritsar is river fish, such as singara and sole. A thin layer of gram flour batter is applied on the filleted and boneless fish, which is then deep fried in mustard oil. Just as the taste of the bhatti chicken was not overpowered by spices, nor was the fish. There was a crunch in each bite that one took and the fatty and indulgent texture of the fish came through clearly.

Located next to Beera, is Makhan Fish and Chicken Corner. While Beera is more famous for its chicken, Makhan is best known for its fried fish. Makhan is a slightly 'grander' restaurant than Beera. They have an air-conditioned section on the first floor and a few tables on the terrace too. It was more crowded than Beera both the times we went there.

I found the chicken fry and the fish fry at Makhan to be a tad spicier than what we had had at Beera and the taste was closer to the tandoori chickens and fish tikkas that one gets in Punjabi restaurants outside of Punjab. A taste the average restaurant diner is more familiar with, so to speak. On both my visits, I preferred the food at Beera, even though Makhan's was also quite tasty.

There was an elderly Sikh gentleman at the cash counter at Makhan who came to speak to us on my first visit, and was excited to know that our group had people from across the country. He insisted that we try the mutton tikka on the house. The dish consisted of goat meat, cut into small pieces and marinated in heavy spices, then fried in ghee. The taste of the dish was indeed heady and I would say that mutton tikka at Makhan's is actually better than the fried fish that it is known for. Interestingly, when I returned to Makhan a few months after my first visit, the same gentleman came up to me with a smile, hugged me and said that he remembered me from my previous visit. Given how packed his restaurant is all the time, this was pretty remarkable.

During my second visit, I asked Kunal Kapoor why most of the fish in the restaurants in Amritsar were fried and why there hardly seemed to be any fish curries around. He had an interesting observation about this, saying that Punjabis are not very intrepid fish eaters. They prefer fish dishes which do not have a 'fishy' taste or texture. He said, wryly, 'Punjabis are not fish-obsessed like you Bengalis. They will eat fish as long as it tastes like chicken!'

Another restaurant that Kunal Kapoor took us to was Surjit Food Plaza on Lawrence Road. This is a largish restaurant located on the ground floor. Both Surjit and Makhan are larger in scale and busier than Beera Chicken House. We tried the mutton tikka here and the biryani, which seemed to be made with chicken curry tossed with basmati rice on a flat tava. Some chefs refer to it as a 'frying pan biryani' to distinguish it from dum biryani, where the rice and meat is cooked together in a sealed container.

We got a warm farewell from the owner here, an elderly Sikh gentleman. He ordered kulfis for everyone in our group and placed his palm on our heads to bless us.

Makhan, Surjit and Beera had all started as hole-in-the-wall shacks about 40 years ago and have grown over time. The menu is similar across the three places, so you can either restaurant-hop or sit at one place and savour the experience. Alcohol is not served at any of these restaurants.

Jaideep Riar has a few more recommendations for non-vegetarian food seekers in Amritsar. These are Pehelwan Fish Corner outside Hall Gate; mutton items (tikkas, brain, trotters, etc.) and tandoori chicken at Pal Dhaba; saag meat at Joginder Dhaba opposite the railway station. These are all hole-in-the-wall operations and would be tougher to find than Beera or Makhan but, as Jaideep insists, are worth a try.

Punjabis are often depicted in popular culture as big-hearted people who are fun-loving and full of life; ready to break into bhangra at the drop of a hat, and who will feed you till food comes out of your ears. I know a lot of this is because of the stereotypes we see in Hindi films but let me tell you, I did come across the famed Punjabi warmth and bonhomie on my trips to Punjab. We were welcomed with a smile wherever we went, whether in a group or alone. Service was warm and everyone was accomodating. Perhaps it has something to do with the holy heart of the city, which inspires and humbles everyone who visits Amritsar and is reflected in their divine food.

FOOD WALK

👣 The green Amritsar trail

Go to Kanha and have puris with aloo sabzi and chhole for breakfast and wash it down with lassi. Step out and have gulab jamuns at Sharma's. Then go to Lubhaya Ram and have aam papad and buy some to take home too. Head to the Golden Temple, where you can savour the kadaprasad. Walk down to Jallianwala Bagh to pay respect to the martys who lost their lives. Stop for jalebis at Gurdas Ram Jalebi Wale on the way. You can shop for papad and wadiya and then head to Kesar Da Dhaba and have kaali dal and rotis for lunch and finish off the meal with gulab jamuns.

👣 The Amritsar meat trail

Go to Beera Chicken House at Majitha Road and have the Beera chicken. Then cross over to Makhan Chicken and Fish and have the mutton tikka and the famous fish fry. Then head to Surjit Food Plaza at Lawrence Road and have the rather unique biryani there. You could also try some more mutton tikkas there. Then go to Lohgar to finish your evening with fruit cream.

A ROYAL AFFAIR IN JAIPUR

I have always been fond of history. It was one of my favourite subjects in school. I used to spend hours poring over *Amar Chitra Katha* comics while growing up in Kolkata, lost in their tales of ancient kings and queens and the battles they fought. Perhaps that is why Rajasthan, the land of the Rajput warriors, is so close to my heart.

I am yet to explore Rajasthan as much as I would like to but I have begun my acquaintance with this magical state through its capital city of Jaipur – to which I have made a few memorable trips and where I have had some brilliant eating experiences.

Warm and friendly people, fantastic hospitality, loads of character and, of course, great food, Jaipur has everything that makes me fall in love with a place and more. My visits to the Pink City challenged many notions that I held of it based on what I had read.

The first time I went to Jaipur was to conduct a market-research workshop. It was the month of November. My colleague from Mumbai and I were dressed in what Mumbai corporates wear while travelling i.e. a formal shirt and a pair of jeans. We got out of the airport, and went to the car which was sent to pick us up. The car started. Then stalled. The engine had conked out and we had to wait for an hour till the resort sent another car, which was fine, except we had come out of the airport and couldn't go back in for security reasons. So we waited in the open and froze under the starry sky. I had forgotten that desert-regions get cold at night, and more so in winter. Muggy Mumbai hadn't prepared us for the cold. My first tryst with Jaipur was anything but as fiery as I had thought it would be.

I didn't eat any local food on my first trip to Jaipur either. Just the usual nondescript resort buffet fare. One morning, I took a rickety bus from the hotel and went to the city centre down bumpy roads (this was in 2005). My bones were still shaking when I got off the bus. I bought a lot of printed long skirts and floral tops for my wife from the local stalls. I was quite thrilled by how cheap everything was but my wife found that everything ran colour, shrank and split at the seams after the first wash. There was a reason why everything was so cheap!

My second trip to Jaipur was again for some market-research work. I had started my food blog by this time, and seeking out local eats had become a big part of my trips by then. I checked out Twitter for recommendations on where to eat at Jaipur. Moon Mukherjee (@moonsez on Twitter) connected me with Gaurav Hajela. Gaurav is based in Jaipur and runs a social-media marketing company. He was very helpful and gave me a lot of recommendations on where to go and eat. I met him a year later at Jaipur when he asked me to speak on blogging at a social-media conference that he was organizing. It was thanks to him that I went to places like Handi and Rawat, where I really enjoyed the food. He also gave me tips on good places to shop at which in, a touristy city, is really important.

It rained on the last evening that we were in Jaipur this time, so much so that the roads were flooded and my colleagues had a tough time reaching the station from the hotel. Rains in a desert? Only then did it really hit me that

Jaipur is not actually in the desert! In fact, my first glimpse of the deserts of Rajasthan finally happened when I drove down to the holy city of Pushkar from Jaipur one morning. Pushkar is a day trip from Jaipur and you can even stop at Ajmer on the way if you have time – which I didn't, as I had to come back to Jaipur and catch a flight to Mumbai. I was impressed by how smooth the roads were and even stopped for a cappuccino at a Café Coffee Day outlet on the way.

I couldn't spend much time in Pushkar as I was on the clock and had to go back and catch a flight. I did manage a little camel ride from the central market to the start of the desert outside Pushkar before we headed back, though. On the way we stopped at a sweet shop where I had the most amazing malpua.

I 'parked' my camel outside the sweet shop at Pushkar and the camel attendant recommended the shop and got me the malpua while I sat perched on the camel. I ate my malpua while still sitting on the camel and took some pictures of the dessert with my DSLR too!

The malpua here was similar to what we get in Kolkata and was vegetarian, unlike the egg-based malpuas that you get in places such as Tawakkal Sweets and Noor Bakers in Mumbai's Bohri Mohalla during Ramzan. Kolkata is home to many people from the Marwari community whose ancestors had migrated there from Rajasthan. I wonder if this is why there is a Rajasthani touch to the malpuas found in Kolkata's Bengali-run sweet shops today.

A TRADITION OF SWEETS AND SAVOURIES

The one place I fell in love with when in Jaipur was Rawat Mishthan Bhandar, and I've made it a point to go there on every subsequent visit to the city. This 45-year-old sweet shop in the heart of Jaipur is extremely popular with the locals and is always buzzing with people. Although it is old, it has kept up with the times and has air-conditioned interiors and décor that's fairly modern. This was one of the places Gaurav told me that I must not miss. The concierge at my hotel agreed too. It is quite the local favourite; even my cab driver knew of the place and took me there without having to stop for directions.

There's a sweet counter at the shop, of course. The sweets seemed pretty popular, as did the savouries, with long queues for both. There were lots of people packing stuff for home but the less patient and more hungry stood by the counter and ate.

My favourite here was the pyaz kachori, stuffed with an incredibly well-spiced potato-and-onion stuffing. The refined flour-based fried crust was nice and crispy. Pyaz kachori is a trademark Rajasthani snack and they make a good rendition of it at Rawat although I have seen pyaz kachoris being sold at almost every street-side stall in Jaipur.

Kachoris are pretty popular not just in Rajasthan but across North India. They consist of different stuffings, onion here in Jaipur, lentils and chillies at other places. This deep-fried treat is made with a refined-flour crust and a stuffing. The outer coating is crunchy and not very thick, while the stuffing is what adds the flavour to the dish. At Rawat Mishthan Bhandar, they have a sweet mava-filled one too. I love the khasta kachori that you get in sweet shops such as Ganguram and Mithai in Kolkata. Back home in Mumbai, I can't get enough of the dahi kachori chaat at Sri Krishna Fast Food in Bandra East.

Another crowd favourite at Rawat is the mirchi bhaji – fat green chillies enrobed and fried in chickpea paste – it is as delicious as it sounds. The chilli is not very fiery for the Indian palate at least. You find a high chilli quotient in many Rajasthani dishes, as it is believed to help cool down the body by inducing perspiration. The mathania chilli is quite legendary in Rajasthan, so you will find its flavour in many dishes here.

I prefer the savoury kachoris at Rawat to the sweet mava kachori but if you have a sweet tooth, you should try that too. And speaking of sweets, you shouldn't miss the Rawat version of the ghee infused, sugar-redolent and honeycombed mithai, ghevar.

 Tip: Don't let the mirchi bhaji scare you. It is not too spicy.

THE ESSENTIAL DAL BAATI CHURMA

Dal baati churma is probably the most famous of all the Rajasthani vegetarian dishes. I have tried it at a couple of places in Jaipur and Pushkar and realized that recipes and renditions can vary from place to place.

In Jaipur, I was lucky enough to try a fantastic dal baati churma at a place called Santosh Bhojanalaya, recommended by my cabbie. It's a no-frills place at the central bus stop. The ground floor is air-conditioned, stuffy and often empty, while the upper non-air-conditioned floor is more popular.

Eating dal baati is an elaborate process for a novice. Luckily, our elderly but very enthusiastic server, Mr Singh, guided me through the process. The baati is a ball of baked wheat flour. You first crush the baati and then add a generous helping of ghee to it. Then there is the dal – black urad in our case – which you pour over the crushed baati. With this we had an aloo curry and a rather spicy, but very delicious, besan kadhi, which is a gramflour-based curry. It was beautifully flavoured, with a touch of tartness from the curd in it. This was to be had with rice. We ended our meal with the sweet powdered churma, which is a mix of semolina, wheat and bajra, ghee, sugar and dry fruits, as Mr Singh explained.

Dal baati churma is an example of how mankind adapts to its environment. This dish is a result of living in the desert where resources are scarce. It is proof that even with limited resources one can come out with dishes that are tasty. There is no reason to not eat well just because one's surroundings are harsh.

I later had dal baati churma at Chokhi Dhani. Chokhi Dhani is a complex outside of Jaipur. It's like a quasi-Disneyland (although much smaller in scale) aimed at tourists. It is a recreated Rajasthani village with all the bells and whistles, including camels and henna painters. You can eat your meals in a dining area under the open skies where enthusiastic waiters in liveried outfits ply you with food while you sit on the ground. The dal baati here tasted different from what I had had at Santosh and the dal was a lot richer in spices and ghee.

At Pushkar I had eaten dal baati churma at a place called Mamta, popular with the local pilgrims. Here, not only was the dish different but the dal was a different colour – a lot more yellow than what I had had in Jaipur!

 Tip: The three dal baatis that I had in Rajasthan were all slightly different from each other. So be prepared to be surprised.

Through conversations with friends such as my former market research colleague, Khushboo Saboo, and chefs such as Ashish Bhasin of the Trident BKC and Chef Minoo of ITC Sonar, who are all originally from Rajasthan, I found out that the constituents of the baati differ from house to house. Wheat flour is used in most houses today, although some still prefer to use the traditional favourite of bajra (pearl millets). The lentils used depend on what's easily available in the region. There are variations in the churma too, depending on taste.

While dal baati churma is now traditionally made at home, historically it has nomadic roots. In the olden days, hunters and pilgrims would carry bajra and dal from home while spending many nights on the road. During stops, they would make the baati with the bajra, roast it and add dal and ghee to the mix to eat. They would add sugar to the leftover baati to make churma. It was a convenient one-pot meal that required very little time and effort.

According to folklore, this dish later became a favourite with the Rajput soldiers, too, while they were out fighting battles.

It's interesting how today we are all raised on the belief that 'food-on-the-go' is a new concept that we've imported from other countries, when in fact traditional 'fast food' like dal baati churma, with its ease of making and its numerous nutritional benefits, have been around for ages – a testament to the culinary ingenuity of our country.

The itinerant life once led by folks in Rajasthan have had a deep influence on their food too. Take for instance the meal I once had at a restaurant called Aapas at the ITC Grand Bharat. The resort is located on the Rajasthan–Haryana border and the chefs there have tried to recreate what they call the Mewati cuisine – dishes which were served to travellers on this road during medieval times in pit stops which were called *serais*. The food was simple in its spices, used local produce and the focus was on making sure that the dishes lasted a long time without getting spoiled, as travellers would pack their meals from these *serai*s and move on. As I have mentioned earlier, chillies were used liberally to make one perspire and thereby cool the body down.

This unique cuisine that developed out of necessity is actually quite delicious!

You also see traces of this culinary intuitiveness in Kathiawadi food from the less-fertile areas of Gujarat. I have eaten Kathiawadi dishes in Soam in Mumbai and have been really impressed by its rich flavours and textural intricacies, which stand out despite the lack of very many vegetables in the region. Like in the Mewati food, chillies, curd, gram flour, ghee and pulses are used in these dishes to create magic.

Some of the dishes that really stood out at Aapas were a bajra-based kebab, a ghee-soaked green moong curry and a light and very subtly flavoured mutton biryani with preserved lime in it.

Even though circumstances might be different today, the Rajasthani food tradition has clearly stood the test of time. I am glad that today's restaurants are taking an interest in reviving and retaining these traditions for the benefit of our palates! Life would not be the same without the dal baati churma.

 Tip: A non-vegetarian version of the baati, called keema baati, is a dish that comes highly recommended by my friends Kurush Dalal and Rhea Mitra Dalal, who had it at a restaurant called Spice Court in Jaipur. The flour dough casing is stuffed with spicy keema and baked into a delicious but heavy dish.

GETTING TO THE MEAT OF THINGS

The popular perception of Rajasthani food among non-Rajasthanis is that it consists primarily of vegetarian food. It is true that a large proportion of the state's citizens today are vegetarians. Restaurants offering Rajasthani thalis in Mumbai, for example, Chetana and Maharaja Bhog are vegetarian. However you will be surprised to know that there's a lot of meat on offer in Rajasthan as well.

Of course, the most famous non-vegetarian dish of Rajasthan is laal maas, where laal refers to the colour of the red chillies used in it. The dish is made of goat meat, which is slow-cooked in red mathania chillies.

The first time I had laal maas was in a restaurant called Handi at Jaipur's M.I. Road. It was recommended to me by Gaurav Hajela. It was a fairly unglamorous place. It wasn't air-conditioned and the seating was quite rustic. The crowd was a mix of locals and tourists, mainly foreigners. The kind waiter was initially a bit doubtful about my ability to handle the heat in the dish when I ordered the laal maas. I assured him that I was used to chillies and that I would be able to take it.

I wondered what the fuss was about even after I took my first bite of the dish. 'It's not *that* volcanic,' I thought. Little did I know that the heat of the chilli creeps up on you slowly and hits you at the back of your throat after the first few bites. Soon, I was sweating like a European in a Turkish hammam. The waiter told me told that laal maas in the more arid parts of Rajasthan is spicier than what is served in Jaipur and that in restaurants they serve toned-down versions, which non-Rajasthanis can stomach. If what I had was the toned-down version, then surely it will take a braver man than me to give the laal maas unplugged version a go!

Dal

Ghee

Churma

Baati

Here I must point out that I don't have a very high tolerance level for chillies so do not let me scare you off from discovering laal maas.

Speaking of the friendly and proactive waiter at Handi, one thing that I observed in Jaipur is that everyone I came across was pretty friendly. They open up readily and try to help you when they realize that you are a tourist, or an outsider, and are interested to know more about their lives. It is truly a hospitable city.

 Tip: If you are not sure about your ability to handle the chillies, you can request them to customize the spice levels for you.

At Handi I also tried junglee maas – literally 'wild meat' – a dish recommended to me by ad legend and proud Rajasthani, Piyush Pandey, when I met him at a work do. It so happened that I was going to Jaipur the next day and I knew that Piyush Pandey was quite well-known for his love of all things Rajasthani. I thought of asking him for some Jaipur food tips but was hesitant, as I doubted whether one of the leading creative gurus in India would bother to spend time with a market-research professional like me, whom he didn't even know. After all, we market researchers are not really favourites of the 'creative types', or so it is believed. I went up to him, and conveniently avoided mentioning that I was a market researcher, and instead asked him about where to eat in Jaipur. He patiently and enthusiastically spoke to me for the next five minutes, giving me detailed advice on where I should go to eat in Jaipur and what I should eat there. Food united us in a way ad pre-testing never could!

The junglee maas at Handi turned out to be a really

wonderful dish and I enjoyed it more than the laal maas there. It consisted of succulent pieces of goat, first slow-cooked in ghee and then finished in a pan over an open flame with dry red chillies, salt and more ghee, making the dish all about the taste of the meat rather than the heavy spices. This is the sort of dish where you keep things simple and let the goodness of great produce do all the work.

The junglee maas at Handi was a dry dish, like the Bengali mangsho bhaaja, which is basically fried mutton. However, the version I had a couple of years later at the ITC Grand Bharat had a gravy. Chef Shivneet, the executive chef of the resort, explained that the version with gravy is called salan and that the non-salan, the drier one, was what was once preferred by the hunters and soldiers of yore when they were on the move.

After my meaty eats at Handi, I stepped out and saw a far more humble food joint across it. I went to see what was an offer. As soon as I got there I met a policeman who was having a thick lassi by the counter. When he asked me where I was from, I explained that I was from Mumbai and was on a mission to discover the best that Jaipur had to offer.

He looked at me while settling his bill and insisted that I try a lassi. It's never a good idea to say no to the constabulary and I ordered a lassi. It was cold, thick, delightfully sweet and refreshing. It could be paired better with the laal maas or junglee maas than any wine ever could, if you ask me.

 Tip: Follow up fiery Rajasthani meat dishes with a sweet lassi.

On my next visit to Jaipur, I met Sudipto Chakravarty. Sudipto is a Bengali gastroenterologist from Jaipur. His claim to fame is his huge Twitter following where he is known as

@ROFLIndian. He is also an avid wildlife photographer. On hearing that I was coming to Jaipur, Sudipto said we must meet. Turned out, the good doctor – a man of big smiles – loves to eat too. I met him on the trip where I had come to Jaipur to speak at Gaurav Hajela's social-media conference. It turned out that Gaurav and Sudipto knew each other well and the love for food united us.

The first place Sudipto took me to was Niros, a place Piyush Pandey had also mentioned to me earlier. Niros is air-conditioned and more posh than Handi. I ordered the laal maas here too and found that the meat was more tender than at Handi and the sauce less spicy. In that sense, it was more 'tourist-friendly'.

Sudipto also took me to Moti Mahal for dinner, where we had some lovely chicken kebabs stuffed with minced meat. Despite living in Jaipur, Sudipto's Bengali diction was quite good and it felt good to chat with him in our mother tongue. The Jaipuri warmth I had spoken of earlier seemed to have rubbed on to Sudipto too. He was quite the cordial host and took time off from his busy schedule to show me around.

Back in Mumbai I caught up with Ashish Bhasin, who is the executive chef at Trident BKC in Mumbai. Ashish is a Punjabi who grew up in Rajasthan and used to spend his school holidays in Jaipur. He had worked at the Uday Vilas in Jaipur at the start of his career. Ashish told me that Rajasthan had quite a heritage of meat-eating, due to its Rajput warriors and hunters. He pointed out that most meat of choice at the time were quail, wild boar and venison, which are illegal to consume in India now. I did have a recreated Rajasthani venison dish in Vivek Singh's Cinnamon Club in London. Vivek told me that he uses venison, which is widely available in the UK, to bring back Rajasthani hunter dishes on the table, which was something that he couldn't do while working in India.

Ashish also told me that there is more to Rajasthani mutton dishes than laal maas and junglee maas. For example, something called safed maas, or white meat, where goat meat is slow-cooked with assorted nuts. He even told me about a dish called khad murg, in which chicken is cooked underneath the ground, just as the bedouins used to cook sheep underground in the deserts of Arabia. This was a practice followed by soldiers in Rajasthan at night when out at battle. Cooking the chicken in pits, dug under the ground, would ensure that the soldier's location wouldn't be given away to the enemy, as there was no open fire by which to be spotted.

More fun than fried chicken in a bucket at a multinational fast-food joint, huh?

Interestingly the imprint of Rajasthan's meat legacy is slowly spreading across the country. The mutton in the Rewati mutton biryani and the junglee maas at the ITC Grand Bharat in Gurgaon comes from goats reared in Rajasthan. As does the goat meat used in the Sunday brunch mutton curry at the Taj Land's End in Mumbai. Anirudhya Roy, the executive chef of the hotel, told me that the goat meat from Rajasthan is of a better quality, as the goats get to graze on open fields – unlike the goat meat available in congested cities such as Mumbai. Exercise leads to happy goats with well-developed muscles and, eventually, better-tasting goat meat. So, somewhat ironically, the goat meat from the predominantly vegetarian state of Rajasthan is now prized by chefs across India.

THE OLD AND THE NEW

During this trip I also tried something called kanji vada, which I hadn't heard of before, at a stall just outside the Hawa

Mahal Palace in Jaipur. I was attracted by the people queuing up at the stall and joined them to see what was happening. The gentleman running the stall was selling something that looked like dahi vadas floating on what looked like a rasgulla sugar syrup from a bucket in a cart. A young couple had just ordered some and some other folks were eating these out of paper cones made with newspapers. On asking what these were, I was told that the dish was called kanji vada.

These vadas are made of ground moong dal, deep fried and then soaked in a water infused with mustard, chillies and tamarind – called kanji.

It detoxes your system and is good for the liver, the gentleman manning the stall told me. This fact was something, Sudipto, later vouched for. After taking photographs, I asked for a serving.

What followed was a five-rupee pop of bliss. The pairing of the spongy moong dal vadas with the tantalizing cold, piquant, tangy, mustard-seed-speckled water was a sheer work of art. The dish was brilliantly refreshing and turned out to be the best thing I had on that trip.

The focus groups that I conducted in Jaipur among the city's young and affluent made me realize that as outsiders, we like to hold on to this image of Jaipur as a quaint, medieval place in which one should have pyaz kachori and then lassi on the streets, in between palace-hopping and buying glass bangles in ancient bazaars.

Well, the youth of Jaipur today would rather go to Café Coffee Days or Costas in malls for cappuccinos and then go to Barbeque Nation for grills or the latest pasta joint for a spaghetti aglio olio.

I realized that there are two Jaipurs – one of its tourists, embedded in the past, and the other of its youth, with global aspirations. But regardless, the city manages to challenge my impressions, each time I visit, and delights me with its varied, and adaptable cuisine.

‼️ The all-day trail

If you have a day in Jaipur, start off at Rawat Mishthan Bhandar for its kachoris for a delicious breakfast. For lunch, you can head to Santosh Bhojanalaya to eat dal baati churma with the locals. Moti Mahal or Handi are good choices for dinner, where you must try the laal maas and junglee maas. Wash it down with lassi from the stalls opposite.

THE RICE BOWLS OF HYDERABAD

Whenever there are discussions on biryani on social media, you have folks from Hyderabad joining in, vociferously claiming that the biryani in their city is the best. I once conducted a Twitter poll to find the best biryani city in India and there was a 90 per cent plus vote in favour of Hyderabad. I had never seen such a polarized Twitter poll before – it almost made me feel that the folks from Hyderabad had galvanized the local support to vote for their beloved biryani! They are indeed really, really passionate about their biryani.

The other dish that Hyderabad is associated with is haleem. This slow-cooked dish, made with wheat, millets, lentils and shredded meat, is difficult to find in local joints in Hyderabad except during the holy month of Ramzan. It is a very heavy dish after all and is best enjoyed after a day of fasting. The recommended places for haleem in Hyderabad, according to food bloggers I follow, are Pista House and Shah Ghouse Restaurant.

I hope to make it to Hyderabad during Ramzan some day to taste the haleem. I had once attended a house party in Mumbai where my friend – and food fanatic – Dr Pradeep Rao had carried back to Mumbai biryani and haleem made by a lady in Hyderabad. The haleem was truly delicious and its meaty flavours were quite hypnotic. I was lost in its taste the entire night.

During my last trip to Hyderabad, I vowed to sample the city's cuisine and was amazed by all the food that I had there. I began, of course, with a search for biryani. What was interesting was that rice played a starring role in all meals.

ON THE HYDERABADI BIRYANI TRAIL

I had been to Hyderabad a few times at the start of my market-research career. In those days, as I had earlier said, I didn't explore the local food scene much while travelling and used to prefer ordering room service.

More than a decade passed by before I returned to Hyderabad. By then I had begun to appreciate local flavours and would head out seeking them whenever I travelled.

I was particularly keen to explore the biryani scene in Hyderabad. I had come to realize by then that each city in India has its own unique form of biryani. I had grown up on the one from Kolkata which was dry and subtly spiced, which is why the Mumbai biryani, which has a wet masala paste running through the rice, doesn't appeal to me. Restaurant owners in Mumbai often label this biryani as 'Hyderabadi biryani'.

Was this claim correct? That's what I wanted to find out when I headed to Hyderabad.

While I waited to board my flight, I put up my plans to explore the biryanis of Hyderabad on Facebook and Twitter and soon suggestions came pouring in. First from the non-Hyderabadis, who all said, 'Go to Paradise'. Paradise is Hyderabad's most famous biryani restaurant after all.

Then the locals from Hyderabad spoke up and most mentioned a host of names other than Paradise. Many spoke of Hotel Shadab in the old city. Other places mentioned were Café Bahar, Green Park, Bawarchi and Dine Hill. Armed with this information, I boarded my flight.

Then, while on the flight to Hyderabad, I had a completely new experience. I actually spoke to the person in the seat beside me!

People talk fondly of the train journeys of yore and the friends one made with one's co-passengers during long-distance train rides – playing cards together to while away the time and sharing food one had packed from home. All of that has changed with plane travel. Today we get into the aircraft and look for our seats, then bury our noses in our laptops or books or the in-flight magazine or just nap during the flight without even looking at who's sitting next to us. If food is served, we quietly suffer through the horrible in-flight food on offer. When the plane lands, we switch on our phones, grab our bags and dash off. No words are exchanged in between.

I had never struck up a conversation with a stranger on a flight before this. Perhaps my doing so this time had something to with the fact that everyone on board the flight seemed to be in such good spirits, beaming away despite the late hour.

My co-passenger sat down and took out a mobile tablet. I asked him whether he found it user-friendly, as I planned to buy my mother one so that she could access Facebook and write her blog. (Yes, she started blogging in her late sixties and now can't get enough of it.)

I found out that my neighbour, whose name was Gaurav, was a Hyderabad local. I took the opportunity to ask him about the food there. From mobile phones and tablets our conversations turned to one on the merits of the biryanis of Café Bahar versus those of Paradise.

Café Bahar at Basheer Bagh was a place that Gaurav said served biryani 'the way locals like it'. Not like Paradise, he said, which apparently had 'sold out'.

'Ask for extra masala at Café Bahar. That's how locals eat it. The biryani is cooked in layers of rice, meat and yakhni (wet masala) in a sealed pot. It's called kachchi gosht biryani. It was invented for soldiers by the army cooks who would march along with them, carrying goats, rice and loads of masala – just to make biryani for the troops while on campaigns. The biryani at Paradise is for outsiders. They cut down on the masala.'

At that point I didn't know whether Gaurav had got his facts right, but it sure did make for an entertaining story. And it's always important to hear the food opinion of others. As it turned out, Gaurav was a food aficionado. He proudly told me that his wife made great biryani at home. He was a Hindu married to a Muslim lady and food was one of the many things that united them. I could appreciate that. As a Bengali Hindu from Kolkata married to a Parsi from Mumbai, my food palate has expanded, as has my world view, through our marriage. Gaurav and I both agreed that being in interreligious marriages had enriched our lives.

Before getting off the aircraft, Gaurav told me that I should go to Southern Spice instead of restaurants such as Angeethi and Rayalaseema Ruchulu for Andhra food. I listened very carefully, for, over the one-and-a-half-hour flight, he had convinced me that he knew his food. However, biryani was what I wanted to try out first.

I zeroed in on Café Bahar for its biryani, thanks to Gaurav. I also wanted to go to Hotel Shadab since it was highly recommended by many Hyderabadis on Twitter and Facebook. And though all the locals said it was no longer the same, I felt that I should try out Paradise too. With these restaurants in mind, I began my exploration of Hyderabadi biryanis.

CAFÉ BAHAR: A PROMISING START

I went to Café Bahar with my market-research colleagues. I couldn't get my lunch-mates enthused enough to sit in the bustling non air-conditioned section, despite the cool weather outside so we headed up to the air-conditioned section.

It was lunch time and Café Bahar was packed and we had to wait a bit for a table. The atmosphere inside the restaurant had the same easygoing warmth which I had begun to associate with Hyderabad. I have had opportunities to interact with local Hyderabadis over the many trips I have made to the city – while conducting focus groups, at client meetings, in shops and restaurants. The people I met in Hyderabad came across as warm and very passionate about food, especially biryani. Once they figured you were interested in food, they would go out of their way to tell you where you should eat. On an unrelated note, they would also tell you where to go and buy pearls (which the city is famous for) from!

The person who took our order at Bahar that afternoon, Bijoy, was a Bengali from Kolkata who had come to Hyderabad for a job interview, had fallen in love with the city and stayed back. He said that he divided his time between his jobs, at a software place, and at the restaurant. He said he was happy to see two Bengalis in our group that afternoon.

Our plates of biryani arrived and the first thing I noticed was that they were topped with boiled eggs. The sight reminded me of restaurants in Kolkata where the 'special biryani' is served with boiled eggs. There was no potato in the biryani, though, unlike in Kolkata or even Mumbai. The amount of rice on the plates of biryani was daunting and we wondered whether we would be able to finish the food. Before anyone at the table could reach for the food, I clicked pictures of the biryani, which made my Bengali colleague from Hyderabad say, 'I have never seen someone take photographs of food before.' My colleague from the Mumbai office, to which I belonged, had eaten with me before and gave him a resigned look. He knew the routine. Photos first. Then you can eat.

After I had photographed the food from every possible

angle, I finally let my colleagues dig into the biryani and helped myself to some too. The first thing that struck me was that each grain of rice was firm and separate. The flavours of the meat and spices in the biryani didn't overshadow the aroma of the good-quality rice used in the dish. The spices of the yakhni were not overtly high on oil or chilli heat. I also noticed that the spices in the biryani appeared in clumps throughout the rice. They tickled my palate but didn't overwhelm me. They imparted a touch of tanginess that flirted with the senses. This was far different from the biryanis in Mumbai, which are often drenched in thick masala. The Hyderabadi biryani was more like a symphony, each component complementing the other. The interesting thing about the biryanis of Hyderabad is that they are served with a crushed peanut-and-chilli-based gravy called mirchi ka salan, and a light yoghurt sauce called dahi chutney.

After tasting the biryani I could understand why Bombay boy Kunal Vijayakar found the Hyderabadi biryani bland and not up to the spicier ones he was used to in Mumbai. He had told me that he missed the masala that was there in the biryanis of Mumbai and 'resented' the fact that he needed a mirchi ka salan to accompany the Hyderabadi biryani. In case you are wondering what Kunal makes of the even lighter biryanis of Lucknow and Kolkata, well, as he once told me on Twitter: 'THOSE ARE PULAOS AND NOT BIRYANI!' In fact, there was one local Hyderabadi at our table and he told us that the Café Bahar biryani was different from 'Andhra biryani', which, according to him, was more like a 'pulao'.

The rice-to-meat ratio in Café Bahar's biryani was similar to Kolkata, with 80:20 in favour of the rice as compared to 60:40 in Mumbai. The Hyderabadis are known to love their rice and can eat it in copious quantities.

The taste of the biryani at Café Bahar reminded me a bit of the biryani at Lucky Hotel in Mumbai. Lucky in Bandra is probably one of the most famous biryani joints in the suburbs of Mumbai. It was founded 60 years ago by the grandfather of the current owner. The founder had come to Mumbai from Iran via Gujarat before setting up Lucky.

I have a hypothesis for the similarity between the two biryanis. Café Bahar, like many other famous biryani places of Hyderabad, is an 'Irani' place. Muslim Irani, not Zoroastrian Irani – I have learned that there is a difference between their cuisines. Lucky is Muslim Irani too. So though the two restaurants, Bahar and Lucky, are in two different cities, they are united by their Iranian heritage. The main difference between the two biryanis is the presence of the boiled egg in the biryani at Bahar and the potatoes in that of Lucky. Lucky does have more masala in the biryani, though, but you can request them to put less masala as per preference.

The biryani at Café Bahar was a reminder of the fact that the dish evolved to its current form after the Mughals came to India and introduced their favourite dish, the pilaf, to the locals. As the dish travelled through the country, it donned a distinctive cloak in each region. As a Bengali who has grown up on the biryani of Kolkata, I must confess that the biryani at Café Bahar did not pull at any emotional heartstrings. However, personal taste and heritage set aside, it offered quite an elegant experience, though the restaurant was pretty simple in terms of décor and pricing.

So did my first taste of a popular Hyderabadi biryani live up to the hype around it?

If I look at it dispassionately, I was impressed by the intricate spicing that burst out in between each bite that I took. The slight tanginess added to the flavour. The rice was nice and firm, the way I like it. The mutton very tender. Though Bahar is a pretty simple, no-frills restaurant, the biryani there spoke of remarkable culinary flair and expertise.

Did I love it? I am too devoted to the biryani of Kolkata for that.

 Tip: Try to enjoy a bit of the biryani by itself before adding the dahi chutney and the salan.

There is more to Café Bahar than just biryani; it has quite a varied menu actually. I ordered the bheja fry or goat's brain fry too. The brain was cooked to a nice and tight consistency, which I liked in comparison to the more amorphous squishy ones that I have had in Mumbai. There was a firmness to the offal which gave way to creamy goodness with each bite. The bheja had been tossed in a simple but interesting sliced onion and green chilli base. This was definitely one of the best restaurant renditions of this legendary dish that I had ever come across.

However, my dalliance with Hyderabadi cuisine had just begun. I was still to visit many of the other local legends and after my experience at Café Bahar, I couldn't wait to try them out.

PARADISE LOST?

I made it to Paradise the next night. I thought that for the sake of honest research I should stop there once, even though the locals warned me not to expect much.

There are restaurants which define cities for the average food-loving traveller. Britannia & Co, the Parsi restaurant in Mumbai, for example; Tunday Kababi in Lucknow; Karim's in Old Delhi; Nizam's in Kolkata; MTR in Bangalore. You could say that Paradise and its biryani would be the equivalent of these for Hyderabad.

Local 'foodies' often rubbish such places and say that there are newer and better places to eat. They say that the old classics are no longer as good as they used to be. Yet, as a tourist, you will feel that your trip has been incomplete if you don't go to these landmark eateries when you visit their cities. Moreover, the places recommended by 'those in the know' could sometimes be deep in the city and difficult for one to reach during a short trip.

My suggestion is simple. Try to go to places suggested by locals if you can. You might find some great food that way. However, don't feel shy of trying out 'touristy' places. There is a reason why they became popular. For all you know, you might enjoy them more than those who have gone there many times and are bored of the restaurants. Most importantly, if you have gone to one of these places, and have had a good time, then don't let others make you feel bad about going there. No one has the right to dictate where or what you eat! At times you will have great meals while travelling, while at times very ordinary ones. With time you will learn how to score more of the former.

My colleagues and I reached Paradise after work. It was close to 11.30 p.m. when we had left work, so we were worried about missing the chance to get dinner there. The gates of the restaurant were shut by the time we reached, which was close to midnight, but my local colleagues managed to get us into the ground-floor section through the back door. The restaurant was packed even at that late hour. Despite it being the fag end of the day, the waiters were going about their job with smiling faces with the hospitality that is so quintessentially Hyderabadi. We ordered the chicken biryani, based on the recommendation of our waiter.

Interestingly, Mr Mohsen Husaini, who owns Lucky Restaurant in Mumbai, tells me that their chicken biryani is more popular than their mutton one. This despite the fact that most biryani 'experts' will tell you that mutton is the way to go when it comes to biryani.

Our Bengali colleague shook his head in disapproval when he heard that our local colleague and I had ordered two biryanis for the three of us. The Bengali gent was right. We had over-ordered. One plate was enough for the three of us!

It is possible that we didn't finish the biryani because it did seem rather average to us. The rice was not very flavourful. There were no bursts of spice, unlike the Café Bahar biryani. Nor were there any boiled eggs in it. The piece of chicken that was in the biryani was gigantic, and had as few signs of flavour in it as are there of life on the moon. It seemed to have been fried separately and put into the rice mix later, and it was definitely not in harmony with the rice.

Paradise is the oldest of the three restaurants I went to for biryani in the trip. It was established in 1953 and I am sure it had seen its glory days. Even now, the restaurant looks crowded but the biryani we tried was the least impressive of all the biryanis that I had during the Hyderabad trip. Those who had warned me that I could do better than Paradise in Hyderabad seemed to have called it right.

Perhaps they were literally scraping the bottom of the barrel that evening in Paradise at that late hour. Maybe mutton would have been a better pick than chicken. Maybe someday I will come across a modern-day fan of Paradise who might convince me to go back again.

You can't put a legend down, though, and I hope the folks of Paradise regain their glory once again.

Tip: If you are looking for biryani at Hyderabad and can't go to the old city, just head to Café Bahar at Basheer Bagh.

AND THE WINNER IS...

I resumed my biryani trail the next morning, but not before a stop at the Golconda Fort. I huffed and puffed my way up the steps of this abandoned fort and my guide, Shiraz, told me that we had climbed 375 steps to reach the top and were 480 feet above where we had started from. The steps were fairly steep and, according to Shiraz, were earlier meant for horses to climb.

I was staying at the Park Hotel during the trip and had had a rather heavy breakfast of medu vada, sliced Gruyére, waffles and cappuccino before setting off that day. The climb up to the fort ensured that my meal was digested and I was ready for biryani by the time I reached the top. According to my cab driver, Shiraz had charged me more than he should have. Well he might have charged me more but he did bring to life the desolate walls of the fort with his stories and opened my eyes to the centuries of harmony between Muslims and Hindus in Hyderabad.

'Everyone from across religions lives peacefully here, busy with their work...these politicians are the ones who spoil everything,' Shiraz had said when I asked him if there were any tensions between the Hindu and Muslim communities of Hyderabad. I couldn't find fault with his logic.

My next stop was Charminar and the 'old city'. Charminar, built towards the end of the sixteenth century, is to Hyderabad what the Red Fort is to Old Delhi, the India Gate is to New Delhi, the Victoria Memorial is to Kolkata and the Gateway of India is to Mumbai. It's a monument that symbolizes the city.

Charminar is located in what is referred to as Old Hyderabad now. Visitors tend to go to the old city only if they come to Hyderabad as tourists. It's less likely that you will visit that part of the city if you have come on a work trip, as it is pretty far off from the newer parts and the traffic can be quite difficult. Thankfully, my work was to take place in the evening so I was free during the day. I hired a car and made use of the opportunity to head to the old city. Though I must confess that it was not the historical monuments that lured me to the old city, but the lure of finding the 'best' biryani in Hyderabad!

I once had a discussion on Twitter with food writer Marryam H. Reshii and others on what attracts us the most when we visit a new city. For Marryam, it is the lure of visiting local markets, especially spice markets. For me, it is the chance to visit small family-run restaurants and street food stalls to get a sense of the city. We were united in our assertion that museums are low on our priority list when we travel. In my case, it is the people I meet and the food I eat on a trip that are more memorable than the statues I might see.

I got off the car at the laq market where Ashok, my driver, told me to bargain furiously for the famous bangles on display. All I wanted, though, was to take photographs of the marketplace. I brandished my camera and captured the faces of people around me, shops, fruits, spices, the Charminar, the Mecca Masjid and, of course, bangles. Somewhere down the line I heard one shopkeeper point to me and tell another, 'He is from the Discovery Channel.'

I can imagine the people in the old city of Hyderabad being used to the sight of media folks taking photographs. Every inch of the street looked as if it were out of a Steve McCurry India photograph. The colours were vibrant, the smiles infectious, the buzz invigorating, the crowds bustling.

The area spoke of an India frozen in time – an India some of us in the more modern parts of the country have forgotten.

I walked past the shops selling bangles, peeped into the shops selling pickles (the fiery Gongura pickles are famous here), looked into grocery shops to see the spices and the varieties of rice on display and also at the utensil shops, which had large metal degs in which biryani could be made.

 Tip: You can buy a variety of local pickles to take home from Hyderabad as well as biscuits at Karachi Bakery.

The only time I stopped was at a bhelpuri cart. This was an unplanned halt. I took a photograph of the cart, bemused to see it in Hyderabad, as I come from Mumbai, which is known as the city of bhelpuri. This street-food dish is usually made with rice crisps, a melange of spices, peanuts, spicy red-chilli-based chutneys and sweet and tangy tamarind and jaggery-based chutneys.

I wasn't sure how the Hyderabad version would taste but Ramesh, the wiry owner of the cart, exhorted me to try his bhelpuri. 'Don't pay me if you don't like it,' he said. Inspired by his pride and passion I agreed to try some bhelpuri, even though I didn't want to eat into the space reserved for biryani in my belly. The plan was to have a polite bite or two, pay him and move on. This was till I took my first bite.

Ramesh's bhelpuri was so different from anything I had ever had before, be it the bhelpuri of Mumbai, or even the hallowed jhalmuri of Kolkata. The simple yet ethereal, light and citrusy mix that Ramesh conjured held me in its spell. Ramesh smiled on seeing my visible delight as I kept saying 'wah, wah' in between bites, just as the erstwhile rulers of Hyderabad must have said when courtesans performed in their palaces. A bon vivant moment, I believe it is called.

I paid Ramesh for my snack and walked into the Mecca Masjid nearby. This is a historic mosque, considered to be one of the oldest and holiest in the vicinity. I walked down the courtyard and then into the mosque, marvelling at its crumbling yet decadent architectural beauty, making a point not to disturb the devotees who were praying there.

I have been agnostic most of my life. I do follow the Nichirin Daishonin sect of Buddhism and am a member of the Soka Gakkai International, but that's more a philosophy aimed at happiness and peace and doesn't have any rituals or priests, as it is an organization of laypeople. Yet, when I walk into places such as the churches of Spain or the mosques of Turkey or the Golden Temple in Amritsar, I always feel a sense of calmness and serenity. I felt that at Hyderabad's Mecca Masjid too.

I was jolted back to reality when our cook Banu called me from Mumbai, asking me what was to be cooked for dinner. She will take instructions on what to cook only from me, as she feels that I run the kitchen at home and not my wife! Banu's call reminded me that I had come to the old city in search of biryani and I realized that it was time to leave the holy mosque and head out on my pilgrimage.

I asked for directions on the streets, which is sometimes a better idea than using Google Maps in India, and headed towards Shadab. Shadab, like Café Bahar, was founded well after Paradise. I was told that it came into its own only after the restaurant at the Medina Building opposite it shut down.

I was eating alone at Shadab, unlike at the other biryani outings where my colleagues were with me. The restaurant was packed and I got a table only after a short wait. I soon had to share it with a gentleman called Umar, who told me he was from Chennai. This experience is typical of old-school restaurants in India, where people share tables during lunch hours. I don't mind this, to be honest, and have often had interesting conversations with strangers over my meals. My lunch at Shadab was no exception.

Mr Umar emphatically told me that the best biryani in India was to be found in Chennai! So much for Hyderabad, Lucknow and Kolkata, I thought.

We both chided our friendly waiter when he got us the huge plates of biryani.

'This is too much rice for one person. Why don't you serve less, even if you don't reduce the price? This will go to waste,' we exclaimed in unison.

Yet at the end of the meal, both our plates were wiped clean. That's how good the biryani was. Yes, Shadab was the winner in my book for the Hyderabadi biryani stakes. It didn't have the boiled eggs that the Café Bahar biryani had. It didn't have potatoes either, but then none of the Hyderabadi biryanis had them.

What tipped the scales in Shadab's favour, over Café Bahar's version, was the excellent quality of the mutton in the biryani. The meat was even more succulent and moist than that at Bahar. The biryani even had the odd marrowbone that one could suck one's way through to er...paradise. The masala in the biryani was once again subtle. It served as the perfect foil to bring alive the beauty of the rice. Another element that distinguished this biryani was the inherent heat of crushed chillies in the rice, which was missing at Bahar. It was a perfect tribute to the chilli- and rice-loving people of Telangana and Andhra Pradesh.

I ended the meal with the satisfaction of having tasted what is arguably Hyderabad's best biryani. I walked down the

stairs after politely declining the smiling waiter's request to try out the special Irani tea, as I was much too stuffed to eat anything else.

 Tip: Biryani portions in Hyderabad are pretty huge. Feel free to pack what's left and take it back home. Some say it tastes better the next day!

On the way out I got to enter the prep kitchen of Shadab thanks to the kitchen-manager – a kindly white-bearded gentleman. This was the kitchen where the rotis were made and the tea of the Irani chai was brewed and then boiled with sugar. This was where the biryani, which was cooked on the upper floors, was taken out from huge metal vessels and assembled when orders came in.

I took photographs inside the kitchen for my blog and then smiled at the elderly gentleman and said, 'Chacha, the biryani that I just had in your hotel ("hotel" being the word used to describe restaurants in India at an earlier time) is the best that I have had in Hyderabad, thank you.'

He broke into an even bigger smile than before and exclaimed, 'Please wait,' then called out to a gentleman sitting at a table close by and said, 'See, you said Paradise is better, this gentleman has come from Bombay and he said ours is the best. Look at his big camera. *Yeh media-wale hain.*'

I didn't bother explaining to him that I was a blogger who had come to do market research and was not from traditional media, as he had just claimed. Instead, I graciously accepted the cup of steaming hot Irani chai that the gentleman offered to his Paradise-loving friend and me.

We sipped our tea together, united in our love for biryani.

THE ANDHRA DELIGHTS OF SOUTHERN SPICE

I headed out from my hotel, in search of the Southern Spice restaurant the day after I had had the epic biryani at Shadab. Nitish, the concierge at the hotel where I was staying and a local, approved of my choice of Southern Spice. The restaurant is older than the other popular Andhra restaurant in Hyderabad, Rayalaseema Ruchulu, according to Nitish. He told me that the branch at Hyderabad's Banjara Hills is the original one. That's where I was headed that day.

Over the years I have noticed one thing about the plush hotels in India. If you ask the staff there – the concierge, chefs, butlers, front desk folks, etc. – about local food, you will find someone who will happily direct you to eateries within the cities.

The weather was pleasant that afternoon and after asking around a bit, I located Southern Spice. The restaurant is located in what looks like a residential area in Banjara Hills, which is quite a premium locality in Hyderabad. It is a bit hard to find the restaurant but once you enter it, the crowds inside will tell you that food lovers know how to find it.

The elderly manager at the entrance told me that I would have to share a table and assured me that Southern Spice did have the best Andhra food in town when I told him that I had come from Mumbai in search of the best food that Hyderabad offered. I like a man with passion and belief in what he does and I was excited at the promise of the meal that was to follow.

I was led to a table. Three waiters came to my table one after another and asked me if I was alone. I smiled back, refusing to be cowed by the judgmental posse of waiters. A while later, they got someone else to share my table – a gentleman who, through his lunch, demonstrated just how much Hyderabadis can eat. Chicken curry, a stack of rotis, fried prawns, a mound of rice...the moderately sized gent finished everything served to him with aplomb.

I steered myself away from the North Indian thali mentioned in the menu, which included cream-of-tomato soup and tandoori rotis. After flipping through the pages of the menu I finally found the section with the vegetarian Andhra thali, which had been recommended to me by many people before I came to the restaurant. The gentleman taking my order offered to tell me how I should navigate my way through the thali when the food came.

In addition to the veg thali, I chose a country chicken dish called natu kodi iguru – chicken in a thick gravy. The maître d'hôtel warned me that the chicken had bones, before he headed off to the kitchen, which was great, because I feel chicken always tastes better on the bone.

Soon, a smiling waiter served me my thali and buttermilk. All the dishes were not brought at one go.

First came fluffy, soft, slightly cold puris with a coconut cream-based vegetable korma on the side. Then came a mound of steamed rice. The waiter told me that I had to eat the rice with each of the dishes brought out sequentially and that he would guide me through this. In case you were wondering, we spoke in Hindi, which is pretty widely spoken in Hyderabad.

The rice had to be eaten first with the fragrant ghee, which had been mixed with an assortment of powdered spices, and a mango pickle that was high on the chilli quotient, I was told. Then the rice was to be paired with the other pickles on the table. Next, the rice was to be had with a thick dal. Two dry-ish vegetable dishes of cabbage and beans followed. The next dish to be brought to the table was a sambar – the staple tangy, lentil-based dish typical of the south of India. This was nowhere as sweet as the sambars served in the Udupi restaurants of Mumbai. The sambar at Southern Spice was rather thick in consistency and was full of vegetables such as brinjal, drumsticks, pumpkin and beans and could be a meal in itself. To end the meal, I was advised to mix a bit of rice with curd and eat it and then a bit of rice with rasam, which is a clear, peppery and tangy lentil soup popular in the south.

I remember I had observed on an earlier trip to Vijayawada, that the people of Andhra Pradesh love to eat huge quantities of rice and my lunch at Southern Spice again reminded me of that, since it was part of every course. I was indifferent to rasams on the whole till I had the one at Southern Spice that afternoon. It was steaming hot, clear, tangy and had a punch of pepper that made it just the sort of thing you could sip on after a great meal.

And what about the chicken? Well, the country chicken curry, or natu kodi iguru, did knock me out with its high chilli quotient and was a lot hotter than the vegetarian food. The chicken was full of bones, as the waiter had warned me. But it turned out to be one of the most flavour-packed and succulent pieces of chicken that I have ever had. Country chicken is reputed to be a lot more flavourful than broiler chicken, but is also supposed to be tough and a pain to cook. The juicy tenderness of the country chicken at Southern Spice was testimony to the culinary skills of the nameless chefs cooking inside its hot kitchens. The chicken had been cooked in a green chilli paste and seasoned with curry leaves. I confess that I can't handle spicy food well and the dish made me shed tears and buckets of sweat. Yet I ate on. I kept attacking the plate of chicken, which continued to make me cry with its spice levels, well after I was full. You are supposed to eat the chicken with the puris and I continued gorging on the chicken even after the puris were over.

I ditched the spoon and fork and ate the chicken with my hands. I separated the meat from the bones and licked my fingers with glee, even though my tongue was seared by the fiery heat of the chillies. The natu kodi iguru transported me to a very happy place.

After the last morsel of chicken was finished, the last bit of the blazing gravy licked off, I was ready to look up and say, 'I have lived.'

 Tip: Follow up the spicy food in Hyderabad with glasses of chilled chhaas (buttermilk).

CHUTNEYS FOR THE SOUL

My objectives during this trip to Hyderabad were to know its biryani better and to try out Andhra food. Little did I know that I had a surprise cameo waiting for me beyond these two.

I am speaking of a dining experience that made me write the following on my blog – 'I had the most incredible idli for breakfast today.'

Regular readers of my blog must have been surprised by this statement. My lack of enthusiasm for idlis had been well-documented on my blog by then. The idlis that I had so far been exposed to were the surgical-glove-textured ones that I ordered from Udupi restaurants in Bandra in Mumbai and then from office canteens as an evening snack. I called for idlis there more out of guilt than joy, led by a belief that they were healthy. I had never enjoyed eating them. I was not fond of the sweet sambar served with them either.

I finally lost my idli ennui when I went to Chutneys, a restaurant in Hyderabad.

Gaurav, my co-passenger on the flight to Hyderabad, had strongly recommended that I go to Chutneys for breakfast.

By this point, he seemed like a guy who knew his food – my Andhra lunch at Southern Spice and biryani tasting at Café Bahar, both of which he had recommended, proved my instincts about him right. Chutneys had been recommended to me by folks on Twitter and Facebook too, so I headed there for my breakfast on my last day in Hyderabad.

Chutneys in Banjara Hills is the first branch of the chain and was opened in the year 2000. It is newer than the other restaurants that I had visited on that trip. There was a queue of people waiting outside when I reached. The manager came out and once again, like in Southern Spice, told me to share a table as I was alone or 'one person', as they say here.

I walked in, sat down and a tray of chutneys was placed in front of me. 'Coconut, sweet, peanut and ginger chutneys,' the waiter explained. The steward who came to take my order said that the steamed dosas were famous here. I asked about the idlis instead and he recommended the Guntur idlis, which I decided to order.

When the idlis were brought to my table, I noticed that they looked thinner than what I was used to. They were covered in a red powder, which the waiter explained was the Guntur masala. It is made with a mix of red chilli powder and four types of lentils – urad, masoor, moong and channa, he told me.

I wasn't expecting much but when I took my first bite of the idli, I did a double take. The idlis were silken and almost cloud-like in texture. The masala had been mixed in a touch of fragrant ghee and then applied on the idlis. The ghee used was the local Hyderabadi one that is so insidiously addictive and the Guntur masala added dimensions of chilli heat which really woke me up. This was a food epiphany – the sort of culinary excellence which seemed so right in this city of nizams. If the natu kodi iguru at Southern Spice was all about fiery passion, then the Guntur idlis at Chutneys were all about love. Apart from the idlis, each of the chutneys on the table was distinctive in flavour and delicious in its own right. My favourites were the earthy peanut one and the very sharp and lively ginger one.

The Guntur idlis at Chutneys made me fall in love with idlis for the first time and I felt the same euphoria a few years later when I had the podi idli at the Murugan Idli Shop in Chennai.

Restaurants in Mumbai need to learn a trick or two from those in the south on how to make idlis!

Another nice dish that I tried at Chutneys was the pesarattu dosa, which is made with moong lentils. The dosa and the idli impressed me so much that I went back to Chutneys that evening, before I left, to have them once again. The restaurant is truly an apt inheritor of the cultural finesse of the nizam's kitchens.

What I did on my work-cum-food trip of Hyderabad was to try out the dishes that are traditionally associated with the city. I explored its legendary biryani places, even though I could not find haleem. I tried out the local Andhra food. I ate at places recommended by locals. This, in my opinion, is the best way to get a feel of a city – by trying out its traditional gems.

However, do biryani and haleem and the Andhra thalis continue to define Hyderabad? Or is the food scene here changing?

I put this question to Siddharth Moghe, a Hyderabad-based food blogger. Siddharth has an interesting take on the issue. He feels that while most tourists make a beeline for the local biryani joints, the biryani here no longer sticks to classic recipes. This is similar to an opinion expressed by some folks in Lucknow too, who feel that the biryani served in the street-side restaurants there is not the same as what was served by the khansamas of the past.

I am sure that they are not entirely wrong in their claim. Dishes evolve or change with time, with changes in people's tastes and aspirations, and in the availability and quality of ingredients.

The biryanis of Hyderabad and Lucknow were prepared in the royal courts first and only later became dishes of the masses. Chances are that they would lose a bit of their decadence in the process. One thing that I noticed about the popular biryani joints of Hyderabad, as compared to those of Lucknow, is that the restaurants in Hyderabad are bigger and comparatively plusher than the Lucknow ones. Though plusher, the biryani joints of Hyderabad are still places for regular familes to hang out and are not as intimidating as fine-dining places.

The original Hyderabadi biryani, according to Siddharth, is not to be found today except in a few select households where the family elders oversee the cooking. The problem is, how does one get an invite to such places as a tourist?

With the entry of expats from across the world to Hyderabad and the changing aspirations of a young Indian workforce, new restaurants are opening up in the city, which offer cuisines as diverse as Greek, Korean, Japanese and Italian, says Siddharth. Asian food in Hyderabad is now going beyond the traditional Indian-Chinese which folks like Siddharth grew up on. Now there are restaurants offering food from Southeast Asian countries such as Thailand, Burma and Malaysia too. You also get pan-Indian cuisines such as North West Frontier food and even Bengali food in Hyderabad beyond the local Hyderabadi and Andhra fare. These are exciting times to be a food lover living in Hyderabad, feels Siddharth.

If you are a traveller to the city, though, I am sure you would love to acquaint yourself with its classic fare first.

At least I did.

FOOD WALK

👣 The Banjara Hill trail

Go to Chutneys for breakfast and start your day with some Guntur idli, pessarattu dosa and coffee. Then head to Southern Spice for a full-blown vegetarian Andhra meal. Another 30-minute ride and you can end your afternoon with biryani and bheja masala at Café Bahar.

 Tip: This is best done by hiring a car.

👣 The Old Hyderabad walk, recommended by Siddharth Moghe, Sankalp Vishnu and Chef Mandaar Sukhtankar

Start with the mutton paya at Hotel Nayaab in Ghansi Bazaar. Then head for mutton biryani and nihari at Shadab. Walk down past the Charminar to Shah Ghouse for more biryani (and during Ramzan, the haleem too.) End your afternoon with chai at Nimrah Cafe or if you are up for the challenge, lassi at Matwale Doodh Ghar.

 Tip: Enjoy this trail on foot as the roads are crowded and the leisurely walk is a nice way to experience Hyderabad of yore, and to build up an appetite.

BACK TO BASICS IN BENGALURU

Often, other cities in India lose out in the debate between Mumbai and Delhi when it comes to which one is the food capital of India. One of the cities which often does not get its due, in my opinion, is Bengaluru. It is one of my favourite cities in India to eat in. The sheer diversity of food available in Bengaluru is mind-blowing. You get food from all over Karnataka – Coorgi, Udupi, Konkani and so on. You get cuisines from other South Indian states here too; some of the Andhra restaurants of Bengaluru are probably more famous than Andhra restaurants in Hyderabad! I have also come across restaurants serving food from other parts of India. This is possibly a function of the high number of immigrants who come to study and work here. Of late, there are quite a few restaurants in Bengaluru that offer cutting-edge international dishes, thanks to the rising expat workforce here.

Bengaluru's relative quietness in the Indian food media is becoming a thing of the past now. Today, it is home to some of India's most popular food bloggers, food journalists and most talked-about chefs, all of whom have helped drive an interest in the food of Bangalore, as Bengaluru was known earlier.

THE BEST BREAKFAST IN BENGALURU

MTR, or the Mavalli Tiffin Rooms, is one of the most iconic restaurants in Bengaluru. Its story is very interesting. It was set up in the 1920s and the legacy of the company is close to 100 years old. According to the company website, it began experimenting with making spices and ready-to-eat products in the 1970s. I have often used these MTR products in Mumbai. Now, MTR is part of a Nordic conglomerate of food companies. There are a number of MTR branches in Bengaluru and I was keen to visit one of the restaurants to sample their food.

I finally made it to the original branch of MTR, which is at Lalbaug, on one of my visits to Bengaluru. I went there for breakfast one morning when I was staying at St Mark's Hotel. I had fond memories of this hotel, as it was the very first hotel I had stayed in when I started travelling for work. I was back after a year and was happy to see that they had renovated the hotel and the service was still as warm as it was a decade ago.

That day, I decided to give the hotel breakfast buffet a miss and headed to MTR instead. The hotel concierge helped me find out if breakfast was being served at that late hour. I reached MTR for breakfast closer to noon, at 11.30 a.m.

When I entered the door of the ground floor of MTR, all I could see was what looked like the kitchen and beside that a couple of rooms, where I saw a few people eating. It looked still and lonely.

I then spotted a staircase and walked up. Things were different upstairs. It was a lot livelier here. There was a long queue of people waiting patiently to get in. Managing the crowds was an avuncular gentleman with a white moustache and a warm smile. He would let a rush of people into the dining area occasionally and then ask the rest to wait. It all looked pretty orderly. Luckily, by the time this Bengali surfaced for breakfast, all the locals were done with theirs and had left. So I didn't have to wait for too long to get in.

I had to share a table with three other 'singles', surrounded by tables full of happy groups of families. We had to wait for a bit till the waiter came to take our order. I took the opportunity to chat with the three middle-aged gentlemen with whom I was sharing the table.

After asking my table-mates for suggestions, I ordered the masala dosa and the rava idli. The food was soon brought to the table, hot and freshly prepared.

The dosa was very different from any dosa I had even seen till then. It was a lot thicker than the standard restaurant dosa I was used to. I found the texture very interesting as well. It was crunchy on the outside. I mean really crunchy. Then soft inside. The secret of the texture, according to my table-mates, was the higher proportion of pulses in comparison to rice in the batter.

The masala was a simple, non-spicy, boiled-potato filling. It worked well for me. As did the ghee, which was served in a tiny bowl placed on the dosa. As instructed by my table-mates, I poured the ghee onto the dosa instead of breaking pieces of the dosa and dipping it in the ghee. The result was a rather hedonistic food experience in the somewhat ascetic portals of MTR. A place which, as one of my table-mates, Mr Dhananajay, pointed out, was older than independent India.

Interestingly, they did not serve a sambar with the dosa, unlike what I was used to in Mumbai or Kolkata, or in most other places. It was served just with a coconut chutney. I asked Dhananjay why this was so. That's when another of my table-mates who had been silent so far, a Mr Prakash, spoke up. 'You don't eat dosas with sambar. Just chutney.' This was quite a surprise for me, but apparently it is a common practice here.

 Tip: First have a bite of the dosa with ghee and then try the chutney to see which option you prefer yourself.

Speaking of interesting dosa pairings, I once had the South Indian dosa served with a very North Indian chhole curry. This was in London's Borough Market at a stall called Horn OK Please run by a couple of young Indian expats. It goes to show that anything is possible in the world of food.

Over subsequent trips, I learned that the thick dosas that I had in Bengaluru are called 'benne' or butter dosas and that they originated in a place called Davangere in Karnataka. You also get them in places such as Vidyarthi Bhavan and Central Tiffin Rooms (also known as CTR), among others, in Bengaluru. I also realized that Bengaluru is strongly divided on the basis of which dosa place one likes, and that the rivalry between CTR and MTR camps could rival that between Real Madrid and Barca football fans.

Getting back to the rava idli, which arrived next at MTR, I found it too to be very different from any idli that I had ever eaten before. This was more like a tightly packed upma than the steamed rice cakes I was used to. The confluence of fried curry leaves and nutty roasted urad dal in the idli packed in a lot of flavour.

I later read that the rava idli was apparently concocted by the owners of MTR during the Second World War when there were food shortages. Rice was scarce then, so they thought of using semolina to make their idlis instead. The popularity of the rava idlis ensured that they stayed on in the MTR menu till modern times. This spirit of innovation was to be seen later too, in their use of modern technology to distribute MTR products across the country and the world in packaged formats.

I ended my breakfast with a frothy milky filter coffee, or 'kaapi' as they say in the South, which had a kick that was really prominent. It was much stronger than the instant coffees one gets from stores.

Tip: Filter kaapi is served very hot. Sip it carefully to ensure that you don't singe your tongue. Specify in the beginning if you don't want sugar.

When I returned to my hotel, the smiling manager who had given me directions to MTR told me that I should have tried the South Indian lunch thali there too. It's a pity that my stomach, unlike my suitcase, is not expandable.

There are some who feel that MTR is 'no longer what it used to be'. A Twitter friend of mine, Sudha Kanago, who lives in Bengaluru and loves to cook, told me that when MTR started off they were apparently the first to provide silver cutlery and tablecloths to their diners, making it a 'genteel' place for the refined diner. According to her, MTR has not kept up with the past and has let things slip.

I guess MTR is a bit like Britannia in Mumbai. Some feel it lives on past glory. Yet, both places are packed with people, eating happily, at any given time. Thankfully, the food in MTR is not as expensive as it is in Britannia!

I have been to various MTR branches on subsequent trips to Bengaluru since then and I always look forward to my dosa and kaapi there. Most MTR shops have a dessert and savoury counter attached to them and you can buy conveniently packed and very tasty food gifts to take back. MTR spices and ready to-cook packaged dishes are available across the country and abroad too.

Thanks to blogging and social media, I rarely eat alone while travelling these days. I just announce the place I'm going to and some contact or the other writes in offering to meet me when I visit their city. I am sure this is true for many of us in our virtually connected world. In my case, my focus on food has meant that I have caught up with people who love to eat. They are the best kind of people, as Julia Child once said.

This has happened abroad and closer home too. There was this time, for example, when I had breakfast with the very effervescent Monika Manchanda in Bengaluru. Monika, a former IT professional, writes the blog Sin-A-Mon Tales and has become an acclaimed food entrepreneur now. I was staying in the Bengaluru suburb of Koramangala and Monika kindly offered to take me to one of her favourite breakfast places there.

We went to Sree Krishna Kafe. It is a tiny old-school place surrounded by a plethora of younger and snazzier restaurants. Koramangla is, after all, a suburb that is packed with new and trendy restaurants. Once you reach Sree Krishna Kafe, you have to go up a narrow staircase to the restaurant on the first floor. The ambience is rather basic. It is non-air-conditioned but not smelly or musty. The weather in Bengaluru is so pleasant that you don't miss the air-conditioning and many restaurants there don't offer air-conditioning, as I found out later. The tables and chairs are pretty functional and they seem to tell you 'eat here, enjoy your meal and move on'. The place reminded me of the old restaurants which big railway stations in India used to have, because of its minimal décor and its rustic ambience.

Monika told me that she often comes to Sree Krishna Kafe on weekends with her husband and child. She ordered an idli vada for herself and suggested that I order a podi dosa, her husband's favourite. It wasn't there on the menu, though, so I would not have known of the dish but for Monika. The smiling waiter, who told me that he had once lived in Mumbai, got us the idli vadas and the dosa in a jiffy.

The podi dosa was not the typical thick Bengaluru benne dosa, being a lot thinner. But one bite of the dosa made me break into a huge smile. I immediately fell in love with the taste and the smell of ghee that bathed the thin, crisp dosa and the red spices sprinkled over it.

Monika, a North Indian who had just completed 12 years in Bengaluru and loves the city, explained that the powdery spice on top of the dosa is called 'podi', which makes it incredibly well-flavoured. I later found out that podi is made by pounding together a dry roasted mix of lentils and chillies. The composition of podi can vary from house to house and a good podi can add wonders to a dish. I bought some locally made podi from a store later and took it home. I smeared it on some chicken which I then grilled and the dish turned out to be pretty tasty!

The podi dosa at Sree Krishna Kafe is one of the best dosas that I have ever eaten in my life.

 Tip: If you ever come across podi in a South Indian restaurant, blend it with a bit of ghee and then dunk whatever you are eating – dosa, idli or vada – into it.

Monika and I chatted about our lives, as bloggers do when they catch up. Monika had quit her job in IT to follow her passion for food. She bakes and retails her baked goods, conducts cooking workshops and has now started restaurant consulting too, so she really knows her food. She is one of the warmest and most positive and enterprising people that I have come across. She's indeed the perfect breakfast buddy.

Monika then offered to order something else from the menu for me and I chose a rava onion dosa. The taste of the dosa was very distinctive and was different from what we get in Mumbai. The difference comes through because of the whole pepper and curry leaves added to the dosa, which give it a lot of character. Monika told me that these additions are standard practice for rava dosas in Bengaluru.

We called for some filter kaapi to end the meal. The coffee was just excellent. It was strong yet silken and creamy. Under Monika's instructions I did the famous South Indian cup-to-tumbler-to-cup swap to cool down the coffee.

The breakfast we had here was really exceptional and the perfect way to start the day and enticed me to come back by myself the next day before my flight.

A BREAKFAST WALK IN OLD BANGALORE'S MALLESHWARAM

I had once visited Bengaluru to review a modern Asian restaurant and was put up at the then newly launched Sheraton Hotel at Malleshwaram. Malleshwaram is called 'old Bangalore' and is famous for its local eats. I decided to make the best use of the opportunity offered by my location and took a car the next morning to hunt for breakfast nearby. I was armed with a list of names of eateries that I had got from some people on Twitter.

On my Malleshwaram breakfast list were Veena Stores and CTR. Sadhvi, a local who worked at my hotel, approved of my list before I set off at around 9 a.m. This was much to the surprise of my wife back in Mumbai, who knew that this hour was quite early for me. The timing was optimum, though, as it is a bit after the locals have had their breakfast in Bengaluru. This meant that I avoided the breakfast crowds and yet was not so late that I missed breakfast.

I was curious to see what 'old' Bengaluru looked like. Old Delhi has its Mughal architecture, old Hyderabad its particular style of buildings from the time of the nizams, old Mumbai has its Victorian buildings, old North Kolkata has its narrow lanes and *rajbaris* of the nawabs of yore while Kolkata's Park Street has the colonial-style buildings in which the British once lived.

What about old Bengaluru? What was its distinctive architectural style?

Well, to me Malleshwaram looked like a typical old-school, urban middle-class Indian suburb, with lots of two- and three-storeyed houses. It reminded me of the neighbourhoods in South Kolkata where I had grown up. There were hardly any high-rise buildings around, so it did not look very modern. While there was the odd South Indian temple dotting the landscape, I didn't see any classical architecture of note. What was there, though, was lots and lots of greenery, the reason behind Bengaluru's 'garden city' label.

My first stop that day was the 40-year-old Veena Stores. It is a tiny shop and not a restaurant. The way it works here is that you go to the counter and place your order and pay for your food. The food is then served to you at the counter. You can either stand on the street and eat the food or pack it and take it away. The food is served in disposable and environment-friendly plates made out of dried leaves.

I started with the much-recommended idli and vada. The idli at Veena Stores is soft as a baby's cheek – my favourite analogy for softness in food. Or as soft as a 'baby's bum' if you go by Bengaluru-based food blogger Nandita Iyer's response to my tweet on the Veena Store idlis on Twitter. The flavours were delicate and the seasoning perfect. The idli was not dry at all and was pleasantly moist and evidently freshly steamed. It combined beautifully with the chilli-and-green-mint chutney that the server standing at the corner of Veena Stores doled out.

The medu vada was quite crunchy and livened up my morning. While I ate it, I saw quite a few folks having coffee. I asked a young couple, who were eating there, for suggestions on what else to try. They suggested that I go for the semolina-based khara and sada bhaats. But my eyes were on something that a young man, who was eating outside the stall, vouched for. The dish was called puliyogare.

I bought a plate of puliyogare and went to the corner to try it. One bite of the puliyogare was all it took for me to fall in love with it. It is a tamarind-flavoured rice in which the rice is light and airy, the tamarind juice gives it a lovely and fresh tanginess reminiscent of the Kolkata jhalmuri and the peanuts interspersed in it give it a nutty taste and texture which contrasts with the rice. It is a fantastically well-balanced dish.

This is what food blogger Anjali Koli wrote on my Facebook page when I put up the picture of the puliyogare: 'The best puliyogare ('puli' is sour and 'oggarane' is tempered rice) I've ever tasted is at a small town called Melkote, 135 kms from Bengaluru towards Mysore. It is a Tamilian, rather Iyengar, settlement in the heart of Karnataka. This town is home to Cheluvanarayana Swamy Temple and there are carts [outside it] that sell the best puliyogare and tempered curd rice. They also sell the puliyogare mix in packets. The secret to a good puliyogare is tempering with sesame oil. Your pic brought back memories of it.'

It was one of the best things I had eaten for breakfast in Bengaluru.

I then drove down to my next stop, CTR, which is a two-storeyed building. This is a 'proper' restaurant with a seating area, unlike Veena Stores. When I asked the gentleman at the counter about the history of the place, he left me a bit confused. He either said that the restaurant was opened in

1950 or he might have said it was 50 years old – I'm not sure which!

CTR's history dates back to the 1920s, according to Wikipedia, and its ownership has changed a few times. It's name has recently been changed to Shri Sagar, which was one of the earlier names of the restaurant. Regulars still refer to it as CTR, though.

The restaurant was fairly full, even though it was close to 10 a.m. The clientele consisted of a mix of family groups and businessmen. I had to share a table with a gentleman who had on a dour expression and who later ate his masala dosa with studied concentration when it was brought to the table.

As recommended by Adrianne, a Singaporean who loves India and CTR, and who had tweeted in response to my query about where to eat in Bengaluru, I asked for a benne dosa. There was no menu card in sight here. Regulars knew what to order, I guessed.

'Aah, butter dosa,' said the smiling waiter and came back a bit later with my dosa. The benne dosa at CTR was much shorter in length than the dosas that you get in Mumbai. It had a spiced boiled-potato stuffing. The aroma of butter in the dosa could be smelled from a mile away. The dosa was very thick, crunchy on the outside and soft inside. And I just loved it. I found it to be crunchier on the outside than the dosas that I have eaten at various MTR outlets.

I know that it sounds hyperbolic but every dosa that I have had in Bengaluru, whether in MTR, Sree Krishna Kafe or in CTR, has become my favourite dosa till date! I miss the dosas of Bengaluru sorely when back in Mumbai.

 Tip: Always follow up a dosa in Bengaluru with a filter kaapi.

I washed down my dosa at CTR with a frothy, sweet and strong filter kaapi. After my meal, I stepped out of the restaurant and went to a store called Ace Iyengar Products. I picked up some packaged South Indian snacks and masalas for friends in Mumbai. They have large pictorial displays of the various food items at the shop, which make it easy for non-locals to decide what to buy.

I was quite stuffed by then, but my chauffeur insisted that I go with him to a place called Raghavendra Stores – a tiny shop located outside Malleshwaram railway station. If he had not taken me there, I would not have known about it. The shop is close to half a century old. It was packed with people waiting for their orders to be filled, even though it was close to noon by then. I had another brilliant idli here and a vada while my chauffeur had an upma. He then wanted to take me to a place where you get thatte idlis (which are like chapatis, he told me) but I was completely stuffed. I could not have eaten even one more idli, so he took me back to my hotel.

OLD-SCHOOL FOOD AT KOSHY'S

Koshy's at MG Road, like MTR, is another Bengaluru legend. Like all legendary restaurants, it evokes passionate opinion and debate. There are those who swear by it, especially by its breakfasts. Then there are those who feel that its glory days are gone and that the hype around Koshy's is misplaced.

I wanted to try out the place for myself, so one night I went to Koshy's for dinner with blogger Naina Jayarajan and her husband. Naina had just moved to Bengaluru from Mumbai then. She had wanted to take me to one of the new European places at Bengaluru's posh UB City Mall. I wanted to go to Koshy's instead.

The moment we stepped in to Koshy's, I knew that it was

my sort of place. The place looked old, the furniture spartan and the customers like regulars. As Naina put it, 'It is not trendy but it is a place for people like us.'

 Tip: The breakfast at Koshy's is pretty popular with meat lovers.

Bengaluru sleeps early and when we reached Koshy's we were told that they take the last order at midnight. We rushed through the food and drinks as it was close to 11 p.m.

We tried the mutton cutlet, which had a lovely peppery taste to it. The prawns in the prawn curry were pleasantly juicy and not overcooked. The pork vindaloo was one of the best vindaloos I've ever had and had an interesting sweet aftertaste to it. But what made the food special was the history and the atmosphere that it came flavoured with.

The food was old-school Anglo-Indian cuisine from what I gathered. Like Kolkata, Bengaluru too had quite an active Anglo-Indian community during the time of the British and this was probably its legacy.

I know that there are people who don't like Koshy's anymore but I must confess that I quite loved what I ate at Koshy's that night. If cheap alcohol, honest food, quiet conversations and a relaxed pace appeals to you then Koshy's is the place to be.

THE MEATY TREATS OF BENGALURU

Since all my breakfasts were vegetarian, I decided to try out some non-vegetarian food for lunch one day. My friend Sushobhan Mukherjee, a Bengali and a food enthusiast, whose recommendations on food have always held me in good stay, first recommended Anjappar to me. He is the husband of

Sudha Kanago, whom I have spoken of earlier in this chapter. The Anjappar in Bengaluru's Koramangla suburb is a branch of the Chennai-based Chettinad food chain of the same name.

I went there with a fellow Bengali, Raunak Kundu. Raunak is an IT professional who is also into restaurant consulting and reviewing. We went to the first floor of this fairly large restaurant and sat by the window, which is always my seat of choice during lunch, as the natural lighting helps me take good food photos.

I had single-mindedly focused on one thing when I came to Anjappar. I had heard that they serve rabbit and rabbit was a meat I was yet to try. To start with, we ordered two Chettinad vegetarian thalis, which had a nice mix of vegetable dishes and a flavour-packed dal. Raunak also called for a very juicy seer fish fry to go with it.

I ordered a dish called 'Rabbit 65', named after the famous Chicken 65 of South India. The dish served to us looked like pieces of chicken, cut into chilli-chicken-sized pieces and coated in a bright red colour. Despite its scary shade of red, which I assumed was a red-chilli-powder-based spicy masala, the dish was not too spicy for me. The chilli kick is a lot more prominent in the Chickn 65 at Buhari in Chennai, which claims to have invented the dish. The rabbit meat, like they say about many exotic meats, did 'taste like chicken'. However, it was juicier than chicken and not as gamey or chewy, as I thought it would be. In the past, I have tried alligator tail in Sydney and frog legs in Kuala Lumpur, which tasted like chicken but where the texture was either too tough or too soft. The texture of the rabbit meat at Anjappar was just perfect.

This was a good introduction to Chettinad food and whetted my appetite to go to Chennai and explore it further, which I did a couple of years later when I went to Ponnusamy in Chennai for a memorable Chettinad meal.

ANDHRA BITES IN BENGALURU

A lot of people had told me to try out the Andhra (from the neighbouring Andhra Pradesh) food in Bengaluru. Some of the more popular Andhra restaurants there are Bheema's, Hotel Nandhini and Nagarjuna. I was quite interested in trying them out, especially since you hardly get any Andhra food in Mumbai. I finally made it to Nagarjuna on one of my trips to Bengaluru, when I stole some time in between meetings to grab lunch.

I reached the restaurant and walked up the stairs to the first floor. The restaurant is a large air-conditioned space and is packed with folks during lunchtime. If alone, like I was, you have to share your table with others.

At Nagarjuna I ended up sharing my table with a gentleman named Sudip who is from the north and who once lived in the suburb of Ranikuthi, very close to my house in South Kolkata. He loves the food at Nagarjuna and told me that he frequented the restaurant often. Unfortunately, his enthusiasm for it didn't translate into much knowledge on Andhra food. He couldn't explain the basic tenets of Andhra food to me when I asked, but for the fact that, like in Bengali meals, it is to be eaten course by course.

I looked askance at my banana-leaf plate, especially when the waiter put down rice, a number of masalas and then some ghee on it. I asked the waiter, in Hindi, about the correct way to eat my meal. He happily explained to me that I needed to mix the masalas to the rice, add the ghee and then eat it.

'I add ghee, you mix,' he instructed me in English.

A dal followed. The dal was rather thick and 'typically Andhra', I was told. I loved the full-flavoured and garlic-heavy taste of the dal.

I enjoyed the vegetarian side dishes that followed but let

me tell you about the chicken dish – ghee roast chicken – that I tried at Nagarjuna. The chicken was served on a bed of deep fried curry leaves, which acted as a nice little taste-breaker in between bites of the meat. It was very well-flavoured and the meat was very juicy. It was a lot less chilli- and heat-packed than the country chicken roast that I had at the Andhra restaurant – Southern Spice – in Hyderabad.

 Tip: The service is pretty friendly in Bengaluru. If lost, don't be wary about asking folks around on what to order and on the right way to eat the food.

On the way out from Nagarjuna, I met Naveen Reddy, the manager of this more-than-25-year-old restaurant. He had worked here for 20 of those. He told me that the owners of Nagarjuna, Mr Mohan Reddy and his son, no relation to Naveen Reddy himself, apparently came to the restaurant every morning and personally supervised the mixing of masalas and the marinating of the food. Naveen said that the spice and heat had been tempered down in the food served there, as Bengaluru locals couldn't take the amount of spice that Andhraites love in their food.

The next Andhra restaurant that I went to in the city was Nandhini Hotel. I went to the St Marks Road branch one night but they hardly had any food left by then, so I went to another branch the next day for lunch. It was packed with people having their Sunday fill of the Andhra thali. I ordered a chicken biryani. It was covered with fried green chillies and curry leaves when it was served. The rice was quite moist and there were no visible bursts of masala, unlike in the Hyderabad biryani.

An important place to remember in Bengaluru is a two-storeyed restaurant called the Empire Hotel at Church Street. It stays open even after most other restaurants in Bengaluru shut down for the night. The local youth consider it to be an after-party eatery. I once went there post midnight when every other restaurant that we tried to go to was shut. The place was buzzing when we reached. We quite enjoyed our meal of a coconut-based Kerala chicken curry and an Arabian barbequed chicken that was served with mayo and pita bread.

 Tip: Head to Empire Hotel for dinner post a pub crawl.

The variety of regional Indian food that I have eaten in Bengaluru, which includes even Assamese food, makes me really admire the food culture here. Bengaluru is one of the most cosmopolitan cities of India – a city where people from all over have come to seek their fortune in the digital age, something which is reflected in its cuisine – a perfect amalgamation of the old and the new.

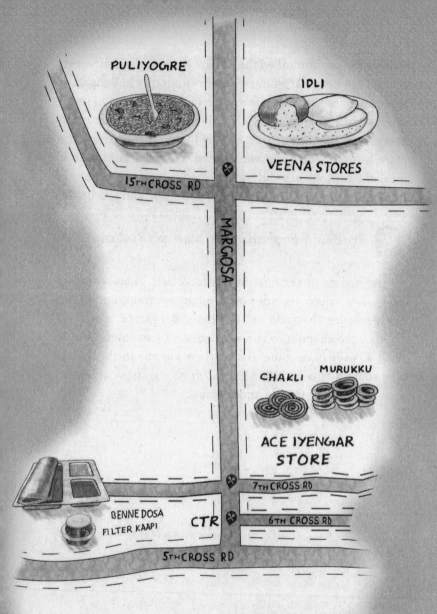

The Malleshwaram breakfast walk

FOOD WALK

👣 *The Malleshwaram breakfast walk*

Start with Veena Stores and have the idli and the puliyogare there. Then go to Ace Iyengar Products and buy South Indian packaged food for home. Then head to CTR. Have a benne dosa and finish your morning with a robust filter kaapi.

TO CHENNAI AND TO
NEW JOURNEYS

I used to travel to Chennai quite a bit at the start of my market-research career. I serviced an American automobile company, which had set up base just outside Chennai at the time.

My colleagues and I would take the early morning flight out of Mumbai for Chennai. We would take a non-air-conditioned Ambassador cab with kitschy interiors and drive off to the client's plant. Lunch would be at the client's massive canteen where everyone would have their meals. The food served in the canteen was local vegetarian food. There were no rotis, much to the consternation of our key client contact – who was a North Indian and who missed having rotis with his meals. All the expats working there, including Americans and Australians, would eat this Tamil vegetarian food. In those days, we would finish our work and then head back to the airport and rarely stay over. My seniors would eat dosas at the airport café while we waited for our flight. I would eat a chicken sandwich.

I used to live in the PG in Mumbai then, where, as I've mentioned before, the food served was vegetarian. Therefore, whenever I was touring on work after I moved to Mumbai, and on an expense account, I would try to eat something non-vegetarian. To be honest, I didn't really look forward to my Chennai trips from a food point of view in those days.

My trips to Chennai stopped after I changed jobs. By then my food palate had evolved. I had begun to appreciate the joys of discovering local food and I was more open to trying vegetarian food. I would rarely eat a chicken sandwich while travelling if I could make it to a local favourite. Unfortunately, no Chennai trips happened after I started blogging and my knowledge of Chennai food was shamefully restricted to the chicken sandwiches at the airport and vague memories of my client's canteen food and a meal a friend's mother had cooked for me when I visited her.

When I began writing this book, I realized that the only metro in India that was not covered in it was Chennai. I had not been there in more than a decade. The book seemed incomplete without a Chennai chapter. I was wondering what to do about this when suddenly a solution presented itself, in the form of a train ride from Mumbai for a promotional activity.

The train ride to Chennai brought back lovely memories. Like most Indians of my generation, I have grown up on train travel and my early trips back home to Kolkata when I had first moved to Mumbai would be on trains. I looked forward to sleeping undisturbed over what was then a 40-hour journey, waking up only to eat. I used to be very fond of the chicken curry that they would serve on the Bombay–Howrah mail in the 1990s. Then, thanks to the opening up of flight travel and the drop in airfares in India, my colleagues and I rarely travelled by train.

My late maternal grandfather, my Dadu, used to work in the Indian Railways. He was an officer in the library services and he was instrumental in inculcating the habit of reading in me. Though a desk man who worked in the Railway Headquarters in Delhi, he was very fond of train travel. He would go on holidays with my granny, my mother and her siblings, using the train passes that he would get at work. They would stay at Railway Guest Houses. My grandfather would go to the local markets and shop and my granny would then cook for the family at the guest house. This was much before staying at homestays on holidays became trendy.

I am quite sure Dadu would have been happy to see me back in a train once again. The high point of a train journey is the people one meets and the conversations one has. Here I got to meet the popular TV food show hosts, Rocky Singh and Mayur Sharma, who were conducting a promotional activity. They turned out to be as fun-filled in real life as they are on television. It was great chatting with them and learning from their experiences in the food world.

 Tip: If you are travelling long-distance by train in India then look for chai- and samosa walas at stations when the train stops for some nice and hot refreshments.

TIFFIN TALES

'South Indian food' for a lot of us, who are not from the south, is often summed up in vegetarian snacks such as idli, dosa and vada. Over the years I have realized that there is a lot more to South Indian food.

My first introduction to dosas happened in the early 1980s, soon after we moved to India and Kolkata when I was around eight years old. I was admitted to a school called Calcutta International School, which was meant for expat and embassy kids as well as Non-Resident Indian children who had moved to India.

There was a teacher there named Mrs Handique who once told my mother that she should buy me a dosa from a restaurant called Rim Jhim (which has now shut down) near the school. Mrs Handique recommended the dosa after my mother told her that I was a fussy eater (and I still am!) and that I refused to eat any Indian dishes even after we moved to India from abroad.

Following her advice, my mom got me a masala dosa from Rim Jhim one day at lunch. I remember perspiring a lot while eating it as I found the dosa very spicy and I was not used to spicy food.

Yet, that was the day I fell in love with dosas. Over the years my mother would take me to Rim Jhim for dosas whenever we went to visit a dentist whose chamber was nearby. Later, when in college, I would go to restaurants such as The Friend's Home and Indra Mahal at Calcutta's New Market and Rana's near the Jadavpur Police Station for dosas.

 Tip: if you are not very hungry I would recommend choosing a sada dosa over a masala one.

I loved the doughnut-shaped, deep-fried medu vadas, once again after I first tried them at Rim Jhim. I was not a big fan of idlis, though that would change once I had the Guntur idlis at Chutneys in Hyderabad, which I've written about earlier.

Dosa joints are aplenty in Mumbai and you get dosas even on the streets, which are sold from carts and small stalls. Some of the most popular stalls in the suburbs of Mumbai are the ones opposite the Narsee Monjee College and Manju Dosa at Santa Cruz.

Over the years, I have come to realize that dosas can be of many types. Take the gossamer-soft, steamed neer dosas of Mangalorean restaurants for example, which are so different from the crisp dosas that most of us are used to.

So the first thing that I wanted to try out in Chennai were tiffin items such as idli, dosa and vada. I wanted to know if the food served here was different from what was served in the South Indian Udupi restaurants in Mumbai, which are mostly run by Mangaloreans and not Tamilians.

Having slept at 2 a.m. the night I checked into the ITC Grand Chola Hotel, I was too sleepy to head out for breakfast in the morning. I requested the hotel to put together a classic South Indian meal for me at their café instead.

Helping me navigate my way through the food of Chennai was a Mangalorean, Chef Ajit Bangera, who had made Chennai his home. Chef Bangera is a soft-spoken, dignified, humble and well-experienced chef who has worked abroad and is now the senior executive chef at the ITC Grand Chola.

The chef told me that the sambar served that morning didn't have vegetables or garlic in it as it was a 'breakfast sambar'. The sambar served for lunch or dinner apparently contained vegetables and garlic.

I noticed that the medu vada, which is just called vada in Chennai, was served separately from the sambar. I have often seen Udupi joints in Mumbai dunk the vadas in a bowl of sambar and then serve them. I prefer to have the vadas served separately, so I was pleased to see this being done here. I asked Chef Bangera about the correct way to eat vadas. He explained that both ways were correct but felt that the practice of immersing the vada in sambar (vada-sambar) might have started as a way to make vadas which were not freshly fried palatable. The vadas here were nice and crunchy outside and soft and flavourful inside. Seemed like one was having them straight from a streetside stall though I was in a hotel which, in my books, is a good thing!

Tip: Have a bite of medu vada and follow it with a spoonful of hot sambar. Makes for a lovely combination!

I then tried the idli. I did this rather gingerly. As I said earlier, I am not too fond of idlis. The idlis here were served with a powder called podi and ghee on the side. This was not the first time I had eaten podi. I remember enjoying the podi-smeared dosa that Monika Manchanda had ordered for me at Sree Krishna Kafe in Bengaluru.

Chef Bangera told me to add some ghee and podi on my plate, break a bit of the idli and dab it into the mix and then eat it. The combination of the idli with ghee and podi that morning was ethereal. The initial taste was slightly buttery, thanks to the ghee. Then the spicy and heaty undercurrent of the podi hit me and woke me up. The idlis were incredibly soft and they just sunk in if you pressed your fingers on them and then sprung back once you removed contact.

The secret behind the softness of the idlis, according to Chef Bangera, is the amount of time that the batter is hand-whipped. Inspired by the idlis his mother used to make, he apparently insists on 45 minutes of whipping for the idli batter in his kitchen.

The dosa that I had that morning was very interesting. It was crisp outside and mildly soft inside. It was not as thick as the Bengaluru benne dosas but the dual texture was pleasantly novel for me. It was definitely different from the Udupi joint dosas in Mumbai's Bandra which can at times make my jaw hurt, thanks to their excessive crunchiness.

There was a potato bhaji as well, made of potatoes tempered with curry leaves, chillies, turmeric and dried lentils, known as the masala, which was served separately from the dosa. Chef Bangera said that some people serve the bhaji separately, especially at home, unlike in restaurants where it is usually stuffed inside the dosa. I am talking of masala dosas here; sada or plain dosas don't have potato bhaji masala with them.

Chef Bangera advised me to scoop a bit of the potato masala with a piece of the dosa and pop it into my mouth. I did so and it suddenly struck me that with one action of mine I had united North and South India. The way I tore the dosa and had it with the potato masala was exactly how someone in the north of India would have rotis and aloo sabzi. The aloo bhaji served with the dosa had a typically South Indian spice palette, thanks to the curry leaves and whole mustard seeds that it was cooked in.

I had another fantastic idli experience later in the evening. I met up with Amit Patnaik, an HR professional, food blogger and budding food writer based in Chennai. He had given me lot of tips on where to eat in Chennai. I was keen to meet him despite my short stay. Thankfully, things worked out and we met up.

Amit took me to the Besant Nagar beach. We had some freshly fried seafood at the shacks on the beach, after which he said that he wanted me to go with him to a restaurant nearby called Murugan Idli Shop to have a local drink called jigarthanda. When I tried the drink it seemed like an ice-cream-based milkshake, which I found similar in taste to the Mewad ice-cream fruit salads sold on the streets of Mumbai. The Murugan Idli chain originally started in Madurai and now has branches in Chennai and other cities, as well as internationally.

I saw a big queue of people waiting to enter Murugan Idli Shop. The crowd was mostly groups of families, consisting of members from many generations. Amit, who had moved to

Chennai from Delhi and loved his adopted city, pointed out that Chennai is one city where youngsters still come out with their parents and grandparents to eat.

We skipped the queue and went into the restaurant saying that we would parcel some idlis but sat down when we saw an empty table. Let me confess here that I was the one who corrupted young Amit's mind and made him break the queue that evening. I sincerely apologize to the well-behaved and orderly Chennai-ites who had to wait longer for a table because of us.

We placed our orders of 'podi idli' as recommended by Amit. The place was packed with people eating away with blissful smiles on their faces. Most dishes on the menu were priced at under ₹20 each. The wait staff would come out of the kitchen with trays full of idlis, vadas, uthappams and so on, and serve these at the table as per the orders. It was past 8 p.m. and yet people were eating idlis by the dozen.

The podi idli was served soaked in ghee and smeared with podi on top. The flavours burst in my mouth, a far cry from the gigiantic, dry and underwhelming idlis I that had been subjected to in restaurants in Bandra, where I live in Mumbai. These idlis were also very soft, just like the ones I had eaten in the morning. The idlis at Murugan are apparently made in a Chettinad style. They were so good that I would travel back to Chennai just for them, and that's saying a lot.

The next day Chef Bangera and I went to New Woodlands, a South Indian vegetarian restaurant in Chennai recommended by many. It is an Udupi, that is, a Mangalorean-run place and not a Tamil-owned place. Most South Indian vegetarian places in Mumbai are run by those from the Udupi community. I was interested to see that this happens in Chennai too.

We reached the restaurant at around 10 a.m. on a weekday.

The place was full but yet very quiet. Like the Murugan Idli Shop, this restaurant too is air-conditioned, though it looks a tad plusher in comparison, and is also a bit more expensive. I found out that New Woodlands is actually the name of the hotel there and it has three restaurants, of which the vegetarian South Indian one, where we headed to, is called Krishna. However, everyone I came across in Chennai referred to the restaurant as New Woodlands and not Krishna.

We ordered everything on the menu – idlis, vada, upma, sada dosa, rava dosa and filter kaapi. The south of India loves their kaapi. Here the kaapi was served without the theatrics with which it was poured out at the ITC Grand Chola's Café Mercara. The sugar was added to the kaapi before serving, which made it a tad too sweet for my taste. You can ask them to give you sugar separately instead.

Our maître d' was from Karnataka, he spoke in both English and Hindi, and served us with a smile. I noticed that most of the restaurants that I went to over the two days in Chennai had wait staff from all over India, including from the north. Most spoke to me in Hindi, so my not knowing Tamil, which is the local language, was not a hindrance anymore. It was different from a decade ago when one felt that it would be difficult to survive on the streets of Chennai without knowing Tamil.

Folks like Chef Bangera, my young blogger friend Amit and others I met on this trip, who had moved to Chennai from other parts of India, said that they loved living in Chennai. They found the locals warm, welcoming and 'very peaceful', to use Amit's words. Chennai now has quite a few international expats living there which, as Amit explains, has led to a number of expat-run restaurants serving international cuisines such as Korean, Japanese, Italian and Mexican.

The idlis at New Woodlands were not as satisfying or soft as the ones at Murugan Idli Shop or the ITC Grand Chola, and weren't served with podi and ghee. The dosas were a different story, however. Both the sada and the rava dosas were wonderfully crisp. They didn't have the soft underbelly of the Grand Chola dosa. The texture was not multi-dimensional, yet the dosas had a pleasant bite and were light and airy. Chef Bangera said that he would have preferred the rava dosa to be more porous but I found them to be way better than the ones I had in Mumbai, which could often get pasty.

I asked the chef about what distinguishes the classic Tamil dosa? Should it be thin and crisp, like at New Woodlands? Or should it be multi-textural, like they were in his hotel?

The chef explained that the average restaurant in Chennai offered thin, crisp dosas, which were easier to make than the dual-textured ones. However, the dosas served at Tamil homes, especially for lunch and dinner, tend to be on the softer side.

This took me back to a meal I had while in high school in Kolkata at the house of a classmate, Narasimha Chari, who was Tamilian and the class topper. His mom made us dosas for lunch. Two things struck me about the meal. First, the dosas were softer and smaller than what one got in restaurants. Secondly, his mom got us one dosa after another fresh from the kitchen. I had six or seven dosas at one go that afternoon, unlike in restaurants, where one restricts oneself to one dosa.

Just as I have seen with dishes such as the biryani or even the samosa, dosas too can be of various types. They evoke equally strong passions and debates on authenticity and supremacy among fans of the dish. Food blogger Nandita Iyer, whom I mentioned in the chapter on Bengaluru, once wrote a couple of articles on dosa places in Bengaluru and in Chennai on a website. Fights broke out among her readers from both cities on which had better dosas!

Purists might cringe at the Schezwan pav bhaji and Mexican dosas of Mumbai, and I for one prefer simplicity over kitsch in dosas, but hey, whatever works! The dosa has definitely evolved into a fusion dish and I don't know if one should call dosas a South Indian dish any more. Their popularity is pan-Indian after all.

I have fond memories of eating dosa, even a keema dosa, as a kid in Kolkata. During my honeymoon in Goa, I had requested the hotel staff to give me my dosas stuffed with ham.

I enjoyed my idli, dosa and vada breakfasts during my stay in Chennai but I wondered if local Tamilians are still as enamoured by these dishes as I was. I know of Bengali households today which have toast and egg for breakfast, instead of the traditional Bengali breakfasts such as luchi and aloo dum. I wondered if, likewise, the average Tamil household still had the idli, dosa, upma, vada breakfasts that I was tripping on or had they moved on to oats and muesli.

According to Chef Bangera, the traditional South Indian and Tamil tiffin breakfast still rules the roost in Chennai and this includes young, Westernized households and nuclear families too.

So you can still hope to get some lovely dosas and idlis and traditional fare if you go to a Tamil household in Chennai for breakfast and filter kaapi to wash this down with.

IS CHENNAI ALL ABOUT VEGETARIAN FOOD?

If you are not from Chennai, then a lot of what you have read so far in this chapter probably coincides with what you have associated with Chennai and its food till now – that it is all about vegetarian food, specifically idlis and dosas.

Well, let me tell you that if you love your meat and fish, then Chennai is the place to head to. It is, after all, the city that claims to have invented Chicken 65, which is so popular across South India. Chicken 65 is present on almost every South Indian non-vegetarian restaurant menu. It's a spicy deep-fried dish, which is often considered to be the ultimate finger food at bars.

I used to think that the Chicken 65 was an Andhra dish as I had seen it on the menus of the bars of Hyderabad and the Andhra restaurants there. Then I came across a version made with rabbit meat, Rabbit 65, which, as I mentioned, I had in Anjappar in Bengaluru.

I read an article by Ashwin Rajagopalan some time ago, in the *Indian Express*, which said that there is a restaurant chain called Buhari Hotel in Chennai which claims to have invented the dish in 1965. I wanted to check out the place during my trip to Chennai and Chef Bangera gamely offered to accompany me. The original branch is at Mount Road and was established in 1951, but I went to the branch at Velachery as it was close to my hotel.

Many of the classic Chennai restaurants today have branched out across the city, which allows one to try the food of these restaurants without having to travel too far. I don't know if one misses out a bit of the atmosphere by going to the newer branches in the suburbs. When it comes to the food though, local food lovers, such as Amit Patnaik, told me that the dishes generally taste the same across branches and are usually prepared in central kitchens.

When I went to the Buhari Hotel at Velachery, I noticed something called a 'special Chicken 65' on the menu, which I was told is the boneless version. I chose the 'original' one.

The dish turned out to be a plate of bright red chicken on the bone, served with slices of lime. The chicken was freshly fried and pretty juicy. A couple of seconds after I began chewing on the meat, a searing surge of chilli heat walloped me at the base of my throat. I have admitted before that my tolerance level for chillies is not very high. I found the dish rather spicy but it did prove the old theory that I had heard many times before – you get a food high on chillies in various parts of India. The belief is that spicy food makes you perspire and cools your body in the process and helps you handle the heat better, as I had learned when I was in Jaipur.

So when in Chennai, keep calm and eat Chicken 65.

 Tip: Follow up a Chicken 65 with a glass of cold buttermilk.

During this trip, I was also introduced to a side of Chennai's local culinary tradition which I had never before associated with the city. This is the tradition of serving freshly fried seafood at its beach shacks. I had heard of places in Kerala where you buy the fresh catch on sale at the beach and take it to nearby stalls to have them fried. It is a popular concept in the touristy spots of Goa too, especially during high season. I had no idea that you could get something similar in Chennai as well.

I owe this discovery once again to Amit Patnaik, who took me to the Besant Nagar beach in Chennai. He told me that there are food stalls there which begin operating at dusk. Some of these shacks sell what is called 'bhajji'. This is similar to what is called pakora in the north and bhajiya in Mumbai. They consist of vegetables such as green chilli peppers, cauliflower and sliced potatoes, which are deep fried individually in a thick coat of gram flour batter. They are served fresh and piping hot on the beachside.

Located beside the bhajji stalls, are a few other stalls which display marinated seafood such as prawns, lobsters, baby crabs, kingfish slices, whole pomfrets and snappers in glass cabinets. The stalls seem to be family-run places. The husband usually stands at the counter to take your order. Once you place your order, his wife comes to the front of the shop, takes the chosen fish, and goes the back of the shack and shallow fries it with house spices on a flat tava.

Though they didn't speak much Hindi at the stall we went to, we had no problem placing our order at the stall. We pointed at what we wanted, they told us the price and started preparing our order once we had made our choices.

Seeing our interest in what they were cooking, they called us into the shack to see the lady fry the fish on a flat tava with spices that she took out from plastic bottles. She tried to explain which masalas she was using. Unfortunately, she could only tell us the Tamil names, so we left none the wiser but were very touched by their earnestness.

I ate fried prawns, baby crabs and a medium-sized red snapper, all of which cost only about ₹180 (in 2016!). The food was delicious and each dish tasted different. I was particularly blown away by the freshness and juiciness of the snapper. The cooking oil was possibly not the best and the food gave me a bit of acidity, but it was nothing that a little fresh lime soda at dinner couldn't fix. We sat on plastic chairs kept on the sand in front of the stall and enjoyed our freshly fried snacks while stray dogs came and snuggled up to me. Amit looked on in amusement as I did a Periscope live video, then shot a video on my phone for YouTube and Facebook, and then a picture for Twitter and Instagram, before eating. I explained that this was all a part of the eating experience for me and this way, I ate a bit less than I would have otherwise! Eating the freshly cooked seafood on the beach was definitely one of my most memorable food experiences from the Chennai trip.

You can get your offal fix in Chennai too. Amit told me that there are soup carts in Chennai where you can have Chettinad-style coagulated goat's blood soup and other offal-based dishes.

I had an amazing liver ghee roast at the Velachery branch of Dindigul Thalappakatti Restaurant, which otherwise is famous for its Dindigul biryani – a type of biryani unique to Tamil Nadu that I will talk about later. The term 'ghee roast' refers to a slow-cooked preparation popular across South India. I have had ghee roast dishes in Kerala and Andhra restaurants with prawns, fish, chicken and goat meat. The spicing differs from kitchen to kitchen. If you are fond of goat liver, which is something Bengalis of my generation grew up on, then the liver ghee roast at Thalappakatti is just the dish for you. The liver is the star of the dish and is accompanied by a surge of heat from the crushed black pepper, which hits you at the base of your throat. The dish is still thoroughly enjoyable, though!

I even had some stir-fried goat's brain and a stir-fried goat's kidney dish at the branch of the Chettinad restaurant, Ponnusamy Hotel. Chef Bangera, who had taken me out for lunch that afternoon, suggested this restaurant purely by chance. We were originally headed to the much-recommended Nair Hotel for a non-vegetarian lunch before I left Chennai later that afternoon. However, the State Legislative Assembly election results had just been declared that morning and there was much dancing on the streets – stuff that would put the bhangra dancers of Punjab to shame. We finally gave up hopes of reaching Mount Road, where Nair Hotel is, and went to Ponnusamy Hotel instead.

Ponnusamy Hotel is a restaurant that serves food typical of the Chettinad community. Chef Bangera explained that the Chettinad community of Tamil Nadu is quite affluent. Their diet was originally dominated by vegetarian dishes but this changed over time when they travelled the world for trade, including to Far East Asia and Burma, and that's where they are said to have picked up their love for non-vegetarian food. Today Chettinad food is quite famous for its array of lip-smacking non-vegetarian dishes.

The branch of Ponnusamy Hotel that we had gone to was large, air-conditioned and clean. The seating was functional and there was a sleepy feel to the place when we reached at around 3 p.m. There was a sari-clad lady at the pass from the kitchen to the dining area who would put together the dishes on plates before they were sent out. The rest of the kitchen and front-of-shop staff were men. The plating of the food was very basic and most of the dishes were in the range of ₹150 to ₹250 and the portions were suitable for one person.

Chettinad restaurants are famous for serving rabbit meat and shark meat, and I wanted to try them that day. However, both the rabbit and shark meat dishes were over as it was well after lunchtime. Chef Srinivas from ITC Chola, who had joined us for lunch, told me that a lot of classic Chennai restaurants such as Ponnusamy Hotel didn't own refrigerators till recently. Their owners apparently didn't believe in keeping leftover food and preferred to start cooking afresh every morning. This concept reminded me of Pancham Puriwala, Mumbai's oldest-running restaurant. The fifth- (or it could have been the eighth) generation owner of Pancham Puriwala told me that they too had not kept a fridge in the restaurant till recently and would not store food or produce overnight.

We almost ordered everything on the menu at Ponnusamy Hotel because the food sounded so good. Crunchy fried goat's kidneys, goat's brains stir-fried with egg, a flavour-packed country chicken curry and a stellar mutton pepper fry were some of the dishes we tried. These are dishes one would not traditionally associate with Chennai unless perhaps one was a local. We ordered flaky porottas to mop up the food with.

I asked the chefs what percentage of folks in Chennai eat non-vegetarian food and both Bangera and Srinivas estimated that the percentage of non-vegetarians would be at least 60 per cent of those living in Chennai. From what I understand, it is only the Tamil Brahmin communities of Chennai who are vegetarian and they don't constitute the majority of the city's population.

The manager at Ponnusamy Hotel, who took our order, was efficient but not the chattiest of people around. But he did recommend we order the Chettinad pepper crab, which he seemed to be very passionate about. I had a flight to catch in a couple of hours and this was the last meal of my trip, so I told myself to go for it and ordered the crabs.

It was one of the best decisions that I have ever taken. The Chettinad pepper crab at Ponnusamy Hotel turned out to be the most memorable dish of a trip packed with wonderful eats. They serve small crabs at the restaurant, which explained the price tag of only ₹260. The famous Mangalorean seafood restaurants of Mumbai, such as Trishna and Mahesh Lunch Home, normally try to entice you with giant crabs brought live to your table and the cost is upwards of ₹2,000 a plate there.

The crab at Ponnusamy Hotel was served in the shell but broken into pieces with the claws and the body separate. Encouraged by my companions, I grasped a crab claw with my hands and proceeded to chew on the shell. The claw broke and exposed the white crab meat inside. The first taste to hit me was the peppery taste of the masala and this was then followed by the sweet taste of the silken crab meat. The heady masala and the fresh crab meat worked in tandem to give me my most glorious taste experiences of the trip to Chennai.

So a restaurant that I hadn't planned to go to and a dish I hadn't planned to order, gave me the most wonderful eating experience of the trip. Proving that you should just go with the flow rather than planning things too much in advance when it comes to travel. Sometimes serendipity can lead to unforgettable discoveries.

 Tip: End a meal at a Chettinad restaurant with some rice mixed with hot rasam.

DISCOVERING THE CHENNAI BIRYANI

A few months before I came to Chennai, I hosted a Google Hangout group chat. The topic was, 'Which is India's best biryani city?' We had people from Hyderabad, Lucknow, Delhi, Mumbai and Kolkata fighting for the biryanis in their city with a vociferous passion that would put guests on the noisiest of news chat shows on TV to shame.

Suddenly Amit Patnaik, our Chennai food champ, tuned

in and made an impassioned plea for biryani in his adopted city of Chennai. He said that people here even ate biryani for breakfast!

I was keen to try out the biryanis of Chennai and find out what was unique about them. I did manage to go to some of the famous biryani joints of Chennai, though these were the comparatively newer branches of some of the city's restaurants. These were all located at Velachery, which made them easy to cover in one afternoon.

I tried the Dindigul biryani at Thalappakatti. The restaurant chain was founded in 1957 in a place called Dindigul in Tamil Nadu by the Naidu family. Their footprint has spread across Tamil Nadu now and they even have a branch in Paris. The biryani takes its name from the hometown of the restaurant. The restaurant takes its name after the founder, who used to wear a *thalapa*, a cloth headgear, apparently to hide his baldness.

They have quite an extensive menu in the restaurant but the Dindigul biryani is what they are best known for. The rice used in the biryani is short-grained, unlike the long-grained basmati used in the north of India or even in Hyderabad. It is called seeragasamba rice, thanks to its resemblance to whole cumin. The rice in the biryani served to us looked sticky but each grain was separate. The mutton was shredded and spread through the rice unlike the large chunks of meat which one sees in other renditions of mutton biryani. The rice in this biryani takes on the flavour of the meat. The aftertaste has a strong peppery heat which can rattle you if you are not used to spicy food. You are supposed to pair the biryani with dalcha, which is a slow-cooked dish of assorted vegetables, dal and mutton bones. I tried the biryani both with the dalcha, which we ordered, and without. Both make for interesting experiences and I advise that you try both. I must admit that if you are used to long-grain basmati-based biryanis then the Dindigul biryani takes a bit of getting used to. So try to appreciate the dish in isolation rather than comparing it with biryanis that you might be used to.

Another popular biryani variant in Chennai is the Ambur biryani, which originated in a place called Ambur in Tamil Nadu, and again takes its name from its birthplace. There is a restaurant chain called Ambur Star Biryani which is popular for its Ambur biryani. Folklore suggests that the founding owners used to first sell biryanis from bicycles on the streets of Ambur before opening their restaurant, which has since branched out to other locations including Chennai.

It had rained earlier in the morning and the entrance to the Ambur outlet at Velachery that we went to was flooded, but Chef Bangera and I managed to get in, thanks to some deft manoeuvring by the driver of our car. With us was Michael, who was from the hotel concierge. He loved food and had volunteered to accompany us and be our guide as he spoke Tamil. The three of us went up and ordered one plate of biryani, much to the bemusement of the staff at the restaurant. The folks manning the restaurant had come to Chennai from Nepal. We placed our order with them in Hindi so we didn't require Michael's Tamil-speaking abilities.

The food here is served on banana leaves, typical of many other traditional restaurants in Chennai. Our waiter gave a banana leaf to each of us, though we had ordered only one biryani. He then got us the bowl of biryani. My lunch mates told me that the local practice is to wipe the banana leaf with some water and the palm of one's hand before eating on it. This is similar to what we used to do in Bengal in my growing-up years in the 1980s when banana leaves were often used instead of plates at weddings and other occasions. I could be wrong but I felt that the food eaten off banana leaves in wedding feasts tasted a lot better than when eaten on regular porcelain plates. There was a certain joy to mopping up the mutton curry and rice from the banana leaf using one's fingers.

The rice in the Ambur biryani was short-grained too, like in the Dindigul one. It was a bit more moist, though. While the Dindigul biryani that we ate was brown in colour, the Ambur one was yellow. The latter had small pieces of tomato in it too. The mutton pieces in the Ambur biryani were whole chunks and not shredded into small bits, unlike the Dindigul biryani. The mutton was very juicy in both biryanis, despite the difference in the way they had been cooked and served. There was a strong taste of garlic in the Ambur biryani, which takes some getting used to. The Ambur biryani was cheaper than the Dindigul one at Thalappakatti. The restaurant looked more humble too in comparison to the Thalappakatti outlet. I can't say that I was too enthused by this biryani as the strong garlic note is an acquired taste and it did put me off a bit.

 Tip: They serve a raita with the Ambur biryani and mixing it into the rice might help you balance the garlic undertones of the dish.

The third biryani that I tried was the Chettinad biryani at Ponnusamy Hotel. Here, the rice used was long-grained basmati. The biryani had a strong garam masala flavour to it, which was more reminiscent of the classic biryani of Hyderabad as compared to the Ambur and Dindigul ones, which had rather distinct identities of their own. Of the three biryanis that I tried, this was my favourite. Possibly because the taste of this was the one I could relate to the most.

There is a reason why I ended this chapter with a discussion on the biryanis of Chennai. As I said earlier, biryani is not something that people outside Chennai associate the city with and yet there is such a strong biryani culture in the city. It goes to show that we often know so little about worlds outside our own.

My trip to Chennai introduced me to food I hadn't tasted before and food that held me spellbound. I knew I had only scratched the surface of Chennai in two days but even that was enough to break any preconceived notions I had had of Chennai's food till then.

It made me want to travel more and explore more of India beyond its main cities. Hopefully, this was the first step of a whole new journey.

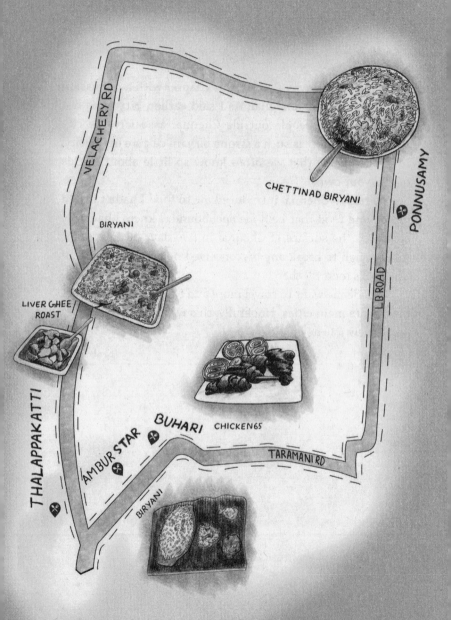

The biryani trail at Velachery

FOOD WALK

👣 *The Besant Nagar Beach walk*

This is best done in the evening. Stroll down the beach and have some sundal, which is a boiled chickpea-based snack, from the hawkers roaming around. Then go to a bhajji stall and have fried vegetable pakoras. Then go to the seafood stalls. Choose whatever your eyes fancy. The food is pretty cheap. End the evening by going to Murugan's Idli Shop, which is on the road by the beach. The podi idlis are a must and if you have a (very strong) sweet tooth, end the evening with jigarthanda there.

👣 *The biryani trail at Velachery*

Start off at Buhari with the Chicken 65 and their unique brand of biryani. Head to Thalappakatti and have the spicy mutton biryani and don't miss the liver ghee roast. Try out the Ambur biryani next door at Ambur Star Biryani. End your biryani feast by going to Ponnusamy for the Chettinad biryani and the crab masala here is a must.

👣 *Amit Patnaik's Mylapore breakfast walk (meant for early risers)*

Start early in the morning and go for a walk on Marina Beach. Then head out at around 7 a.m. for a taste of classic Chennai at the restaurants there. Rayar's Mess has vadas that are crisp outside and soft and airy inside and the pongal is recommended too. Mylai Karpagambal Mess has a variety of delicious dosas. Idlis at Geetha Café are a must-have too.

FINDING YOUR OWN GOA

It was the eve of my birthday and my wife and I were in Goa. Sitting on Goa's Baga beach, reading a book, looking out at the sea, sipping on a glass of watermelon juice or a beer along with a simple ham sandwich for breakfast, then heading to Britto's for prawn chilli fry, walking back to our hotel to nap, then walking by the flea markets of Calangute in the evening before heading to Infantaria for pork chilli fry and rum was my idea of a perfect birthday.

The evening I am talking of was different from our usual Goa evenings. We had not gone out to a restaurant. Instead, we were at the house of Sanchita Banerjee Rodrigues in a village near Panjim. Sanchita is a Bengali Hindu married to a Goan Christian, who has settled in Goa. We got to know each other through common Facebook friends in the early days of Facebook. Food was the common connect. On hearing that my wife and I were in Goa, Sanchita invited us home for dinner. She had cooked up a dinner of local Goan favourites, including chicken cafreal and prawn curry. This was the first time I had actually visited someone's home in Goa, even though this was my sixth trip to the state. Even the staff which was there in most restaurants and shacks had come from elsewhere to make a living during the tourist season. Which meant that we had rarely met locals during our trips to Goa.

Sanchita went to the kitchen to fry some fish to start off the party while we were left in the room with friends of the Rodrigues.

'We love Goa and especially Goan food,' I said to ingratiate ourselves with the folks in the room.

'Really? What do you like?' asked a lady with a big smile, who was dressed in a North Indian-style salwar set.

'Goan sausage fry, pork vindaloo, pork sorpotel, pork chilli fry, beef chilli fry, beef croquettes, oxtail roast...' I replied proudly, thinking they would be impressed by the extensive list I had rattled off.

Instead a silence shrouded the room. It was almost as if I had admitted to being a mass murderer.

'We don't eat pork. Or beef. We are Hindus. We love our fish, though.'

Which was when I realized that the world of Goan food was not as straightforward as tourists like us seem to think it is.

As a tourist who had spent most of his time at Baga beach, I had been exposed to dishes which have come to define 'Goan food' to outsiders. Coincidentally, most of these belong to the Goan Christian community. This community mainly consists of folks whose ancestors were Hindus who converted to Christianity when the Portuguese colonized Goa. They had adopted some of the food habits of the Portuguese and this explained the prevalence of pork and beef on the table. The Goan Christian community had applied a spicy subcontinental dimension to Portuguese dishes. So the vindaloo and sorpotel are packed with chilli and garam masala and the Goan sausage is way spicier than the original Portuguese chorizo from which it was inspired.

The Goan Christian ethos came to define the Goan culture for many of us non-Goans, whether it was in terms of the food served in restaurants or characters who played Goans in Hindi films. The famous cartoonist, the late Mario Miranda, whose drawings often summed up the Goan life for the outside world, was Christian too.

The evening at Sanchita's reminded me of the fact that the

majority of Goans are actually Hindus. Their love for fish is visible even in Mumbai, where I live, in the form of a series of tiny restaurants famous for their seafood. These restaurants are called Gomantak restaurants. The most famous one is Highway Gomantak in Mumbai's Bandra East. Then there are the very popular Pradeep Gomantak Bhojanalaya in Fort and Gomantak at Dadar. Saayba Gomantak Hotel at Bandra West has its fans too. These restaurants offer Hindu coastal Goan food in Mumbai and are very popular among locals, including Maharashtrians, as the food is very similar to Malvani food from the coasts of Maharashtra. The food in these restaurants is relatively inexpensive, the décor functional – most are not air-conditioned. They almost always have a queue of people waiting to enter.

Yet, when non-Goans talks of Goan restaurants in Mumbai, the name that often comes up is that of a tiny place called New Martin Hotel, better known as Martin's at Colaba, which serves the vindaloo, sorpotel, sausages and steak fries that the Goan Christian community loves.

Ironically, Martin's is owned by a Mangalorean gentleman and not a Goan!

Of course, it's not as if the Goan Christians eat only pork and beef and don't eat fish. A friend that I made through food-blogging, Gia Fernandes, is a Goan Christian from Mumbai. She is as adept in cooking pork as she is in making fish curries or xit codi, as it is called in Konkani. Gia tells me that the curries made by the Goan Christian community are different from that of the Hindu community in terms of spice and sourness levels.

Gia occasionally goes to Goa with her parents to her

ancestral home. Every morning a fish seller comes to their door with fresh catch from the market. Gia buys fish from her and makes fish curry for her family. Sometimes she asks her local Goan house help for recipes. Gia tells me that the common way for people to greet each other in the village is to ask, 'What curry is cooking in your home today?' They actually want to know what fish has been bought that day when they ask this question.

This reminded me of my native Bengal where people often greet those returning from the fish market by asking, '*Aaj ke bajare ki maachh kinlen*?' (What fish did you buy at the market today?)

Gia rarely goes to the beach during her time at Goa. When she told me this, I realized that there are several Goas when it comes to food and culture. There's one Goa for those who call Goa their home. Then there's one for tourists. And one for regular visitors who call it their home away from home. Which Goa you want to go to depends on you really. Each can be equally enjoyable.

I have often wondered if there is an uneasy relationship between local Goans and tourists. The locals in Sanchita's house, for example, felt that restaurants in Goa depended on people like them who offered steady business through the year, and not on tourists who visited only during some parts of the year. They even spoke of outsiders who ran up a tab at local bars and homestays and escaped without paying!

I have also observed that one of the surest ways to get berated and mocked by Goans on social media is to mention that you ate at one of the popular places in Goa, such as Infantaria or Britto's. There are those who will scornfully say, 'That's touristy'. This is, of course, not always the case but I do understand the emotion behind it, as I've found that smaller, unknown food joints are often the heart of the state's cuisine. But I have come across Goans who like the food at these 'touristy' places.

There is no denying that if there is one state in India that owes at least some of its affluence to tourism, it's Goa. I can sympathize that having your hometown flooded with strangers for parts of the year can be trying, though!

As for me, I just love Goa. For many of us in Mumbai, Goa is Riviera and Vegas rolled into one. Thanks partly to Hindi cinema, Goa's popularity spread all across the country including to Kolkata where I grew up. Going to Goa was on the top of the list of my priorities when I moved to Mumbai.

My first trip to Goa was a sanitized office off-site spent in a five-star hotel resort and completely cut off from the local scene. All my meals were buffets at the hotel. I don't remember anything about food from that time. Over the years, my wife and I stayed at many luxurious hotels and resorts in Goa, including on our honeymoon. These places are pretty expensive during high season (November to February) but you get good deals during off-season and so Goa is a favoured monsoon getaway for the Mumbai corporate crowd.

What I considered the 'real' Goa experience came alive for me during my second trip there. I had gone there with a few friends from college during the Diwali break. Our destination was Baga, which one of the folks in the group had recommended. So we took a bus and headed to Goa, landed at Baga and checked into an inexpensive bed and breakfast. I proceeded to have some of the most amazing few days of my life during the trip. I fell in love with Baga. To me, it represented the freedom I had sought when I left my sheltered life in Kolkata and came to Mumbai.

I took my wife to Baga for the first time on her birthday and she took to the place immediately. Even though the visit was during the monsoon, when the seaside shacks were shut, as were many of the restaurants, she was taken in by the spell of Baga, just like I had been.

We returned next spring for my birthday, and then for three more years after that. For a while I couldn't think of celebrating my birthday anywhere else. Then we stopped going there for a few years because of work commitments. We returned to Baga in February 2014. Though we had come back after a couple of years, we saw that everything seemed more or less the same. After a day, we realized this was not so. To start with, there were tonnes of new restaurants. Quite a few of these were vegetarian Gujarati thali joints. I found this a little disconcerting. Goa for us, after all, is the promised land of pork and prawn. The vegetarian restaurants seemed out-of-place, given the image we held of Goa. There were other changes too. It seemed more crowded and dusty. There were also more tattoo and massage parlours and cashew shops and some malls too. Baga, for me, had lost a bit of its charm.

Yet, there is something about Baga that is still alluring. I know that there are many who prefer the quieter beaches of South Goa, but my wife and I are clearly 'Baga people'.

Unsurprisingly, we have a few favourite restaurants in Baga and, thankfully, they have remained unchanged. Even the staff looked familiar when we visited these in 2014, although Goa has a huge floating work population during the holiday season. Most importantly, the food, tasted exactly the same as it did in our earlier visits.

Here are the Baga classics that my wife and I always go back to.

OF INFANTARIA AND 'ROSARY' SAUSAGE

I still remember our first visit to Infantaria. My wife and I had landed at Goa. She was not very happy with the room in the resort that we had checked into at Calangute. It was the rainy season and the walls were damp and the roads outside were muddy. We decided to step out in search of a place to eat. We walked on to the road which led to Baga. Suddenly my wife pointed to a restaurant and said, 'This is Infantaria. We had gone here during an ad film shoot at Goa. We can eat here.'

We stepped into the rather sleepy restaurant. There were two storeys but everyone was sitting downstairs. We ordered an ox tongue roast to start with. The dish was brought to our table and we were delighted to find that the meat was juicy, supple, soft yet not mushy and that the sauce enrobing it was very robust. It was the beginning of a beautiful friendship. With Infantaria and with Baga.

From that afternoon onwards, Infantaria became our favourite restaurant in Goa. The pork chilli fry here – with its delectable pieces of belly fat, whose richness is cut through by the spice from the fried chillies – is our favourite dish.

They also make a delicious Goan sausage fry here, which is spicy and not too sour. I love the Goan sausage fried rice too. I find it so bewitching that I order it every time I go to Goa. There is something about the marriage of rice with spring onions, eggs and crunchy bits of fatty Goan sausage that makes this dish very addictive. So much so that despite resolving to have just a few spoons, I wipe the bowl clean every time I order it. The Goan sausage pulao is a more traditional rendition of the dish.

Goan sausage has a very sharp taste. It is a bit like a pickle, as Kunal Vijayakar once told me. It is a dish that was originally inspired by the chorizo, except that the Goan version is spicier and tangier. It is traditionally made with pork, though I have spotted the occasional beef version too. Some people used to be wary of the pork used for sausages and other Goan dishes, as they were made from pigs that scavenge on waste at Goan farms. Now there are farms where pigs are raised for consumption and these are considered safer to eat.

You get packaged versions of Goan sausages in Christian-run meat shops in Mumbai's Bandra where I live. They are fairly easy to cook and my wife makes a lovely version. She slits the sausage casing and puts the meat into a hot pan. She adds some finely chopped onions, split whole green chillies and peeled potato cubes and lets the whole mix cook in a covered pan for about half-an-hour. You don't need to add any salt or spices as the sausages are already spiced. We eat this with pav, which is the bread that the Portuguese introduced to Mumbai.

 Tip: If you go to a Goan restaurant in Goa, ask for poi, the local bread. The Mumbai equivalent is pav. Both have Portuguese origins but the former is crustier on the outside. You might find it difficult to have Goan sausage without bread or rice on the side as it has a very sharp taste.

Those in the know will tell you that the best Goan sausage are the 'rosary' ones sold in the local Mapusa market in Goa. They are sold on strings and look like rosary beads, and that's why they are called so. I have found the meat from these sausages to be less acidic and pungent than the ones sold in branded packets in Bandra shops, even though the latter come from Goa too.

There has been a bit of a Goan sausage revolution in Mumbai of late, with folks running modern restaurants in

Mumbai introducing it in their menus. Non-Goans have responded positively to it too. Anil Kably at The Bagel Shop in Mumbai's Bandra offers a cream cheese and Goan sausage bagel at his café, which is very popular among foreigners too as the cream cheese helps tone down the sharpness of the sausage. Chef Glyston Gracias offers a sandwich at Smoke House Deli where he uses multigrain bread, Goan sausage bits and potatoes to make a delightful Goan sausage-and-potato sandwich.

Glyston is an East Indian but uses Goan sausage at his restaurants. The East Indians were among the many original residents of Mumbai. They too were converted to Christianity by the Portuguese, just as the Goans were. They have their own version of the Goan sausage, which uses East Indian bottle masala instead of garam masala for the spicing. You can find this in East Indian Chef Aloo's Villa Vandre in Bandra.

Then there is Chef Irfan Pabaney's Sassy Spoon, which offers a mac-and-cheese with Goan sausage, quite the hedonistic treat. I also enjoyed the Goan sausage 'tiffin box combo' at Goan chef and one-time Bandra boy (based in the US now), Floyd Cardoz's The Bombay Canteen in Mumbai. I found the meat in the Goan sausage to be toned down in the dish and not too intimidating. It was mixed with boiled potatoes and salli, fried potato straws. Chef Thomas Zachariah of The Bombay Canteen told me that they added minced pork to the Goan sausage in the dish to make it less daunting for the non-Goan palate.

The efforts of these restaurants to use indigenous produce such as Goan sausage is an encouraging one. I am sure that it is just the start of the Goan sausage wave. Plus it helps reduce the carbon footprint involved in importing European chorizo.

To get back to Infantaria, we once ordered a fish curry

there and found that the curry was perfectly balanced. The fish used was a semolina-crusted fried kingfish, which my wife and I both agreed was the juiciest and best fried fish we had ever had. We liked the curry much more than the curry at a local Hindu restaurant called Reis at Mapusa that we went to, where the curries seemed spicier and heavier and less tangy. When I told Gia about this, she said that the Infantaria version was probably cooked in the Christian Goan style versus the Hindu Goan style at Mapusa, and perhaps our tastes were more attuned to the Christian style. Gia approves of the red and tangy Goan fish curry that we get in the Goan Christian family-run Candies restaurant in Mumbai. As does my mother-in-law, but Gia is Goan so her words carry more weight in this case!

Apart from the great food, there is a sense of calm and warmth that permeates Infantaria that tugs at our hearts. This has not changed one bit in the last eight years. The restaurant often hosts live musical performances on the first floor at night. My wife and I prefer to sit downstairs, though, to take in the sights and sounds of the road in front of us as we eat. For those looking to have a drink, alcohol in Goa, and in Infantaria, is cheaper than in most other parts of India. The service can get a bit slow here when the place is crowded but the food more than makes up for it.

 Tip: Infantaria gets crowded during the day during the tourist season, so it's best to go at night. The beef croquettes, which taste so good that my wife is addicted to them, are rarely available. They get over very soon, so order them quickly if you ever see them.

A SYMPHONIC PRAWN BAFAT

Next on my list of favourites in Baga is Britto's, which is said to have started in 1961 as a four-table affair but is now a largish beach shack with both a covered and an open section.

Like Infantaria, Britto's too hasn't changed much since we first went there in the early 2000s. The look of the place hasn't changed, nor has the menu. Since it's located right on the beach, you can get tables fairly close to the sea when it is not raining. You can sit at the cemented and covered restaurant section closer to the road and away from the sand. My wife and I prefer the latter.

We keep going back to Britto's for their prawn chilli fries. The chilli fries here are sweeter – they have more tomatoes and cubes of parboiled potatoes –than those at Infantaria. Gia tells me that Goans rarely add garam masala to a seafood chilli fry.

Another classic here is the prawn bafat or bafad. The curry is a symphony of flavours that hits all the right notes – it is coconut-milk-based and I find it similar in style to the Bengali prawn malai curry. The prawns are cooked just right – juicy and delicate on the inside. I wonder if both the Goan and the Bengali dish have a bit of Portuguese influence in them. The Bengali malai curry came from Malaysia, which explains the word 'malai' in the name. The Portuguese, who have influenced so much of Goan cuisine, were in Malaysia too!

I once found a bafat masala packet at Marks Cold Storage, a meat shop at Pali Market in Mumbai's Bandra, which I frequent. I excitedly showed this to Mrs Nancy D'Sousa at the cash counter and told her that bafat was one of our favourite dishes in Goa. Mrs D'Sousa has married into the family that opened Marks Cold Storage 60 years ago. She is often at the counter now, when her husband is not there, greeting customers with a big smile. We have seen her sons grow up from little kids who wore shorts to school to young collegians in frayed denims. Nancy aunty (she chides me with a smile for calling her aunty) will happily dish out recipes if you go to her and ask her how to cook the meat that you have bought at her shop.

Nancy is a Mangalorean Christian originally from Karnataka. The Mangaloreans have a lot of dishes – such as the vindaloo and sorpotel – in common with Goan Christians and Mumbai's East Indians, and yet these dishes differ in terms of flavour and spice notes across the three communities. Such is the complexity of Indian food. It's a bit like the Vedas. You can keep diving into it and yet never claim to be an 'expert' who knows all that there is to know about Indian food.

Nancy told me that bafat is actually a Mangalorean dish. It is traditionally made with pork and not prawns and is a must on festive occasions. I used the bafat masala to make a prawn bafat and felt transported to Britto's in Goa while sitting at home in Bandra.

 Tip: Do try the prawn vindaloo at Britto's. Prawns are stir-fried in a vindaloo masala and makes for a delicious meal.

As I said before, many Goans on social media run down Baga and Infantaria as being 'touristy'. Well yes, they are touristy, to the extent that they are situated in areas flocked by tourists. Once again, I turned to Gia and asked her what she thought about Britto's.

She said that in her younger days she would often go to Infantaria after church for Sunday lunch with her family. They would apparently order the 'continental' dishes there.

'Goans don't go to Goan restaurants to eat Goan food,' she explained.

 Tip: If you're looking for a good breakfast option, Lila Café, with its fresh juice and baguettes, is a good choice. It was set up by a Swiss family who came to Goa decades back and has changed location a few times.

FRANCISCO'S CASA PORTUGUESA

If you were to ask my wife, she would put Casa Portuguesa as her number one recommendation in Baga. Our first visit here was in 2008, at her insistence, and it turned out to be fabulous. We were back six years later and, thankfully, nothing had changed. Casa Portuguesa is situated in a 300-year-old Portuguese house run by Francisco, the ever-smiling owner of the restaurant who is also a lawyer. He's one of the most hands-on restaurant owners I've seen. On a busy day, you will find Francisco taking orders, rolling up his sleeves and joining his staff in serving guests and cleaning up tables. Finally, he will take out his guitar and soulfully croon Portuguese songs from the Fado genre.

The ambience of the place is very old-world aristocratic, right down to the candlelit dinners. The food is great too. The first time we went there, we had the duck cooked with clams, a novel combination, and the pork curry. We loved both dishes. On our next visit we tried a Portuguese seafood stew, which was made with clams, squids, prawns and a local fish called tamoshi, which is a kind of mackerel. The stew was served on a bed of caramelized onions. We followed this with slices of the delectable roasted suckling pig. And then, of course, there was the complimentary bread, baked in-house, which came at the start of the meal, along with butter and a lovely olive spread.

The service here is so special that the waiter told us that the stew would be enough for the two of us and when we ordered the piglet, he himself offered to get this as a one- by-two portion, since there were two of us. And what's more, unlike in Mumbai, they don't charge an extra service charge here when they give you the bill.

If you want to feel special, or are looking for a celebratory meal, then this is the place to go to. The food is always delectable and you will never leave disappointed. Francisco will pour you a glass of port on the house at the end when he is in a good mood. Which is always.

HITTING THE SHACKS OF GOA

You can't go to the beach and not hit the shacks if you are in Goa during the season, which is from February to March. On our last visit in 2014, it was terribly hot, even in early February, and we could only enjoy the beach in the evening. Still, it felt good to take a break from Mumbai, reading a book while lying on a deck chair on the beach or lazily watching the waves.

One of our favourite snacks to have on the beach whenever we visited Goa was fried pork cocktail sausages. But they were hard to find during our last trip.

We went to a shack called O'Pinhal which served some nice beef sausages one day but the next day, they had neither beef nor pork so we went to Love Shack, which assured us that they had pork sausages, and then came with a plate of Goan sausages, much to my wife's annoyance. She had forgotten to specify she wanted 'English' sausages, which is how Goans distinguish sausages from the local Goan sausage.

 Tip: While ordering sausages in Goa, always specify whether you want 'English' or Goan sausages.

Service at the shacks can be a bit quirky and uneven. Most of the folks are busy trying to convince foreigners to order fresh seafood, which is brought out on platters for inspection. You are also assailed by an army of hawkers selling everything from cut fruits to junk jewellery – even beachside massages.

'The shacks are no longer what they used to be,' was my wife's verdict after our little sausage fiasco.

However, there is no denying that for the first-time traveller to Goa, a visit to its shacks during the season is a must.

 Tip: The trick to hitting the shacks in Baga is to take the Vila Goesa Beach Resort entry to the beach, which puts you between Baga and Calangute, where the crowd is a little sparser.

THE OTHER GOA

Earlier in the chapter, I had referred to the 'real Goa'. Over the years, I have realized that the Goa I was referring to was the land of freedom, beaches and cheap alcohol that collegians and young working crowds in Mumbai dream of. That alcohol-doused version was my first experience of Goa, after all. That, of course, is not what Goa means to Goans.

After a decade of trips to Goa and Baga I decided that I wanted to explore more of the 'local Goa'. The best way to do so would be to hire a car (I don't know how to ride a bike so I can't suggest it) and drive down with locals, going to places that they frequent or to eat in their homes. That's how an ideal food trip would be. However, in real life that's not always possible. Here, trips are made for work or for leisure with meals tucked in between. Unless you are a food journalist, or a food freak, who has gone in search of a food story with a single-minded focus, an ideal food trip rarely happens by accident.

We did have a brush with a different Goa during our most recent trip there in mid-2015. This time we didn't stay at Baga but stayed in Goa's capital city, Panjim, instead.

We were staying at the Goa Marriott, right on the beach. We could hear the waves from our room. The hotel is also close to the heart of the city of Panjim and a lady at the desk connected us with Jack Makhija who takes people on heritage walks at Panjim's Fontainhas. Jack took us through the bylanes of Panjim where each building was painted in bright colours including green, red, yellow and blue. This was a very different and colourful Goa from the dusty lanes of Baga that we were used to. One normally associates such colourful suburbs with places like Pondicherry. The beauty of Panjim was a revelation to us. Jack told me that not too many tourists come to Panjim, which probably explains why the architectural beauty and heritage of Panjim is not too well-known outside of Goa. The soft-spoken Jack is very passionate about the city he grew up in and patiently answered all our questions. The walk is customized and is built around what the participants in the walk are looking for. I asked Jack about which restaurant he would go to for the best Goan food in Panjim.

His answer was typical. 'You get the best Goan food in Goan homes.'

I had plans of exploring local restaurants on this trip and went in search of a place called Bhatti Village, which is the 'secret' Goan food place that everyone on social media had been telling me about. The cab ride (₹1,500 to and from our hotel) cost more than our meal. The restaurant is located in a nondescript lane in the village of Bhatti Waddo. Once you reach close by, locals guide you to the place.

Bhatti Village is a dimly lit place located in a Goan house, which at some point housed a distillery or *bhatti*. It takes its name from its history and the owner, Patrick, has kept a few century-old implements from the original distillery on show at his restaurant. The seating is pretty basic and is spread across the different rooms of the house.

Patrick's wife, Merciana, cooks recipes from their family's repertoire. The menu changes daily. He is very proud of the food that they put out and is annoyed when he hears that other retaurants have begun to include some of the home-styled dishes that they offer at Bhatti Village. Once you are seated, Patrick comes and tells you what's there for the day and you place your order with him. There is no menu card so we didn't have an idea of the prices when we placed our order. We had some lovely semolina-coated fried whitebait and meat croquettes to start our meal. This was followed by a plate of roast pork lined with pieces of delicious fat and a prawn curry called guizad, which was very thin and delicate and took on the flavour of the prawns. Later when I told Gia about the dish, she said that she often makes it at home. The subtlety of the dish made it so different from what we would normally eat in Goan restaurants. The entire meal with a dessert and soft drinks cost us ₹1,000 in 2015.

Tip: Ask for the prices of what you are ordering so that there are no surprises at the end.

We didn't explore any other place in search of Goan food during that trip and there is a reason for that. We went to the Marriott coffee shop to have lunch on the day we landed. There was a buffet laid out which had the usual buffet favourites – cheesy pastas, kung pao chicken and dal makhni. Then I spotted a counter which said 'Goan corner'. No one else was taking food from there. I went and chose some squid grilled in a green xacuti masala. I was blown away by the dish. The squid was fresh and juicy, perfectly cooked and the spices coating it were delicious. When I went to the counter at night I found a flavour-packed pork vindaloo.

The next morning I met the executive chef of the Marriott, Anupam Gulati, and got to know the secret behind the simple, uncomplicated and robust flavours of the Goan food I had sampled.

It turns out that they have a local lady as chef, whom they call Aunty Jyacinta, who comes from the local village twice a week to the Marriott. This soft-spoken lady came to the hotel to work when her husband passed away more than a decade ago. She grinds the masalas and trains the young chefs there with her original Goan recipes. The Goan food that came out of her kitchen is phenomenal. It is fresh and quite different from what one finds in restaurants in terms of the punch of the spices used and their fragrance. You can also tell that the fish and meat are cooked with much love and care. She is a woman of few words but her pride in her work was evident and led to some pretty lovely meals for us.

I found out that they also have some young Goan chefs at the Marriott such as Samantha Nunes, the pastry chef. She comes from a local village to work at the Marriott early in the morning as she gets crusty butter croissants and amazing bacon-and-honey waffles ready for the breakfast buffet. However, she also recreates traditional Goan desserts that she has learned from her grandmom. While I knew of the Goan classic desserts, bebinca and dodol, I was mesmerized by the Goan desserts that she introduced me to – bolo sans rival, vonn and doce bolo chocolat caju. I had not come across them in all my years at Baga.

Thinking about my Goa visits made me wonder about the much-bandied phrase in the world of food travel writing – 'eating like a local'.

Trying to eat where the locals do and showing an interest in their food is a great way to know a place. But is this always possible? If you are not besotted by food and if you have come to a place for just a day or two, then can you really go into the interiors seeking out the places where locals eat? If you don't know anyone at the place you have visited, then how can you go to someone's house and eat?

During a recent trip of ours to Italy in 2016, Jonaki, my college friend, who is married to an Italian chef, would send me detailed Facebook mails on where to go and eat at the cities we visited. The problem I faced was that on a short visit where time was at a premium, in a place where language was an issue, it was not always possible to go find some of these places.

Then comes another question, how does one define a 'local'? In the case of Goa, would it be a Goan Christian or a Goan Hindu? Their cuisines are different, after all. Would it be old-timers in Goa who would never go to a restaurant to eat what they can get at home? Or would it be the young

IT professionals working in Goa who want to go to the new places there that have been set up by foreigners and offer international cuisine?

The thing is, if you go to a place to eat while on a trip, enjoy your meal and then share an update on social media (which we have to, right?), there will always be someone to tell you, 'You went to the wrong place, you should have gone to this other place instead.'

So here's my take on this problem. Do your research before you travel on where to eat. Ask folks on Twitter or Facebook for suggestions. Ask people at your hotel, cabbies, shopkeepers and even people on the road about where they like to eat once you get there.

Once you have landed somewhere and had a meal then try to enjoy the moment and savour what you had without letting anyone spoil the experience for you.

Life is all about living in the present, after all.

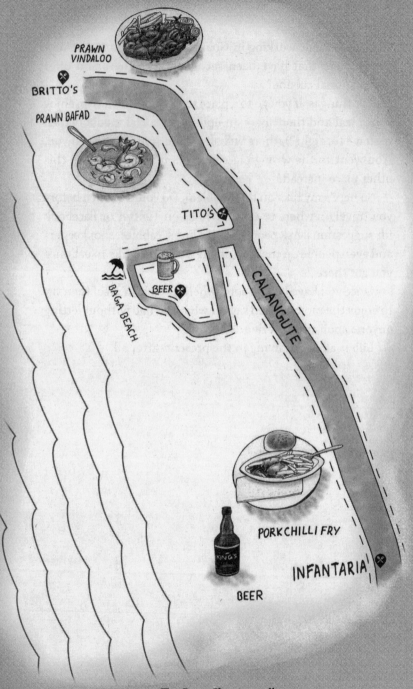

The Baga Classics walk

FOOD WALK

👣 The Baga Classics walk

Start your evening at 7 p.m. and walk into Infantaria near Calungute. Have some pork and squid chilli fry with the local King's beer. Walk down the lane to Baga and stop at the flea market on the way for some shopping. Take a turn up ahead and step into Tito's for a beer. After you're done drinking, hit the beach and walk further down, with the sea by your side, to Britto's. You can sit by the sea or go to the covered portion further up and end your evening with prawn vindaloo and prawn bafat. Or go to Casa Portuguesa for a romantic dinner.

👣 Panjim evening walk

Start your walk at 7 p.m. and head down the Fontainhas area and take in the beauty of the local architecture. Head to Panjim Church at 8 p.m. and have omelette pav at Sandip's stall. Then go to Ritz Classic Restaurant N Bar for a seafood thali. You might have to queue up here. End your trail by going to the Marriott Goa for an Aunty Jyacinta Special chorizo pav and a nightcap.

MUMBAI, I LOVE YOU

I

Of Courtship, Colaba and Old Loves

Would you be able to remember the exact time and place when you fell in love?

I fell in love with Mumbai during my second trip to the city. I had come with a group of classmates from my MBA institute to work on placements. I was staying with Tokaidi, the niece of Biswaranjan Jethu, a neighbour of mine from Kolkata. Her place was at Colaba and this, for a week, was my base in Mumbai.

Every day after work I would head back to my host's place, which was at the end of the Colaba Causeway. It was an interesting time in my life – still a student and about to step into the corporate world.

As I walked down Apollo Bunder past the Gateway of India, with the rush of breeze from the Arabian Sea whistling past me, somewhere in my subconscious, the germ of an idea – of wanting to move out of home and explore the world – was planted.

When I returned to Mumbai a year later as a market-research trainee – a white-collar worker and no longer a student – Colaba continued to play a big part in my life.

This was the late 1990s. Bandra was yet to become the restaurant hotspot that it is today. No one spoke about Oshiwara or Powai which, since then, have grown to become major restaurant hubs too. My colleagues and I used to work around Dadar, stay in PG digs at Bandra and hang out in what we called 'Town' in Mumbai, specifically Colaba.

Heading out to Colaba meant evenings spent in Leopold Café – a long time before *Shantaram* made it famous and the attacks of 26/11 made it infamous. Leopold Café, or Leo's, was a place for us out-of-towners to hang out over beer and other drinks with names as intriguing as Black Russian, and feel all grown-up. The local Mumbaikars would go to Mondy's or Café Mondegar next door. When we wanted to eat, we would head to the Bade Miya stall down the lane from Mondy's and gorge on kebabs, perched precariously on plastic chairs with cats brushing against our legs. We also used to have cheap alcohol with fried prawn balls at Gokul, another establishment in Colaba. Or, when we were feeling posh, we would go to Cafe Churchill down the road at Colaba Causeway for what we called 'continental' food.

A lot has changed since then. Bade Miya now has a restaurant with seating at Fort, though the stall at Colaba remains a favourite with tourists. Gokul is still popular for cheap alcohol but as the city has moved northwards, places like Bandra's Janata Lunch Home is giving it stiff competition. Plus, there's Bar Stock Exchange which has become another trendy new player on the *sasta daaru* front. Cafe Churchill still has queues lining up outside, but with fancier new-age European restaurants opening everywhere, the once-trendy little café is now a tad anachronistic; our palates have learned to distinguish between Italian, French and Spanish cuisines and our 'continental' sensibilities have changed. Leopold Café is still touristy and is a hangout for *Shantaram*-clutching foreign tourists and Mondy's continues to be more popular among the locals.

I don't hang around at Colaba every evening now as I once used to, but my wife and I do head there when we get the time.

It is still our favourite part of town to visit. Colaba, after all, was once the backdrop of our courtship and the place where we used to spend evening after evening. We would have dinner together and I would then drop her home before I headed back to my PG. Our romance was built on prawn fried rice and mutton chilli at Leo's, sausage with firecracker sauce and penne in Newburg sauce with prawns at Cafe Churchill, Goan sausage fry and steak fry with chips at New Martin Hotel, prawn balls at Gokul and seekh kebabs and rumali rotis at Bade Miya. A couple of other places that we would frequent in South Mumbai were the now-shut Just Around The Corner at Churchgate for salads, Kobe Sizzlers at Girgaon where we would share a sizzler, and Crystal for rajma, kali dal, sukha aloo, paneer bhurji and fresh rotis.

After a year of eating out, we were completely broke when we got married. Dining out was no longer an option. That's when I taught myself to cook in the tiny veranda of our apartment, which acted as our kitchen. But that's a story for another day.

GOING GOAN AT NEW MARTIN HOTEL

I have always been flummoxed by the paucity of Goan eateries in Mumbai. Mumbai, after all, is considered to be the stepping-stone to Goa by outsiders. There is a sizeable Goan population in Mumbai but hardly any Goan restaurants.

I must clarify that by 'Goan' I mean Goan Catholic – which, to me, means the porcine world of sausages, vindaloos, sorpotels and roasts. Goan food also includes Gomantak cuisine, which is the Hindu food of the coastal region and a cousin of the Maharashtrian Malvani food, as I've mentioned earlier. It takes an insider to know the difference between them, if you ask me.

The most famous of the Goan Catholic eateries is New Martin Hotel on Colaba's Strand Road. 'Famous' has to be accompanied with quotes here. Experience has showed that many, including 'foodies', haven't heard about Martin's, especially those who are new to the city. Martin's is tucked away in a by-lane in Colaba and it took me a year to find the place after landing in Mumbai in 1997. It was thanks to a newly made Bengali friend, who lived in the YMCA at Colaba, that I managed to locate Martin's. The best landmark now is Theobroma after Cusrow Baug on the Colaba Causeway. Take the lane opposite this popular bakery and the first right after that to hit this tiny and unpretentious little eatery. The restaurant has five tables with spartan benches. It is clean and rarely smelly, despite the strong aromas that Goan food emits at times.

My wife and I used to go there at least once a week when we were dating. In the early 2000s a meal for two there would rarely cross ₹100 and it's not much more even now.

We have a clear favourite at this restaurant. That is the buffalo steak fry with chips. It's nothing like the pink on-the-inside, medium-rare steaks you will see on foreign TV channels. The 'steak' here is a thin, stringy piece of water-buffalo fillet deep fried to oily oblivion, encased in a bed of caramelized fried onions and the odd green chilli and tomato. Let me assure you that this tastes a lot more special than I made it sound.

 Tip: Reach before 9 p.m. if you don't want to miss the steak fry.

They serve a pretty nice, sharp and piquant Goan sausage fry here too. The thing about Goan sausage is that it has a very sharp taste. It is difficult to have this dish without some pav (or pao) bread. Pav is more a Mumbai speciality while in Goa, you get a bread called poi instead.

Both pav and poi were introduced in India by the Portuguese. These breads were adopted first by the local Christian, Irani and Muslim communities. The Hindus of Mumbai were slow to adopt pav, as Saee Koranne Khandekar points out in *Crumbs!: Bread Stories and Recipes for the Indian Kitchen*. Toddy was used to ferment the dough for the bread in the Catholic- and Muslim-owned bakeries of Mumbai, which the Hindus were wary of. It was only in the 1960s, with the introduction of vada pavs on the streets of Mumbai, that the use of pav became ubiquitous in Mumbai.

My wife is quite fond of the pork vindaloo at Martin's. The juiciness of the pork and the tangy spiciness of the curry works for her. She loves to dip her pav in the vindaloo to mop up the curry. The vindaloo, like the Goan sausage, is of Portuguese origin, which got a local makeover.

 Tip: Mop up the sorpotel and sausage fry with pav and remember that the Portuguese have spawned each of these dishes, so three cheers to fusion cooking!

I have seen families feasting on the bangda curry at Martin's. That is usually the only fish dish that they offer. Mackerel or bangda is usually the most economical fish to eat in Mumbai restaurants. The custard-and-jelly is a popular dessert at Martin's and on my last visit I tried it. One indulgent bite and I knew the secret of its well-earned popularity. It is a lovely dessert which harks back to happy childhood memories for most of us.

Ironically, this popular Goan restaurant is owned by a Mangalorean gentleman. Mangalorean and Goan Catholics share a lot of dishes such as sorpotel, vindaloo and choriz as part of their repertoire, though the spices used differ a bit. The food at Martin's is Goan though.

Another Goan restaurant that hardly any non-Goan knows about is the sleepy Snowflakes near the Metro Cinema. The food here is more homely than Martin's and the atmosphere even quieter. The hours of opening can get a bit unpredictable and you might land up there and see that it's shut. They make a pretty nice vindaloo and lovely mince chops too.

 Tip: On your way back from Martin's, do try the gooey brownies at Theobroma.

'CONTINENTAL' AT CAFE CHURCHILL

In the late 1990s and early 2000s, if you saw a queue on the footpath roughly opposite Cusrow Baug – the Parsi colony on Colaba Causeway – you would know that they were people waiting for a table at Cafe Churchill.

Cafe Churchill at Colaba and Pot Pourri in Bandra were the two famous outposts for accessible and non-five-star 'continental' food in Mumbai in those days.

Since then Pot Pourri has given way to the Asian restaurant Lemon Leaf, run by the same owners. Now the Bandra Lemon Leaf is shut too and there is a a Café Coffee day outlet in its place. Cafe Churchill has been repositioned by the spate of trendy, albeit more expensive, modern European places that have sprung up all over the city. Yet, for its regulars, Cafe Churchill is full of soul, and stories that are unmatched.

Let's go back 15 years when my wife and I used to hang around at Colaba. My wife is a Parsi. It is often said that Parsis are more British than the British themselves. She loved continental food while I preferred Chinese food. So every evening, there would be a tussle between whether to go to Leopold's for noodles or to Cafe Churchill for pasta.

After we got married I learned how to cook pasta for her and today can churn out quite a few varieties of rather excellent (if I may say so myself) pastas to keep her happy.

Fifteen years ago, on a Sunday, it would take more than half-an-hour to get a table at Cafe Churchill for dinner, sometimes even an hour. Yet we would wait. We were regulars then.

When we went back recently, we waited for less than ten minutes to get a seat at 9 p.m.! I would never have believed it if someone told me this was possible back in 2000.

Once you step inside Cafe Churchill, you feel as if the place is frozen in time. The arrangement of the tables is the same as it was in the late 1990s when I first started going there. The American-deli-style board displaying the fare is the same. The menu card is the same, barring the prices. The 'specials of the day' have not changed for years. The range of iconic desserts in the fridge also remain the same. As do the papermats on the table with the sketch of a smiling sun licking its lips.

Mr Gandhi, the affable and plump gentleman who mans the cash counter, continues to sit at the till a decade later, looking bemusedly at the CCTV feeds. We always used to order iced teas when we went there and Mr Gandhi would send out sachets of tea to the kitchen to make our drinks. Those were more innocent times.

The thick, cream-coloured, ceramic plates on which the food is served haven't changed. There is no pretence of fine dining or gourmet trappings here. If you order a dish with sauce, then the meat or fish will be served in a sea of sauce with a blob of mashed potatoes on the side. There are no artistic squeeze-bottle patterns on the china. The hearty and uncomplicated taste of the food remains the same too. So does our order whenever we return to Cafe Churchill. Peach iced tea (no longer served in beer mugs though), followed by sausages in firecracker sauce and garlic bread and then a penne Newburg sauce with prawns. For dessert it has to be the gooey chocolate cake that we so love.

Back in the old days, we would usually be sent to a table for two by Mr Gandhi at the cash counter. If you looked up from your food, you would see happy faces with a slight triumph at having finally secured a table and diners digging into their meals of carbohydrate- and sauce-laden, generous-on-meat meals.

Going back to Cafe Churchill today is like going back to your grandmother's house. The food made you feel special while growing up. Since then you may have moved out and experienced a lot more that the world has to offer. You may have expanded your palate and learned to be discerning. You may have formed erudite opinions on food. Yet, when you visit Grandma, and when she comes out with the dishes she has made specially for you, you know there is nothing else in the world you would choose over this. After all, it is food served with a hug on the side. As Anthony Boudain puts it in his book *Medium Raw,* this is the 'Grandma Rule' for travellers.

 Tip: Try the garlic bread at Churchill. For many of us, it was our first introduction to garlic bread and we just couldn't get enough of its buttery goodness.

LEOPOLD CAFÉ VS CAFÉ MONDEGAR: AN OLD WAR

You could say that Leopold Café was the start of my Colaba experience. That's where my summer training project guide had taken me for a beer when I was still an MBA student from Kolkata. Leo's was also where I used to go with my friends from work for a drink. We were all new to Mumbai, away from home and full of dreams.

This is the place the world got to know later as Shantaram and Karla's Leopold's, thanks to the book *Shantaram*. However, my wife Kainaz and I claimed Leo's well before that, with our Friday lunches of meat chilli with prawn fried rice.

Leo's has an air-conditioned section upstairs. However the vibe in the non-air-conditioned section is what makes it unique. It could get a bit hot and stuffy downstairs but that won't bother you when you are with a group of friends, or are in love.

To be honest, you should go to Leo's for the ambience and the character. The food can be patchy and the taste ranges from good to average. I think I enjoyed the food more back in the 1990s than I do now. I'd say stick to the draught beer and salted peanuts if you go there now. Try some of the Chinese starters if you want to get adventurous.

The thing is, when you are at Leo's, you get a taste of an institution which is more than 100 years old, with all its quirks – the fairly strange tall pitcher of beer, the old posters on the wall, the graffiti, the high ceilings, the big doors which open on to the street.

Do spare a thought, when at Leo's, for those who died in the terror attacks of 26/11. There are bullet holes in the wall from that night when terrorists opened fire at the café during their siege of Mumbai.

You can't come to Mumbai and not go to Leo's, but there

is a place around the corner that you should check out too. This is Café Mondegar or Mondy's, which is owned by Iranis, just like Leo's. Neither can be counted as 'Irani cafés', though, as the vibe, and the food on offer, is nothing like that of traditional Irani cafés.

My introduction to Mondy's happened shortly after I moved to Mumbai in 1997. I soon discovered the rivalry between the fans of the two most famous pubs at Colaba – Mondy's and Leo's.

The main difference between the two, as I saw it, was that Mondy's was where those who had grown up in Mumbai hung out. Leo's, on the other hand, attracted out-of-towners and a sprinkling of foreigners. This is possibly why I rarely went to Mondy's when I was new to Mumbai. I started going there after I had settled down in the city and began to consider myself a Mumbaikar.

Mondy's loyalists swear by the food here, especially the steaks and roasts. I must say that on recent visits I have found the food at Mondy's to be better than Leo's. My picks at Mondy's would be the roast beef and the mixed grill. The 'beef' is water buffalo, of course. It is well done, smothered with barbeque sauce. You won't find any micro greens or edible flowers on the plate here!

A big part of the Mondy's experience is the jukebox. I remember one afternoon when I had gone to Mondy's with a couple of friends. There was a gentleman in his 50s sitting at the table beside us. He had four empty bottles of beer in front of him. He was sending song requests for the jukebox and tapped and swayed to the beat of songs from the 1970s and '80s. He was lost in his own world, smiling, clapping and throwing his arms up in joy when he liked a particular section of some song. He was very happy when I complimented him on his choice of songs later. We shook hands when I left. We were two happy men in the middle of Colaba that afternoon. One high on beer and music, the other on great food and good company.

So head to Mondy's on a lazy afternoon and, who knows, you might find the elusive secret to happiness.

GROWING UP IN GOKUL

Gokul was a big part of my early years in Mumbai. My Gokul memories are those of evenings spent looking for cheap alcohol to celebrate one's coming-of-age, namely moving out of home. Gokul was considered to be the only place in South Mumbai where the booze was cheap and which was suitable for a mixed crowd – both men and women.

Gokul was always packed in the evenings. There were two sections in those days – the larger section was non-air-conditioned and the crowd there was more blue-collared; the smaller section was air-conditioned and, unlike the section outside which was largely male-dominated, it had both men and women inside.

This section was where agency folks would hang out. Most ad agencies in the 1990s were in South Mumbai then, as were a smattering of market-research agencies. I worked in Dadar but we would come to South Mumbai after work.

It was pretty smoky and noisy inside Gokul. The prawn fries were quite good and were served with the Schezwan sauce Mumbai can't seem to get enough of. I noticed that people would eat boiled eggs with their drinks, which seemed strange. Sometimes we would smuggle in packs of peanuts, as they were cheaper at the corner shop outside than at Gokul. We would bring these out after the peanuts we had ordered in Gokul were polished off.

It was a happy place back then. Drinks at Gokul would be followed by dinner at the Bade Miya stall before hurrying back to catch the last train home.

I went to Gokul after years in 2016, but this time to eat and not drink. I had met the owners of Gokul and got to know its story. A young Mangalorean named Jaya Pujary had come to Mumbai, started a little idli-dosa counter in the spot where Gokul stands today. This was in the mid-1970s. His hard work helped the stall become the popular restaurant that it is today. He has since passed away and Gokul is now run by his sons.

They told me that that you get good Mangalorean food there, apart from the crowd favourites – Punjabi and Indian Chinese food. I had the surmai fry, chicken sukha and the prawn gassi and was very impressed by the quality of what I ate. The restaurant still attracts crowds of people. There is an upstairs section too, and you can still smoke inside. There are more women than before and youngsters as well. I spoke to some of them and they all said they felt safe at Gokul, that they loved the cheap prices of alcohol, the tandoori chicken and the Chinese starters. There were some office folks having a drink here before heading home and I saw a few foreigners as well.

It is still a happy place, I was glad to note.

 Tip: Try the chakli with green chutney to start your evening at Gokul. Friday evenings get very busy and you might have to wait a while for a table.

THE BREAKFAST OF CHAMPIONS AT OLYMPIA

Olympia is a Muslim-owned restaurant at the beginning of Colaba Causeway. They belong to a community originally from Gujarat and referred to as Chilias. The Chilias own quite a few no-frills restaurants across Mumbai that serve economically priced Mughlai food.

The smiling owner of the restaurant once told me that his family has owned Olympia for more than 60 years. His father had bought it from the original owners back when it used be an Irani restaurant. This explains the Irani café-like ambience in the ground floor of the restaurant. It has the round tables and wooden chairs typical of Mumbai's Irani cafés. The place is usually packed with diners right from early morning.

The section upstairs is labelled the 'Women and Family' section. This is air-conditioned unlike downstairs, and the food is more expensive here, though the menu is the same. They have 'modernized' the upper section, which I wish they hadn't, as it now looks like a nondescript wedding hall with none of the charm of the regular section downstairs.

One of the specialities of Olympia is the keema for breakfast. Lazy sloth that I am, the breakfast keema eluded me for a while. Who would wake up that early and go all the way to Colaba for breakfast? I finally made it when I had to go to meet my uncle Jamshed one morning. I had the keema with roti, followed by chai, at Olympia first.

The keema is made with goat meat and the smell can take some getting used to if you are not familiar with it. It is quite typical of the keema curries of Mumbai's Irani cafés. You can have this with pav too. There is a variation of it called keema ghotala, where an egg is scrambled into the keema. The keema is high on grease and spice and makes for quite a hearty breakfast.

My favourite at Olympia is the mutton fry masala. The gravy in which the mutton is served has me in its spell every time that I have it. There is a silken feel to the gravy which I love. The mutton pieces can be a tad tough at times, though. You can try the chicken fry masala instead, which is also good.

I am fond of the kacchi biryani here. It is, of course, not something that a Kolkatan would recognize as 'biryani', if not for the placard stating so. But I have long made peace with the fact that biryani can be of many kinds. What works for me in the biryani at Olympia is that the rice is long-grained, the meat tender and that the masala doesn't dominate the rice.

I normally wash down my meals with lassi here, which is extremely refreshing and not too sweet.

FOOD WORTH TRAVELLING FOR

What do I say about what is now possibly my favourite restaurant in Mumbai? It's a restaurant which has come rather late into my life. I didn't go there in my early years in Mumbai as I thought it would be too expensive. Once I began blogging, Manisha, a friend I made through my blog, took me to lunch at Ling's Pavilion.

Since then Ling's has won over my heart, that of my wife's and of every single person whom I have introduced it to. It is one of the two restaurants in Mumbai for which I am willing to travel to the other end of the city (the other is Bhojohori Manna in Oshiwara). It is the restaurant whose co-owner, Baba Ling, welcomes me with a hug whenever he sees me. When he is not there, the waiters still get us ice cream on the house, 'because you are Baba's friend, sir'.

Baba Ling is the co-owner of Ling's Pavilion, which he runs with his elder brother, Nini Ling. If you look at the roly-poly Baba Ling in his safari suit, and the ramrod-straight, very thin, always-in-a-printed-beach-shirt Nini Ling, you would not guess they are brothers. There is a clear division of labour between the two. Baba stands at the gate while Nini is inside, going from table to table to make sure that you are well-fed.

Their father had come to Mumbai from China in the 1940s. He set up a restaurant called Nanking in Colaba. Old timers in Mumbai swear by Nanking, which stood where Indigo Deli is today. In the mid-1980s, the Ling brothers opened Ling's Pavilion, which was bigger and grander than Nanking – the latter had become a bit decrepit by then. Nanking shut down soon after and its legacy has since been carried on at Ling's Pavilion.

On my first visit, I had seen a big Chinese delegation eating there. Over time I got to know that this restaurant is where the Chinese in Mumbai head to when they're looking for home food. A number of recipes here are family recipes, including some from the repertoire of the brothers' grandmother. The hard work put in by their father has not gone to waste. Even the fish and meat suppliers used by the restaurant today are those identified by him, who have been their suppliers since the Nanking days. The great quality of produce, most of it locally sourced, used here, really comes through in the food.

The restaurant doesn't qualify as a 'street eat' but it definitely is a place with a lot of soul. In terms of ambience, it is a large cavernous property with two floors. Inside, it is dimly lit and the décor is a bit dated and hence comforting. Members of the family are usually present on the floor and this reflects in the good quality of the food. Regulars like us rarely look at the menu when at Ling's Pavilion. We have our favourites or we ask the brothers what to order.

I love the simplicity of the flavours of the food at Ling's Pavilion, which are best seen in the salt-and-pepper prawns or crab. The crab version is one of the few crab dishes to be had in Mumbai which is all about the taste of the crab meat, and not that of the masala in which it is cooked, unlike what the norm is in Mumbai's coastal restaurants. Some of the great pork preparations that they have here are the roast chilli garlic pork, the stewed pork belly with shitake and bean curd, the pork soup dumplings and the bacon pot rice. Then there are the pan-fried noodles with Chinese greens and the shitake prawns/buffalo tenderloin, which are so addictive. I love the crunch of noodles and the delicately flavoured sauce. The pomfret and snapper served in chilli garlic are pretty good too. They are expensive, though, and the basa dishes are cheaper options when on a tighter budget. I know that fish snobs look down upon those who order basa but hey, whatever works for you.

It is almost as if anything that they serve in Ling's Pavilion is magical. How else would you explain the fact that we even like the bitter gourd with scrambled eggs here? My Ling's Pavilion picks would include the pork soup dumplings, the salt-and-pepper prawns or crab, the chilli garlic pork, the roast pork belly, the mixed meat fried rice, the pan-fried noodles with tenderloin, Chinese greens and shitake, the chilli garlic pomfret and, if you order a day in advance, the very authentic Hainanese Chicken rice.

I could go on and on about this restaurant but let me just say that it is the one eatery which has ruined all other Chinese restaurants in town for me.

 Tip: The best way to have a good meal at Ling's is to go to either Baba Ling, or his brother Nini Ling, tell them what you like and request them to order for you. Be assured, they won't make you over order.

Once again, I must leave the last word to my wife. She is not fond of Chinese food and yet she says, 'If I lived in Colaba, I would order every meal from Ling's.'

The story of the Ling family is that of immigrants who came to Mumbai seeking a new home. They were welcomed by the locals and built a new life by dint of their hard work and today, they are an integral part of the city's fabric.

This to me is the most enduring Mumbai story.

 Tip: *Walk across to the Le 15 Patisserie after a meal at Ling's Pavilion for some dark chocolate macarons.*

II

Setting Up Home in Bandra

If Colaba was the scene of our courtship; Bandra is where we set up home.

I shifted out of my PG and my to-be wife and I rented a tiny apartment in Bandra when we were about to get married. Its narrow balcony was our first 'kitchen'. It was so small that the two of us couldn't stand next to each other at the same time but we still used the kitchen a lot. You see, a year of eating out while dating had left us broke. So our only option was to cook at home. We would download recipes from sites on the Internet (this was before there were blogs). I would ask my grandmom and my mom for tips on cooking. My wife would look up recipes from her grandmom's recipe book. We began experimenting because our bank accounts were barren but we were happy like never before.

I loved cooking and would look for opportunities to cook when I could. My wife hated cooking and still does. Yet, she would gather recipes for me as she knew I loved good food.

If the streets of Colaba were where we fell in love, then this tiny kitchen in Bandra was where the foundation of our married life was laid.

Over the years, Bandra became a restaurant hotspot. Our circumstances improved, we changed houses and we could afford to go out to eat again.

Today, we love going to Salt Water Café for the grilled John Dory and the eggs Benedict. To Sassy Spoon for the scrambled eggs and scones and the spaghetti with lemon butter sauce and almonds. To Smoke House Deli for the creamy mushroom omelette and chocolate-chip pancakes. To La Folie Patisserie for the hot chocolate and the chocolate cake. These are new and posher additions to Bandra's eating scene and are a big part of our lives today. However, what we are most grateful for are the classic Bandra restaurants that have made Bandra feel like home over the years.

CANDIES, OUR SECOND HOME

You will find me at Candies at Mac Ronells in Pali Naka on most mornings. I go there to have breakfast and work. In fact, most of this book was written at Candies. On weekends, my wife joins me there, where we have our favourite bench by the entrance. I love to have the chicken sandwiches and the egg sandwiches (grilled) for breakfast. At times I order the fried eggs. I go there so often that Sylvia at the counter makes sure that my toast is not served cold because she knows I hate cold toast.

If I look sleepy, or if I am alone, she asks me, 'What happened, sir, missing madam today?'

I take my first sip of the double-shot cappuccino and beam at her. She feels reassured and gets back to her work.

If I go there in the evenings, I usually have the mutton puffs.

I don't know what to call Candies. Our second home? Our equivalent of a club? Or should we just say that Candies is a happy place for us and leave it at that?

Judging by the smiles that break out on the faces of those who enter Candies, I would say we are not the only ones.

Allan Pereira started Candies about 25 years ago. He named it after his elder daughter, Candice. It started as a tiny outpost in Mumbai's Andheri before he shut that and set up his first shop at Bandra's Pali Hill. Then he added the larger, and now-renovated, Candies at Bandra Reclamation. The third branch is at Mac Ronnels and that's where we go to now. This is nestled in the lanes behind the crowded Pali Naka junction and was opened, rather fortuitously, when we moved into the neighbourhood.

When he started Candies, Allan used to sell dishes based on recipes from his wife's Goan kitchen. There were mince chops, mutton puffs, chicken mayo sandwiches, roast chicken, lemon sponge cakes, lemon tarts and chocolate tarts on offer.

The menu has expanded over the years to include dishes such as Thai green curry and khao suey and, most recently, some really traditional stone-oven pizzas, which would be quite at home in Rome too.

 Tip: Weekday breakfasts are the best time to go Candies. You can hang around till lunch, have lunch and then move on.

If you do go to Candies at Mac Ronnels, you might spot the oldest customer there, who comes over every morning in her cotton shirt, straight-lined skirt and bandaged knees, hobbling to the counter to pick up her salad. You might see the schoolkids from Learners' Academy next door bouncing in, very chuffed to be able to open the glass door by themselves, running straight to the dessert counter. Or you might see groups of college kids streaming in and plonking down with their orders of milkshakes and fat overstuffed rolls and mayo-salad plates, often climbing the stairs and going up, unlike lazy old me. Then there are the couples who find nooks and corners to whisper sweet nothings into each other's ears. You may even spot tall Caucasian supermodels sashaying in for their sushis and lemongrass coolers. I once saw Salman Khan there, standing patiently in line for his food. Yes, Candies is a microcosm of life in Bandra, the queen of Mumbai's suburbs.

Now to get down to what should you eat at Candies. The chicken sandwiches, the mutton puffs, the fried eggs, the grilled egg sandwich, the Thai green curries, the Goan fish or prawn curries, the sorpotel, the roast chicken, the four-cheese pizza, the tea cake, the jelly slice, the petit fours, the sugar cakes, the cookies my wife is partial to and, of course, the double-shot cappuccinos or my wife's favourite, the wild berry iced tea. It may seem like a lot to try but it's completely worth it.

KHANE KHAAS, BANDRA'S HOME KITCHEN

While on the topic of home away from home, here is another one – Khane Khaas.

It was started by four partners in 1989, which makes it fairly old by Bandra standards. Today, two of the original band remain, Atul Sahni and Hardeep Chadha. Coincidentally, they started their careers on the same day in the President Hotel (Taj Vivanta today) in 1989. Then they were working at a landmark restaurant in Mumbai called Mela (which is now shut), they decided to start Khane Khaas in Bandra together.

I was first introduced to this restaurant by my Presidency University classmate, Promita. We ate black dal, tandoori chicken and rumali rotis that night. It later became the place from which my wife and I would order a single serving of rice when we inaugurated our first kitchen in our first house. I would cook chicken with packaged masala on an electric stove given to us by my mother-in-law and call for rice on the side.

We don't go to Khane Khaas to eat as often now but order from there if our cook is on holiday (which she often is) and we don't want to cook. It's the place where my friend Anchal from Chandigarh finds Punjabi food that reminds her of home. It's the place that my British friend, Sue, whom I first met in Bandra, talks of wistfully when in London.

Khane Khaas is a home away from home, not just for us, but for many in Bandra who consider it their 'back-up kitchen'.

If you were to go to Khane Khaas on 16th Road, rather than call in, you'd find it to be a small place with dhaba-like plastic chairs, tables and even plastic flowers. The place is neat and clean, non-air-conditioned; the service efficient and courteous.

Their menu consists of a mix of Lucknowi and Punjabi dishes. My picks at Khane Khaas are the tandoori chicken, the black dal, the jeera (cumin) chicken, the rajma, the tangdi kebab, the rumali roti and a chat with the warm and hospitable owners. Oh, and you can specify that you want only the 'leg piece' in chicken dishes, like I do!

 Tip: If ordering chicken dishes here, ask for the chicken drumsticks, as they are particularly tasty. They charge a premium for this.

THE REAL MUMBAI BIRYANI AT LUCKY

I knew of Lucky Restaurant, or Lucky Biryani as it is known, well before I discovered Khane Khaas or Candies. I discovered it on my first day in Bandra. It is a Bandra landmark after all, and you often hear people use the restaurant's name to give directions. It is the suburban answer to Jaffer Bhai's Delhi Darbar and Café Noorani in South Mumbai.

I used to go to Lucky every Sunday for lunch when I first moved into my PG in Bandra. Since the food at the PG was vegetarian, I would head to Lucky in search of meat. Sunday lunches back home in Kolkata consisted of chicken curry and rice, week after week. At Lucky I would have the biryani to satiate my cravings for non-vegetarian food.

I was flummoxed the first time I had the biryani at Lucky. The grease and the masala in it made it dialectically different from the demure, delicate, masala-free biryanis of Kolkata that I had grown up on. The quantity of the serving, the amount of meat in the dish and the price were all more than those in Kolkata. My first brush with the high-octane Mumbaiya biryani overwhelmed and overpowered me.

Over the years I began to appreciate the slight tartness in the taste of Lucky's biryani. I loved the fact that it included potatoes, even if they are not the near-baked potatoes you get in the Kolkata biryani. I learned that you could 'customize' your biryani at Lucky – you can ask for 'less' masala and you can ask for leg pieces of chicken, which are always juicy and falling off the bone. And you can ask for extra potatoes. Mumbai, unlike sulkier Kolkata, is where the customer is king.

I slowly became a Mumbaikar from a Kolkatan and began to appreciate the biryani here. Though, to be honest, my heart still sings if I get hold of a Kolkata biryani from Peetuk or Hangla in Mumbai.

I recently returned to Lucky after many years to eat, instead of ordering in, like I do nowadays.

Everything seemed to have remained the same. There was the same dimly lit cavernous non-air-conditioned section inviting me in, the same fan swirling languorously, the same high ceilings, belonging to a time well before there was air-conditioning, ensuring that it was pleasant and balmy inside even as the sun raged fiercely outside. People still shared tables in this section. The same waiters who have been working here for years, ensuring the people were fed, were bustling around. This was a place for serious, no-nonsense, unapologetic eating.

I noticed the same fair-complexioned and smiling gentleman at the gate, whom I remembered from my earlier visits, shepherding people to their tables. He ran up to me when he saw the look of bafflement on my face when my biryani was served and asked if anything was wrong. I told him that the biryani was served in a copper pot, which surprised me as they would earlier serve it on a plate.

The gentleman explained that they served the biryani in the pots now to ensure that it remained hot and quickly offered to take it back and serve it on a plate. I declined the generous offer.

Well, the price and dinnerware might have changed but what hasn't changed since 1997 is the taste of Lucky's landmark biryani. It was as tasty as ever.

I found out that the smiling gentleman's name was Mohsen Husaini. He and his family own and run Lucky, a restaurant that his grandfather, the late Mr Sayed Aliakbar Husaini, had opened around 75 years ago, 'at the time of the British' as Mohsen pointed out, which explains the roomy architecture of the restaurant. I wonder how much the biryani, which cost ₹60 in 1997, cost back then!

Mohsen's grandfather had come to Mumbai from Iran –

a country I had lived in for a year when it was still very Westernized, before the Islamic Revolution; a country that Mohsen visited in the 1990s well after the Revolution and came back from unimpressed. Mohsen has taken over the reins of Lucky from his father, Mr Safar Ali, whom he still looks to for guidance. Though Irani by heritage, Mohsen and his father consider themselves to be proud Mumbaikars and Bandra-ites.

I asked Mohsen about the style of biryani at Lucky. He didn't have any romantic or legendary tales to wow me with. No, this was not his grandmother's recipe. Nor was it the recipe of some unrequited love that his grandfather had to leave behind in Iran. There was no romance or razzmatazz in the story of his biryani, just a passion to feed people and a dream to set up a new life in a new country.

Mr Safar Ali is quick to point out that this is 'real biryani'. Biryani where the meat and rice is cooked together with spices, unlike in biryanis where the two are cooked separately and assembled together. The biryani at Lucky is made in large vessels, each of which can feed 60 people at a go. Chicken biryani sells more than mutton biryani here.

 Tip: If you are a Kolkata or Lucknow biryani fan, ask for 'less masala' in your biryani. They are also happy to give you an extra aloo too, if you want.

On the way out I spoke to Mohsen about something that I had observed over the years – the fact that Lucky is not shut during daytime or the fasting month of Ramzan, unlike some other Muslim-owned restaurants such as Olympia.

'Look around you. Our customers are from all communities,' said Mohsen. 'This is Bandra. It is cosmopolitan. Everyone comes to eat here. We can't afford to keep the place shut at any point.'

Yes, Lucky, at the mouth of S.V. Road where Bandra begins, is as good a welcome as any to Bandra.

FINDING MUMBAI'S BREADMAKERS

American Express Bakery or Amex – no relation to the bank – is another Bandra landmark. The original branch is at Byculla but the Bandra one is pretty old too.

The Bandra outlet is a simple shop. There is a bench kept at the entrance in case you want to sit there and munch on something you've bought from Amex. I had spotted the shop first while heading to Bandstand in search of the sea in Bandra. Having just come from Kolkata, I used to find the sandwiches at Amex outrageously priced in the 1990s. The prices have hardly changed over the years at this bakery, which now makes it one of the cheapest eating options around.

No tale of Amex is complete without mentioning my late father-in-law, who loved the mutton sandwiches here. There was a branch at Kemps Corner and my wife used to pick up sandwiches for him from there when she worked at an ad agency next door. The Kemps Corner branch was since shut down. Later, when he and my mother-in-law came to Bandra for visits to the doctor, he would go to Amex and buy mutton sandwiches to take home.

If you are lucky, you can find the lovely Mrs Carvalho sitting at the cash counter at Amex.

She and her family own Amex. She loves to talk and will tell you many stories in between dishing out change at the counter. Yet, she says she prefers to be behind the scenes. She once told me that her husband Ross, and her sons Emil and Yvan, are the ones who run the show. 'Cooking runs in the blood of the men in the family,' she explained. Mrs Carvalho said that the 'only' dishes she cooks are paya or trotters, oxtail and mulligatawny soups.

Mrs Carvalho pointed out two staff members in the shop to me. 'The boys do all the work. I just help them.' She was very clear that any photos about the eatery should be of the staff. 'I am shy,' she said as she graciously allowed me to click a silhouette of hers.

Having married into the family, Mrs Carvalho is a bit hazy about the history of the bakery, as it was started before her time. She told me that her sons are the fourth generation of the family running the business. The bakery had started as 'Wiseman and Company' somewhere in Colaba and then became 'American Express Bakery' in the late 1920s. The name came about because they used to deliver bread to American war ships docked at Mumbai at 'express' speed in those days. She showed me some of the old advertisements of the shop, which had been photocopied and printed from newspapers given by regular customers.

According to Mrs Carvalho, the American Express Bakery ruled the packaged bread market in Mumbai till Britannia bread was launched. Amex used to provide bread to the posh clubs of Mumbai till the clubs set up their own bakeries. The product range has changed with time and now they have rye bread, brown bread, multigrain bread, soya bread, tomato and basil bread, muffins and whole wheat crackers too.

I told Mrs Carvalho about my love for the prawn patties that they stock during Christmas.

I told her about how much my mother-in-law liked the quiche from Amex and how it reminded me of my favourite quiche, which was one that I had outside Geneva station.

She smiled and said, 'Our quiches are good but I cannot say whether it will be as good as what you have had at Switzerland.'

I told Mrs Carvalho about how much I liked their chocolate cookies and how I had one every morning with my coffee.

She smiled at my enthusiasm and responded to all my food questions with warmth and patience. Before leaving, I asked her a question which had bugged me since the time I was 12 years old – why are chicken patties in India comparatively more bland while mutton patties are spicier and have more masala?

Mrs Carvalho broke into a smile and said, 'That's because they used to be called mutton curry puffs earlier. I wonder why people have stopped calling them that.'

The chicken puffs, on the other hand, were flavoured with a version of the French bechamel sauce.

Ah, well. One of life's mysteries solved.

 Tip: My picks at American express bakery are the quiche, the chicken puff, the chocolate cookies, the lemon pie, the plum cake, the chocolate chip cake, the salami sandwich and, in memory of my father-in-law, the mutton sandwich.

I will leave the last word to Mrs Carvalho who pointed out that the American Express Bakery headquarters is one of the stops in the Mumbai heritage walk. I hope that the heritage of American Express Bakery remains as fresh as its bakes.

 Tip: Located beside the American Express Bakery in Bandra is the A1 Bakery where you get fresh pav and very inexpensive cutlets. Opposite is Hearsch Bakery which also offers inexpensive food.

III

Of Chai, Bun Maska and the Nostalgia of Irâni Cafés

One of the most distinctive facets of Mumbai's restaurant scene is its Irani cafés.

The Iranis are largely Zoroastrians who came to India from Iran in the 19th century. They are distinct from the Parsis, who are also Zoroastrian immigrants from Iran, but who had come to India much earlier, possibly more than 1,200 years ago. There has also been a long-standing tradition of Muslim traders from Iran, who used to come to India on work even before the Parsis did, points out Dr Kurush Dalal, a Parsi himself. Some of the Irani restaurants of Mumbai such as Lucky and Good Luck Café are owned by non-Zoroastrian Iranis.

The Zoroastrian Iranis had to make a fresh start when they came to India; they had left their fortunes behind. Many of them set up new businesses and shops, which is when the idea of making arrangements to serve tea and bread and meals came about.

Going out to eat was not prevalent in Mumbai then. The main options that existed for eating out in Mumbai were what were called *khanawal*s or small stalls where travellers could come to eat and move on. One of the few remaining examples of a *khanawal* is Pancham Puriwala at Fort. It was set up in the 1940s by a gentleman named Pancham who walked to Mumbai from Uttar Pradesh over a period of 39 days. He set up a stall selling puris, then converted the stall into a small restaurant. This still exists outside Mumbai's Chhatrapati Shivaji terminus and is possibly Mumbai's oldest-running restaurant.

The eateries set up by the Iranis are considered to be the

genesis of Mumbai's modern restaurant culture. This concept was fairly new for Mumbai at that time. The local Hindu customs encouraged people to eat at home, so going out to eat was an entirely new paradigm. The Iranis, being smart businessmen, set up shops at the corners of buildings. Hindus found these locations inauspicious, so they were available at a low price. To encourage families to come out and eat, the Iranis introduced family rooms with curtains.

The Irani cafés acted as melting pots in the city with people from different communities coming in to eat. Some Irani café owners, it is said, had coloured cups to serve people of different religions, in deference to local customs. Good business is all about customizing and adapting, after all.

The culture of Irani cafés grew and in the 1950s there were about 350 of them, all largely in South Mumbai. Today, unfortunately, you can count the number of Irani cafés left in Mumbai on your fingers.

Irani cafés are family-run establishments and are kept alive largely by family elders. Many in the new generation of Iranis look for more profitable and easier means of livelihood and many have migrated out of India too. As the elderly owner of B. Merwan & Co. at Grant Road once told me, waking up at 3 a.m. every morning to run a bakery is not an easy job.

However, we Mumbaikars love our Irani cafés and bakeries and hope that this is a story that never ends.

Being married to a Parsi myself, I feel an even stronger connection to Irani restaurants. So let me tell you about some of the wonderful times I have spent in these establishments.

CAFÉ MILITARY: THE LAND THAT TIME FORGOT

One of the most enduring myths about Irani cafés is that of their grumpy owners. They often have the reputation of being no-nonsense establishments where you came in, ate, had your chai and left as soon as you were done. This is very different from the free-Wi-Fi, air-conditioned, sit-endlessly-over-a-cappuccino, modern cafés.

Sample this story that Freddy Kerawala, my wife's maternal uncle, once told me about an Irani café owner. Freddy Mama is Parsi and worked at a bank in Fort before he retired.

This happened sometime in the 1970s or '80s in an Irani café in South Mumbai's Fort District. Freddy Mama doesn't remember the name of the café but it was a place which employees of the State Bank of India nearby used to frequent.

It was early evening. People had stepped in for a break after a slow afternoon at work. All the tables were occupied. There was the sound of muted conversation enveloping the place.

Suddenly a jovial shout broke the silence of the café.

'Behram, chai ma khaan aj nathi.' (Behram, there is no sugar in the tea). They spoke in Gujarati, which many Iranis and Parsis adopted after they came to India.

Behram, the owner of the café, continued looking at the cash box, counting coins.

'Behram, samjhaich ke? Chai me khaan aj nathi.' (Behram, did you hear me? There is no sugar in the tea.)

Behram looked out towards the entrance, oblivious of the term 'customer service'.

The customer got up and walked to the till.

'Behram, chai ma khaan aj nathi.' (By now even you know what this means!)

Behram looks up at the big bulbous Parsi nose pointed at his face.

'Main tumhe bulaiya? Ke aa, maari dukan ma chai piye jaa? Tum tara mere aai pagathiya chadiya aayechh. Aaj koine kaai complaint nathi. Baddha chup chap chai peene chali giya. Koi kai

bolta nahin. Tamune kai kai nakhra sujechh... [He takes a breath]
Kaun jaane tara bairi tara saathe kem rahta hose? Chhe ke haju
taare saathe, ke chorhine naasi giyechh?'

(Did I call you? Did I say, come to my shop and drink tea?
You are the one who climbed the steps and came in. Today
there are no other complaints. Everyone's quietly had their
tea and gone. No one said anything. What are these tantrums
that you come up with... God knows how your wife stays with
you. Is she still with you or has she run away?)

And here the story ends.

I guess we can count our blessings the next time we are at
a restaurant and the service is slow. That's nothing compared
to facing the wrath of the Irani café owners of yore.

Years later, I was able to trace the café that Freddy Mama
was talking about. It is a restaurant called Café Military in
Fort. I did meet Mr Behram (from the story), the owner, who
still runs the place with his wife. Age has softened him and he
is now what one would call a 'sweetu' which has, in fact, been
my experience with most Irani restaurant owners that I have
met. Their owners are some of the nicest people that I have
come across. They can be quite quirky and unpredictable, but
chat with them and they will soon open up.

I discovered Café Military when I had gone to an area close
to the Bombay Stock Exchange with a couple of colleagues. We
decided to look for someplace new to go to that afternoon so
I tweeted asking people for suggestions and this was the one
we took up. My colleagues and I found Café Military rather
easily once we reached Kala Ghoda. We walked in and found
that it had all the trappings of a traditional Irani joint. It was
cavernous, with high ceilings, and was airy, cool and dimly
lit. There were red-and-white checked tablecloths covering
wooden tables, with accompanying wooden chairs, across half

the restaurant while the other half had basic w
and chairs. There was a content hum resonati
restaurant as people ate in studied silence. The
to be a mix of government office folks, elderly Parsi cu
lawyers in black gowns and bank employees with ID cards
strung around their necks.

Unlike many other Irani places which don't have a liquor
licence, they serve beer at Café Military. And unlike the
caricatured image of Irani restaurants, it didn't have a cat, or
a board with stern instructions on how to behave. Nor was
there the archetypical grumpy Irani café owner, which, as I
have begun to believe, is an urban legend.

The owner, Mr Behram Khoshravi, the same Behram from
Freddy Mama's story, whom I met on the way out, was in fact
the polar opposite of grumpy. He punned on his surname
(*khush* – happy, *ravi* – stay) as he introduced himself to us with
a toothy grin and said that he was always happy. He told us
he had been running the restaurant that his father, the late
Khordad Khoshravi, started in 1933.

I met Behram's equally sweet wife, Shireen, who was
helping him. I asked her if she supervised the kitchen. She
made no fancy claims of doing so. She just smiled and said
that she had come to help her husband so that he didn't get
tired. 'We have a cook who cooks all the food here. We even
serve Mughlai food.'

There was no pomp or hype here. Just good food that is
easy on the pocket.

Mrs Shireen waved goodbye when we left and said, 'Khush
raho' (be happy) and closed her eyes in prayer.

And that's what our afternoon at Café Military was all
about. It was all about finding happiness and feeling at home
– a feeling that started the moment we sat down and our order

as taken by Mohan, an elderly waiter who served us with a smile that reflected his boss's toothy grin.

Sulky service at Irani cafés? Well, Mohan ran up and down that afternoon getting each dish the moment it was ready.

There was just so much good food to try at Café Military. We started with the red aerated drinks so typical of a Parsi *bhonu* or meal. Then came the akoori. This was served with soft slices of bread which they get from Roshan Bakery at Mazgaon.

Akoori is the Parsi version of scrambled eggs and it has quite a bit of soul. The akoori at Café Military consists of eggs beaten to a creamy consistency, flavoured with finely chopped tomatoes and the odd bite of chopped green chilli.

The other great dish here is the keema ghotala, described to us by Mohan as an 'egg and keema' dish. What we ate that afternoon was probably one of the best keema dishes I have had in my life. The dish consists of pre-prepared keema into which eggs are scrambled in when a customer places the order.

Chinmai Prabhune, food lover and my former colleague, who was with me that day pointed out the true test of a restaurant is its keema. I agree. Many places in Mumbai disappoint when it comes to keema, but the keema ghotala at Café Military was sheer culinary wizardry.

There was more to come. The keema ghotala was just the crescendo that rose to a climax with the caramel custard. One bite of the custard and we could hear angels sing. The sugary, cold, caramelized, milky and delicious custard filled our souls.

Since then, I have been to Café Military quite a few times. I have fallen in love with it each time I've been there. The food has been consistently good and I never tire of it.

 Tip: *The keema ghotala and caramel custard are must-eats at Café Military.*

HAPPY WITH THE CLASSIC BRUN MASKA AND CHAI

Yazdani is not a restaurant. It is a bakery. Or a boulangerie, as the hand-painted sign at the shop proudly proclaims. You know you have reached Yazdani Bakery when you come across the intoxicating aroma of bread being baked. Yes, they are as passionate as the French when it comes to bread here.

The bakery is divided into two sections. The inside section is the kitchen where the baking begins every day from before the crack of dawn. The 'chefs' are dressed in singlets and lungis. They measure out flour by instinct, roll the dough and put shaped pav into the deep, cavernous wood-fired oven to be baked. There is a separate electric oven for the biscuits. Years of experience and honest sweat rules this kitchen. Recipe books are nowhere in sight. Yet, perfection is delivered consistently in every loaf that comes out of the bakery.

The section outside is where people sit to have tea with the baked goods on offer. The place is not air-conditioned but the high ceilings ensure that the air is well circulated and that it doesn't get hot and stuffy inside. There's no free Wi-Fi here – Mr Tirandaz, the second-generation owner of the bakery, has heard of the Internet; he proudly tells me he has an email ID. I doubt if he has ever used it. This is the lost world of Irani cafés, after all. It has basic sunmica-topped tables which you share with strangers, and benches with no backrest. You can plonk your weary self and refresh yourself with some life-infusing sweet Irani chai combined with bun maska or brun pav, or perhaps both, with some buttery khari biscuits thrown in.

Maska means butter. Specifically, Amul (salted) butter. This is the answer to all of life's problems, according to most Iranis. It is applied liberally to the breads here. The bun pav is soft while the brun is crusty. The crusty brun is the favourite of

Parsi grandmothers, according to my wife. They dip it in tea and eat the soaked bread with their toothless gums, enjoying the taste of the bread and the chai simultaneously.

 Tip: Do dip your brun or pav in tea – it tastes better that way. Pack khari biscuits to take home.

Yazdani Bakery and other Irani cafés are pit stops and not lounges. You come in, refuel yourself at a very nominal price and then move on. That's the difference between them and modern coffee shops. Plus they have character, which a chain coffee shop can never offer.

Most people don't get to see the kitchen inside. It is a unique experience and a temple for anyone who loves breads. I got to see the bakery on my first visit when a Parsi colleague of mine, who was with me, asked Mr Tirandaz if we could go in.

Mr Tirandaz runs the bakery today with his father Parvez Irani and his uncle Zend Irani. I have had the pleasure of meeting them both during my visits to the eatery. The family had come from Yazd in Iran and hence the name Yazdani, Tirandaz tells me. It was started around 60 years ago in the mid-1900s. Tirandaz tells me that he often feels like modernizing the place a bit but finds it difficult to convince the family elders.

Is Tirandaz and his family grumpy like Irani café owners are reputed to be? Far from it.

Quirky? Yes.

There was this time that my sister-in-law, who was with me, went in to see the bakery and Tirandaz's father screamed, 'No ladies inside'. Then there was the time when Tirandaz grabbed hold of one of his workers by the throat to re-enact for me the story of an ad film which my wife and her team had once

shot at Yazdani Bakery. I have often gone into the eatery and sat and chatted about life in general with Tirandaz over cups of chai. We belong to very different worlds and yet connect so well. The love for bread unites us, you see.

One of the most inspiring experiences at Yazdani is seeing Mr Zend Irani, Tirandaz's uncle, sitting at the bakery every day. He suffers from Parkinson's, has speech impediments and his body is shaky. Yet, he sits daily at the counter of the bakery without fail. At times he might show you newspaper clippings of him taking part in the local marathon, despite his physical limitations, to drive awareness about his disease. Once I had reached Yazdani Bakery with a food walk group when it was about to close. The staff politely asked us to leave when Mr Zend came out with the assistance of staff members. He reached the gate, pushed away his helper, stopped and kept gesturing to us. We realized that he was telling his staff to let us in and not turn us away. He then joined us as we had bun maska and chai. Mr Zend showed us that there is no reason to let the limitations of our bodies hold us back.

In case you go there and wonder why Yazdani Bakery looks like a pagoda from the outside, it is because this 60-year-old bakery stands on what was once a Japanese bank. The owners didn't know about this till a Japanese gentleman dropped in at the bakery a decade ago, says Tirandaz's father.

'He came up to me and bowed. I bowed. He bowed. I bowed. I thought we would keep on bowing,' said Parvez Irani. 'Then he told me there used to be a Japanese bank here once.'

If you want a place to sit down and write a book, head to one of the more modern coffee shops of Mumbai. But if you are looking for a story, head to Yazdani Bakery.

OF RASPBERRIES AND BERRY PULAO

Britannia is possibly the most well-known of all the Irani restaurants in Mumbai today. It is open only during the day for lunch and is shut on Sundays. You will see a huge queue of people waiting to enter if you go there at lunch time. If you are a tourist looking for a Parsi meal, this is where you will be sent. The restaurant is not air-conditioned but is a fairly expensive place. It is packed with both locals and tourists on any given day.

Once you have gone to Britannia you will realize that the experience there is all about meeting the grand old owner, Mr Boman Kohinoor. His sons sit there too but Mr Kohinoor claims that Britannia will be open only till he is alive. He can't guarantee what happens after that, he says. Real estate is an expensive asset after all.

Chances are that once you sit down at a table in Britannia, the nonagenarian Mr Kohinoor will quietly come to your table and take your order himself. If he approves of your order he will say 'good boy' or 'good girl' as the case may be, even if you are silver-haired. If you are Caucasian then he will take out clippings that he got from Queen Elizabeth's office when he wrote to her. The queen of England is Parsi, after all, as the joke goes. He is besotted with the British royal family. Some time ago, Prince William and his wife, Catherine, were in Mumbai. A local media team worked on a social media campaign to reach out to the hosts of the royals and to get Mr Kohinoor to meet them. They actually succeeded at the last minute and Mr Kohinoor got to meet the royal couple for a short while at their hotel.

While Mr Kohinoor appears to be the sweetest grandpa around, try wrangling a raspberry drink out of him and you will see how obstinate he can become. Raspberry is a fizzy soda that looks and tastes like cough syrup. It is an acquired taste, which I am yet to acquire. My wife loves it, though. She has been brought up on raspberry sodas at Parsi weddings, new year parties and navjote ceremonies.

Mr Kohinoor has a pathological fear that raspberry sodas will get over if everyone orders it and he might some day face an irate Parsi customer with no raspberry to offer. So he tries to persuade non-Parsis to have the fresh lime sodas instead.

Nilaakshi, a Bengali who loves Parsi food, and I went to Britannia and experienced this first-hand. This is how our conversation went with Mr Kohinoor:

BK (Boman Kohinoor): Are you ready to place your order?

N (Nilaakshi): Yes, one berry pulao please...and a salli boti.

BK: Very good combination, good order. [*He writes the order down studiously.*]

N: And two raspberries.

BK: No raspberry. [*He says this with the same soft voice.*]

N: But I want raspberry. [*She'd apparently been through the drill before, she later told me*]

BK: Have a fresh lime soda. Britannia's fresh lime soda is number one. [*Does a thumbs-up*] Very good. Will go well with your food.

N: But I want raspberry...I have come all the way from Delhi specially for it.

BK: No raspberry... [*After a short pause, he whispers conspiratorially.*] If I give you raspberry, it will get over...then some Parsis will come and ask for it and I won't be able to serve it.

Me: But I am married to a Parsi... Doesn't that makes me half-Parsi?

BK: [*still very genial*] No half-Parsi, no quarter-Parsi, no conversion, no raspberry.

N: But I am staying with a Parsi friend... I love raspberry.

[*Finally, I fished out a print-out of my last blog post on Britannia.*]

Me: I am a big fan of your restaurant. This is an article I wrote about it when I came here last time. My wife and I heard that you were closing and we had rushed here. We were so happy to hear that you weren't closing down. [*There are often rumours of places like Britannia shutting down. Usually unfounded, thankfully.*]

BK: Aah, I remember... Can I keep?

K: Of course. This is for you. In fact, my wife could not come today and asked me to pack cutlets for her.

BK: That won't do... You must ask her to come here.

[*He still looks unconvinced. No sign of the blessed raspberry. That's when I suddenly had a flash of inspiration.*]

Me: I even made salli per eedu (a Parsi breakfast dish) myself for breakfast today. [*This was true.*]

BK: [*breaks into a big smile and nods*] Salli per eedu... [*He looks at N, then at me.*] Hmmm...he is Parsi.

BK: [*He turns towards one of the waiters*] Manish, two raspberries.

BK: [*looks at me*] You are a very good boy.

BK: [*looks at N*] And you are a veryyyy good girl.

My picks at Britannia would be the mutton salli boti, the mutton berry pulao, the egg masala, the mutton cutlets and Mr Boman Kohinoor personally taking your order. Opinions on the quality of the food are divided but many would feel that a visit to Mumbai is incomplete without going to Britannia. I feel that I have eaten nicer and more reasonably priced food in other Parsi restaurants in Mumbai but sometimes a memorable meal is about more than just the food.

IN SEARCH OF 'REAL' PARSI FOOD

I discovered Ideal Corner the day I moved into Lakshmi Building at Fort for a period of about six months. It has become my favourite Parsi restaurant in town since then. This too, like Yazdani, is a regular stop during the food walks I conduct at Fort. Folks on the walk can't seem to get enough of the akoori, salli boti and dhansak here. Cyrus Broacha once told me that he is a fan of the akoori here and is very fond of Ideal Corner.

Ideal Corner is a tiny, non-air-conditioned place with a mezzanine floor. The seating is fairly cramped but the food is so good that you will forget your surroundings as you feast on food that matches the best of what you get in many Parsi houses. Many Parsis – and they are a very picky lot – have told me that Ideal Corner is a place they would go to for authentic Parsi food.

My search for the apocryphal grumpy Irani café owner turned to naught here too. Ideal Corner is run by Parvez Patel, a silver-haired, soft-spoken gentleman with the quietest of voices. He always greets me with a super-sized smile. As do his staff, who remember the faces of all their regulars.

Ideal Corner once used to be a motorcycle servicing garage run by Parvez. The Parsis love their bikes and cars. Mumbai folklore says that you would be really lucky to lay your hands on an automobile which was owned by a Parsi, given that they take such good care of their vehicles.

A couple of decades ago, Parvez set up Ideal Corner to serve

Parsi food in lieu of the garage. He has gone from strength to strength since, has won awards, has been invited to train chefs on Parsi cooking in five-star hotels, and yet remains one of the most unassuming people you can meet.

Parvez now keeps his restaurant open on Sundays (Mondays are shut) and at nights too. Many places in Fort, including Ideal Corner, used to be shut at night as it is a commercial area. But efforts like these – made by traditional restaurant owners like Parvez – to become more user-friendly and move with the times are necessary. We need more of this kind of initiative.

Once a regular came in when I happened to be lunching at Ideal Corner, and told Parvez, 'You look younger every time I see you. What's your secret?'

'Two eggs in the morning,' replied Parvez and then with an impish smile and a dramatic pause, he added, 'Two pegs at night,' much to the amusement of everyone around.

 Tip: My picks at Ideal Corner would be the mutton dhansak, the akoori, the mutton pulao dal, the salli boti and the railway mutton.

MY FIRST WEDDING FEAST AT JIMMY BOY

Jimmy Boy is one of the youngest Parsi restaurants around and one of the oldest too. Puzzled? Let me explain.

Jimmy Boy traces its roots to India Café, started by Jamshed and Boman Irani (not the actor) in 1925. India Café was an Irani café in the truest sense. It served brun pav, bun maska, eggs and keema and Irani chai, of course, but not full meals.

The next generation renamed and relaunched India Café as

Jimmy Boy in 1999. Jimmy Boy, it is said, was a play on the Westernized name 'Jimmy' used by Jamshed Irani to explain his name to trunk-call operators while calling his family in Australia in the 1990s.

Jimmy Boy was launched as a full-fledged air-conditioned restaurant in 1999. It was one of the first and rare attempts by an old-school Irani café to remodel itself for the new era. A decade-and-a-half later, Jimmy Boy is now only partly air-conditioned. The upper section is air-conditioned while the lower section is not. It is open seven days a week for both lunch and dinner. It is popular with foreign tourists who come to Fort and Parsis who want to bring their non-Parsi friends for a Parsi meal. Parsi patrons often step in and give their feedback on the food that they were served. Young Sherzad Irani, the manager at Jimmy Boy, tells me that they take note of the suggestions and sometimes incorporate them in the kitchen.

Sherzad has been a family friend of the owners since his childhood days. You will often find him, with his sleeves rolled up, running around the restaurant and looking after the customers. The attention he pays shows in the big smiles of those eating at Jimmy Boy.

The thing to try out at Jimmy Boy is the *lagan nu bhonu*, which is the Parsi wedding feast. *Lagan* means wedding and *bhonu* means feast or meal. The idea behind relaunching Jimmy Boy for the owners, Aspi and Dara, was to offer a place where non-Parsis could try out these delicacies.

Some of the classic Parsi wedding dishes that you can find on the menu here are saarya (a sago papad) and lagan nu achar; in fish – patrani machchi or saas ni machchi, in chicken – a choice between salli murgi and chicken farcha. Then there is mutton pulao dal followed by kulfi or lagan nu pudding for dessert.

Jimmy Boy is where I had my first taste of a Parsi wedding feast. My wife and I were dating then but not 'officially', so I had not yet been invited to any of the family functions. So she took me to Jimmy Boy to get a taste of a Parsi wedding feast. What I remember from that night was the owner telling us that we could order one set meal and share it between the two of us. This was music to our ears in those cash-strapped days.

We had a civil (court) wedding with only our immediate family joining us for lunch at a local Mumbai restaurant. We had neither a Bengali nor a Parsi wedding feast for our wedding. However, now that I've married into a Parsi family, I have been invited to many family weddings and navjotes and had the Parsi *lagan nu bhonu* numerous times. However, that first meal at Jimmy Boy, and the kind gesture of the owner, will always remain special.

My picks at Jimmy Boy would be the *lagan nu bhonu* and, in à la carte, the dhansak. Dhansak is not part of the *lagan nu bhonu* as it is not served on auspicious occasions but on the fourth day after a funeral. Pulao dal, which is pulao with meat and dhansak dal on the side without the meat, is served instead.

I sometimes feel that Irani café owners of today don't always show the same innovative spirit that their forefathers did and there is very little improvization to be seen in the cafés. It's almost as if they are caught in a time warp. Today's customer expects amenities such as air-conditioning and clean toilets, for example, which are rarely found in such places. The cafés in Paris, for instance, are great examples of century-old establishments retaining their old-world charm and menus, and yet offering modern amenities. I hope that the Iranis take up the challenge too and that the world of Irani cafés is not lost to our children's generation.

IV

Tracing the Spirit of Mumbai at Fort

Fort was one of the original CBDs (Central Business District) of Mumbai. People from all over India and beyond would come to work at Fort. Restaurants sprung up to feed them and many offered the native cuisines of the new immigrants. Most of these restaurants were set up by immigrants too.

There is Pancham Puriwala at the start of Fort. This restaurant is located opposite the CST station and, as I have mentioned earlier, is possibly one of the oldest-running restaurants in Mumbai today.

Moti Halwai, located opposite Yazdani Bakery, was set up by a Punjabi family. The family had migrated to Mumbai from Karachi, and had to start life from scratch after they lost everything during the Partition. Setting up Moti Halwai helped the family rebuild their lives. You get lovely, thick full-cream lassis here as well as Punjabi-style parathas, Sindhi dal pakwans and Punjabi vegetarian thalis and mithais. It is packed during lunchtime though rarely written about in the media or in guidebooks. The food is homely and delicious.

If you like jalebis then go to Vidya Dairy Farm, opposite the Fort Post Office, and have the freshly fried jalebis there with some khasta kachoris. Its owners had come to Mumbai from Uttar Pradesh in North India.

Fort is also where you can explore a world of Irani restaurants beyond the more famous Britannia located at nearby Ballard Estate. Ideal Corner, Jimmy Boy, Café Military and Yazdani Bakery are all located here.

I am quite fond of the Swagat Restaurant near the Strand Book Stall. It is an old-school South Indian Udupi restaurant. I used to stop for a dosa and a filter kaapi here every evening before setting off for home for the six months that I had the privilege of working out of an office based in Fort.

For Keralite food, go to Hotel Deluxe, which a Malayali reader of mine had recommended to me. Try the sadya – a vegetarian meal served on banana leaves. You can also try the fish fry, especially karimeen when available, and Kerala fish curries. Or go for the mutton or buff chilli fry and have them with porottas. Do try the Kerala biryani made with short-grained rice, which is different from the other biryanis you get in Mumbai. Some of the other popular Keralite restaurants here are Taste of Kerala (on the same lane as Hotel Deluxe), Rahmaniya Restaurant and Fountain Plaza.

If you come to Mumbai, chances are you'd be looking for places to try seafood. Trishna and Mahesh Lunch Home are some of the most famous restaurants for this. Both are run by Mangaloreans and the original branches are in Fort. These restaurants started as simple 'lunch homes' offering reasonably priced food for those who worked here. Both these restaurants have become pretty posh over the years, though. You can still go to places such as Harish Lunch Home and Modern Lunch Home and have some beer with surmai fry and chicken kori rotti and get the old lunch home vibe. My favourite among Mangalorean restaurants is Apoorva in Fort, which is run by a Mangalorean family. I just love the prawn gassi and neer dosa there. They do quite a nice surmai fry and the quintessential Bombay dish, butter garlic fry. I prefer the version with squid.

There aren't too many restaurants offering Mahrashtrian food at Fort. Food writer and blogger Saee Koranne Khandekar once told me that this is because most Maharashtrians used to work in the mills of Central Mumbai and not in Fort in the post-Independence era – which is why you will find more Maharashtrian eateries in areas such as Dadar and Parel.

Keeping the Maharashtrian flag flying is the Bedekar Sales Shop tucked inside the by-lanes of Fort. It is an outlet of a 100-year-old company which manufactures an array of Maharashtrian spice mixes, condiments and snacks and is quite popular with the locals.

You can also go to a tiny restaurant called Pradeep Gomantak opposite Ideal Corner. You get inexpensive non-vegetarian thalis offering dishes from the Hindus of Goa. Manisha, the owner's daughter, sits at the cash counter everyday and there is a long queue at lunch time.

There are no Gujarati thali places of note in Fort. You could go to Chetana at Kala Ghoda at the end of Fort if you want Gujarati food. Chetana is a multicuisine place and offers Rajasthani food too.

Do try to spot a tiny shop called Narendra Farsan Mart at Bora Bazar. You can buy homemade Gujarati farsan or snacks such as dhokla, kachoris, pattice and puris here. It is a takeaway place. Or go to Suresh's bhajia shop (in the lane down Ideal Corner) to have bhavnagri mirchi fry, which are big green chilli peppers coated in a gram flour batter and deep-fried.

Dr Kurush Dalal, who has grown up in Fort, recommends a shop called Zaverchand Morajee Mangrolwala for packaged Gujarati farsan items at Bazar Gate. You get Jain-friendly food here too.

 Tip: My favourite Gujarati restaurant in town is Soam Restaurant opposite the 200-year-old Babulnath Temple. It is not a thali joint and it takes a while to get a table here so go there when you have time to wait. Must-trys here are the handvo, cheese and palak samosa, satpadi paratha with gatte ke sabzi, dhebra puris made with bajra, yogurt and methi and freshly fried jalebis washed down with ganna ke juice.

Fort has quite a few street food options too. Most of these are vegetarian places. The food served here is cheaper than the street food joints on the beaches of Mumbai. They mainly cater to office-goers and not tourists. The time to go to these places is at lunch time or after work. The pav bhaji, puri bhaji, batata vada, toast sandwiches, bhelpuri and sev puri that I have eaten here are better than what you get in most other parts of the city.

Fort is no longer the core CBD of Mumbai. Most offices have moved away from this area. The buildings here, which are from the British era, look grand from the outside but are not very well maintained inside. Yet, Fort is still full of life and the sense of history you get here is amazing. The best thing about the place is that the restaurants that feed the denizens of Fort are still going strong. Their food is still consistent in taste and the prices are easy on the pocket. The owners are just as friendly as ever. Plus you have to share tables at most of these places so you might end up making new friends over your meal too.

What I like most about Fort is that it symbolizes what to me is the spirit of Mumbai – a city where people from different parts of India have come and built their lives. To me the spirit of Mumbai is about harmony, hospitality and hope. There is no better place for a food lover to experience this than in Fort. Which is why I say that I am 'Fort Enchanted'.

υ

The Wonders of Bohri Mohalla

One of my favourite places to eat in Mumbai has to be Bohri Mohalla, or Bhendi Bazaar, as it is commonly known.

It took me a decade-and-a-half in Mumbai to discover the inner lanes of Bhendi Bazaar. After all, it falls in the part of the city that we cross over on the JJ Flyover and has been forgotten by all except those who live there. One might at the most go to Noor Mohammadi Hotel, which falls on the main road, or to the Minara Masjid Lane for the Ramzan stalls. I was oblivious to the delights of this place till a few years ago.

I owe my discovery of Bohri Mohalla to my friend Dr Kurush Dalal. I have learned so much about Mumbai's heritage from him. Kurush is an archaeologist and son of legendary Parsi caterer, the late Dr Katy Dalal. He and his Bengali wife, Rhea, run the Parsi catering business, Katy's Kitchen. They are two of the band of great friends that I have made through blogging.

Kurush grew up in old Mumbai and is a walking-talking encyclopaedia of the city's food. He is a gifted raconteur and is great fun to hang out with, even though we differ on our opinions about biryani. I love the Kolkata one while Kurush plumps for the Mumbai biryani, much to the bewilderment of me and our other ex-Kolkatan friends.

One day Kurush said that he would take me to his favourite part of town to eat. We headed out with him. The other two in our group that day were Soumik and Shanky, fellow food lovers.

After much confusion – Kurush is horrible at giving directions – we finally reached Bohri Mohalla. The locality is not easy to spot and even Google maps might fail you. The landmark is the Saifee ambulance stand below the JJ Flyover, before Noor Mohammadi Hotel, when you are coming from the suburbs. You get off and walk down the lane opposite, past the Saifee medical office. This is also the entrance to the famous Chor Bazaar of Mumbai which is open during the day and shut on Fridays. Those who stay here refer to the Bohri Mohalla as 'the Mohalla'. The time to go there to eat is after dusk, 7 p.m. onwards.

The interesting thing about Bohri Mohalla is that the food that you get there is not necessarily Bohri food. The Bohris belong to a sect of Islam whose followers trace their origin to Yemen, from where they came to Mumbai via Gujarat. They have their own set of practices, which are slightly different from other sects of Islam. There are hardly any Bohri restaurants in Mumbai, but at the most you might find takeaway stalls such as Jeff Caterers and Safe Caterers on Bandra's Chapel Road. The Bohris run the sweet shops in Bohri Mohalla while the restaurants and food stalls are mostly run by non-Bohris.

I have gone back to Bohri Mohalla many times since then. I once took Simon Majumdar to Bohri Mohalla. Simon, who has been my mentor over the years, then suggested that I do these tours professionally, which led me to launch my food walks.

The area is supposed to go in for redevelopment and you never know how long the restaurants will be in operation. So a Bohri Mohalla food experience comes with an expiry date and I would strongly recommend that you go there as soon as you can.

I thought I could chart out a little Bohri Mohalla path for you.

I usually start my Bohri Mohalla food walk at Firoz Farsan, which shuts by 8 p.m. This is a Bohri family-run place. A must-have here is the very unique 'patrel biryani', made with buffalo meat cooked in colocasia leaves instead of rice. The family that runs the place says that this dish is their innovation. You get chicken on weekdays and buffalo on weekends. They have a great range of farsan or crunchy, fried snacks here of which, again, the patrel farsan is arguably the best. You can also find non-vegetarian snacks such as Russian cutlets and seekh kebabs here, specially during the month of Ramzan.

Next, walk down to the India Hotel. Don't be misled by the word 'hotel'. It is an open-front shop which specializes in tava fries. They have a few plastic tables and chairs for diners to be seated. It is owned by the Methuselah-like white-bearded Haji Chacha who sits at the counter, keeping a sharp and proud eye on the food being served. He is Muslim but not Bohri. He is a hands-on owner and his passion shows in the excellent quality of the food here. The pan-Asian range of food prepared on the tava of this very humble, hole-in-the wall 'hotel' is rather astonishing. The chicken and mutton ('don't ask what goes in it', says Kurush) rolls in his shop – delectable stuff – are in the style of the rolls of Karachi, Haji Chacha told me once. What they call 'Rangooni' rotis or 'Burma' rotis look like the martabaks of the Malays and the Moghlai parathas of Kolkata. They are also known as baida roti in Mumbai. Friends of mine who worked in Rangoon tell me that similar dishes do exist in modern day Yangon and they are called palatas there. The other great eats here are the gurda kapuda (goat kidney and testicles) masala and the bheja fry masala. You should also try the cubed potatoes fried in oil – not technically vegetarian as the meat juices spread across the tava flavour the potatoes.

 Tip: While the bheja fry is a more iconic dish, I would recommend the gurda kapuda here.

Tear yourself away from the India Hotel and cross the tiny lane to the Haji Tikka kebab stall opposite. It was started by the late Haji Mohammad. He had a kebab cart at Bohri Mohalla but had a few run-ins with the local constabulary about licensing issues. This is when, according to folklore, the local Bohris advised this non-Bohri gentleman to take up a permanent space in the mohalla so that he could get rid of his police woes. Thus, about a decade-and-a-half ago, the Haji Tikka kebab stall was born. You can spot it in the evening by the crowd of people surrounding it, munching away happily on kebabs, often using the scooters and motorcycles parked around it as makeshift dining tables. Haji Mohammed passed away recently and his son now carries his father's legacy ahead, and does a great job of it.

The khiri kebab here is an absolute must-try, which is made from the udder of the buffalo. I first had khiri in the rolls of Kolkata's Nizam's in the early 1990s. You do get khiri at a few kebab places in Mumbai. It is one of the the most amazing meat experiences that you can have, in my opinion. Slighty firm outside with a pleasant crispy bite and creamy and luscious inside with intense smoky flavours. I have yet to come across anyone who makes it better than the kebabwalas at Haji Tikkas. Everyone I have introduced to it has fallen in love with the khiri kebabs here. Having recently eaten a khiri roll in Kolkata's Nizam's once again, I can definitely say that they do their khiri better at Haji Tikka.

They also do a pretty decent kofta kebab here. These are balls of juicy minced water buffalo meat, skewered on an open charcoal grill, which beats the dryish mincemeat shammi kebabs that you usually get in Mumbai. If the thought of udders make you queasy, the kofta is a good second choice. The koftas go very well with the thick, deep-fried maida parathas that they make here.

If neither the khiri or the kofta work for you then do try the chicken tikkas. Everything they offer at Haji Tikka is brilliant.

 Tip: Bade refers to beef, usually water buffalo, while chhote refers to goat meat.

Another great find is Surti Bara Handi Payawallah. Don't be scared of the dark, empty, tiny lane that takes you there. This tiny shop is one of the last exponents of the lost art of 'bara handi', which originated in Iran. This place is around 80 years old. It was set up by the ancestors of the current owner, who had come to Mumbai from Surat in Gujarat. Hence the name.

Bara handi literally translates to 12 vessels, though you will actually see nine at the entrance of the shop. They claim that there are another three pots inside. What you get to try here are slow-cooked marvels at their very best. Pulses and wheat cooked in different proportions over a period of six hours, and the meat cooked separately for the same amount of time. The meat consists of what once used to be discarded cuts of buffalo and goat, such as trotters, rump, tail and so on. This was considered to be the poor man's food. The slow-cooking technique of bara handis came to Mumbai via Gujarat, and converted these tough and often inedible cuts of meat into the most delectable meat experience that you can have.

The cuts of meat that you select are served along with a mix of curries from the handi, topped with silky marrow, taken out of marrow bones, and josh, or animal fat, that came out of the meat while cooking, alongside freshly made rotis. It is one of the most hedonistic meat experiences that you can have in Mumbai.

The Bara Handi shop that Kurush loves is Vallibhai Payawallah and I have had many lovely meals with him there. It had shut down recently and then opened again at nearby Null Bazar. If you love meat, then either of these places is a must-visit.

Tip: Visit Bara Handi by 9 p.m. as the food gets over soon after that. Pair the meat with khamiri rotis fresh from the tandoor.

After Surti, trace your steps back to the Haji Tikka lane and walk past the largish tea shop and take the first left, where there is a lane of pulao shops selling Delhi-style pulao. A stop at the first tiny shop with no name for a very delicate, well-balanced and flavoursome Delhi pulao is well worth it. Salman's shop down the lane serves a great pulao too. You would do well to close your eyes to the surroundings and take in the beauty of the delicately cooked rice and meat instead. The style of pulao here orginated in Moradabad in Uttar Pradesh. That's where the stall owners at Salman's are from. The pulaos are inexpensive and are quite different from the oily and rich biryanis of Mumbai. Don't expect to be given spoons here; you have eat with your hands.

You could also walk down a bit and try the wares of the man known simply as 'channawala'. He has a stall selling the popular Mumbai street snack of ragda pattice (a variation of aloo tikki), but with a twist. Instead of the usual pattice made of potatoes, he serves his channa or ragda with a unique combination of kalejis and gurda (liver and kidney).

Done with your meat fest? Head for the mithai now. This is where the sweet Bohris are waiting with their equally sweet treats. Have the jalebis at Noor Sweets opposite Salman's. Ask them to fry the jalebis fresh for you. This makes a big big difference.

Then go back down the Haji Tikka lane towards India Hotel. Stop at Taj Ice Creams. Taj Ice Creams is a simple shop with spartan tables and chairs, which has no connection with the plush and posh hotel chain it shares its name with. It is now run by the third and fourth generations of the Bohri family that founded it. Everyone I have taken to Taj Ice Creams, following Kurush's footsteps, has agreed that it serves the best ice cream in Mumbai. The ice cream here is made with milk and fresh fruit, hand-churned every morning in *sanchas* (canisters) in a process that has remained unchanged for close to 130 years. Ask for the seasonal ice creams here. Mango, strawberry, sitafal or mixed fruit – you could never go wrong in the creamy world of Taj Ice Creams.

 Tip: If you have had your fill at Taj Ice Creams and yet want more, you can pack some to take home.

The other stop that you can make is at the Bohri-owned Tawakkal Sweets, especially at Ramzan. Kurush claims that the malpuas made at Ramzan here trump those in the more famous Sulaiman at the glitzy Minara Masjid Lane in Mohammed Ali Road.

As always Kurush is right. You get the malpuas only during Ramzan but do try the phirni, aflatoon and halwas during the rest of the year. Tawakkal Sweets started as a small corner shop which has been expanded over the years, as the owners won more and more hearts with their sweet treats.

The encouraging thing about Tawakkal Sweets is that the new generation is actively involved in the business started by their fathers and uncles and are growing it and maintaining its success. We see this also in establishments such as Haji Tikka, Surti Bara Handi and Noor Sweets. The redevelopment plans spell uncertainty for these popular family-run businesses that dish out wonderful food, and are such a big part of the city's heritage. I do hope that the culinary wonders of Bohri Mohalla are not lost to future generations.

Bohri Mohalla and its shops have some of the nicest, warmest and most honest people around. Its lanes are full of lip-smacking food stories. It has some of the most marvellous meat dishes on offer. And some of the best ice creams in town. Is it any surprise that Bohri Mohalla is one of my favourite places to eat at in Mumbai?

VI

The Maharashtrian Soul of Mumbai

If you think that the local food of Mumbai starts and ends with the iconic vada pav, or that you have to go to Mahesh Lunch Home to enjoy Mumbai's 'local seafood', then think again.

There is a lot more to Marathi food than vada pav, even if it is yet rarely spoken about. Restaurants serving Maharashtrian food are not new to Mumbai and some of them have been here for almost half-a-century and even more. Places such as Mama Kane and Prakash Restaurant at Dadar have been serving Maharashtrian Brahmin vegetarian food for decades. They are immensely popular and packed with locals and yet, chances are, you would not have heard of them or been there if you are not a Maharashtrian. This may be because I find Maharashtrians to be some of the quietest and most self-effacing people around and they have not showcased their culture to the world enough. Things are changing though. The growing popularity of Marathi cinema across the country is a testament to that.

Over the years, especially after I started blogging, I have made a conscious effort to find out more about the food of the people of the city I call home. I have asked Maharashtrian friends for pointers, sometimes serendipitously landed at local places. I have always had great meals at all these places, been touched by the warmth and pride of those who run these restaurants and those who eat here.

There are a number of family restaurants in areas such as Girgaon, Dadar and Bandra East which serve Maharashtrian vegetarian fare and their menu has a lot more than vada pavs.

Here's an interesting story. Vada pavs possibly didn't even exist in Mumbai till about 50 years ago. Surprised?

Batata vadas would be made in Maharashtrian homes, of course. However, pav – the bread introduced by the Portuguese – was not consumed in local Hindu homes till much more recently. It was in the 1960s that a movement began – some say it was led by the Shiv Sena – which encouraged the unemployed Maharastrian youth to set up stalls in the streets of Mumbai and sell batata vadas stuffed in pavs to earn a living. Thus was born the vada pav. There is also a vendor called Ashok Vada Pav Stall near Kirti College whose owners claim to have invented the vada pav.

There is a lot of debate on where to get good vada pavs in Mumbai. I am fond of the ones sold at Shri Samarth at Dadar and Shree Krishna at Bandra East. In my experience, if you find a stall frying fresh batata vadas, and if there is a crowd of people there, you are likely to get good vada pavs at that stall!

A HEALTHY PLACE FOR A HEALTHY MEAL

I had not gone to Girgaon in Mumbai to eat till I started writing this book.

One of my blog readers left a comment saying I should go to Girgaon in South Mumbai to check out the Marathi food there. This was not the first time someone had said this and I realized it was time I headed there. Girgaon, after all, is one of the original Maharashtrian bastions of Mumbai. That's where the first Govinda *dahi handi* festival was held and even today Girgaon is famous for the *dahi handi* festivals and the Ganesh *utsavs*. The Khotachiwadi hamlet in Girgaon offers some interesting old school architecture to look at too.

I rustled up a troop for my Girgaon exploration. Joining me were Indophiles Sue and Nathan Cope, a British couple who lived in India for a while, fell in love with it and who keep coming back even after returning to London. We connected through my blog and have become great friends since. We were also accompanied by food blogger Nandita Iyer of *Saffron Trail*, who was visiting Mumbai from Bangalore.

We headed out together to Girgaon from Bandra one sunny morning. We went by road but if you go by train then Charni Road is the closest station. Vinay Lunch Home, B. Tambe (also known as Sujata Uphar Griha) and Shree Ram Boarding House were some of the places on my radar, as suggested to me by people on Twitter.

We reached Vinay Health Home soon enough and walked in. The first thing that struck us when we entered was that the place was spick and span, and bright and airy. It had a little air-conditioned section too. We sat in the non-airconditioned section but didn't feel too hot thanks to the ventilation.

There was a group of ever-attentive and polite staff waiting at the corner, one of whom came and took our order. I was impressed to see Nandita place our order in Marathi. She had apparently picked up the language when she lived in Mumbai and had a domestic help who spoke only in Marathi. Sue and Nathan had taken Hindi lessons when they lived in Mumbai, so they were not too lost either.

Our order that morning was a mix of Maharashtrian snacks. We ordered misal pav (a sprouts-based dish with namkeen/farsan added in), thalipeeth (a multigrain roti) and a dish called patal bhaji usal (a legume-based curried dish) which seemed rather ketchup-y. All the dishes were a tad sweet as

Nandita pointed out and she wondered if this was to pander to the tastes of a Gujarati clientele. We got some answers before we left but there was more food to come first.

I ordered a pohe (made with flattened rice and spices) and was a bit surprised at the soggy texture. The dish tasted good though the look of it had put me off initially.

Our last order was the sabudana vada (made with sago beans). This dish was perfect. It was hot, crunchy and not sticky at all. It was so good that we ordered seconds – definitely one of the best sabudana vadas that I have had.

On the way out we spoke to the elderly cashier at the cash counter who pointed us to one of the owners, septuagenarian Mr Chandrasekhar Tembe. His cousin and co-owner Mr Ajay Tembe was there too. The cheerful and lively Mr Chandrasekhar sat us down, treated us to delectable mango lassis and chatted with us for a while.

He told us that Vinay Health Home was around 75 years old. His father had started the restaurant and that he (Chandrasekhar) has inherited from his father.

Nandita, who blogs about healthy vegetarian food, asked about the secret behind the 'health' in the name of the restaurant. He explained that in the 1940s, when Vinay Health Home opened, the prevailing practice was to name Maharashtrian restaurants after their owners. So you would have names such as Tambe and Mama Kane. Chandrasekhar's parents decided to break from tradition by giving the restaurant a non-family specific name.

They decided to name the restaurant after Ganesh, the elephant god and the favourite deity of Maharashtrians. However, they felt that Ganesh would be too generic a name, so they picked the name 'Vinay' instead, which is another name for Lord Ganesh. The 'home' part of the name came from Chandrasekhar's parents' desire to make their restaurant a place where everyone feels at home. I must say that the way our waiter politely answered our questions and the overall pleasant atmosphere at the restaurant did make it feel like home.

Health, Mr Chandrasekhar explained, finally answering Nandita's question, meant that the food served aimed to be hygienic and good for one's constitution. He said that according to Girgaon folklore, Vinay's food was something even doctors recommend when you are unwell! The extremely neat kitchens and storerooms that Mr Chandrasekhar proudly showed us were ample testimony to the hygiene of the place.

We then asked Mr Chandrasekhar about the sweetness in the food. He explained that Maharashtrian food can be of different types, according to the region they come from. The food in places such as Kolhapur and Sangli is spicy. The Brahmin food of the Konkan region, on the other hand, where Mr Chandrasekhar's family hails from, tends to be on the sweeter side. The addition of jaggery is what sweetens their dishes. He also said that the food at the restaurant used to be a bit spicier till recently but had been made less so at the request of customers.

There's a bit of a story about the changing demographic of Girgaon hidden here. Mr Chandrasekhar said that the area of Girgaon is no longer a Maharashtrian dominated area. According to him, many Maharashtrians sold their houses here as their families grew in size, and moved to the suburbs. Those who came in their place, and could afford the new real-estate rates, were apparently the Gujarati and Rajasthani diamond traders. The palates of the new settlers of Girgaon also explains the tempered spice levels of the food at Vinay Health Home.

 Tip: My picks at Vinay Health Home are the sabudana vada and the mango lassi.

PRAKASH RESTAURANT

Prakash Restaurant is one of the oldest of the Maharashtrian vegetarian restaurants near the Shiv Sena Bhavan at Dadar. You will always find it packed with people wolfing down the homely Maharashtrian food on offer here. The service is efficient and warm and they never let the crowds get to them. The loyalties of Dadar food fans are divided between Prakash Restaurant, the traditional favourite, and comparatively newer places such as Aaswad and Gypsy Corner.

I often duck into Prakash Restaurant in the evening for sinful bites of freshly fried puris and a sukha aloo bhaji. Their misal is also delicious. They don't serve it with pav as the misal, like the batata vada, was not eaten with pav earlier in Maharashtrian homes.

The sabudana vada here is quite the crunchy treat too.

 Tip: Most Maharashtrian places offer sukha *(dry) and* gila *(wet) bhaji with puris. I prefer the former versus the curry, but you should specify which one you want when you order.*

A WINNER IN THE MIDDLE OF SENA BHAVAN

Aaswad at Sena Bhavan is another favourite of my blogger friend, Sassy Fork. I fell in love with Aaswad when she first took me there.

Aaswad was started in 1986. It was a small 16-seater restaurant then. It expanded in 1996 and added air-conditioning in 2006. Aaswad is another of those places that you can recognize by the crowds queuing up outside it. It has a sweet shop attached to it serving popular Maharashtrian sweet dishes such as puran poli and shreekhand peda.

The founder of Aaswad is Mr Shrikrishna Ganesh Sarjoshi. He came to Mumbai from a village in the interiors of the Konkan in 1968. He initially worked in the now shut Trupti restaurant, in Dadar, as a salesman and worked his way up the rungs to open his own restaurant in 1986. The foundation stone of Aaswad was laid by the late Shiv Sena chief, Bal Thackeray. Aaswad is now run by Shrikrishna's son, Suryakant Sarjoshi, a most friendly and helpful gentleman. His warmth is infectious and spreads to his staff, who are very hospitable even within the confines of the 'quick service' format.

Suryakant keeps trying out new things at Aaswad. He introduces new dishes to the menu, often from his wife's kitchen at home. He has tried to take Aaswad out of its confines in Dadar by opening an outlet in Ghatkopar. He then opened a branch at the Mumbai T3 International airport, which has made Mahahrashtrian food accessible to a larger and more diverse audience.

I have tried out various snacks at Aaswad and have always been impressed by the simplicity and the honest flavours of the food. The pohe, sabudana vada and misal at Aaswad are leagues ahead of anything I've had elsewhere. You can also get Mumbai street stars such as batata vada here and indulge without any worries about hygiene or compromising on taste. Then there are dishes such as the multigrain thalipeeth, which is robust and nourishing. The service here is very efficient as well. You sit, share seats with strangers if required, order, eat and move on, making place for the next hungry customer.

I had nominated the misal pav at Aaswad for the 2015 Foodie Hub Global Awards in the Best Vegetarian Dish category. (Foodie Hub is a group of global food bloggers and writers where I represent Mumbai.) The awards are given every year based on recommendations given by local representatives.

The misal pav went on to win the award and the queues at Aaswad have doubled since then.

I once took celebrity chef and friend, Ranveer Brar to Aaswad. He liked it so much that he went back there the next weekend with his wife.

My picks at Aaswad are the misal, the pohe, the batata vada, the thalipeeth, the amba dal, the aam panna, the sabudana vada and the masala chhaas.

 Tip: Queues get pretty long at Aaswad, so going before noon helps.

A SWEET DOLLOP OF HISTORY AT PANSHIKAR

Another Maharashtrian institution that I was introduced to by Sassy Fork was Panshikar Sweets. I had first gone with her to the Dadar outlet but soon realized that there are several Panshikar sweet shops in Mumbai.

One crisp morning, right before Diwali, I went to meet Prakash Kamlakar Panshikar, the owner of the Panshikar Sweets outlet at Mahim to uncover the mystery behind the many Panshikar sweet shops of Mumbai.

Prakashji told me that the original Panshikar outlet was located at Thakurdwar at Girgaon in South Mumbai. It was started by Prakashji's uncle, the late Mr Bhalachandra Narayan Panshikar, in 1921. That shop still exists and is very popular in the area.

Mr Panshikar has been in the family business all his life. He used to sit at the Panshikar shop near Dadar Station, founded by his father, the late Mr Kamlakar Narain Panshikar, in 1931. He then set up his own shop near the Citylight Market in 1984, which is the outlet I visited. He comes here every day to oversee the running of the shop.

When I asked him about the other Panshikar outlets across the city (Girgaon, Dadar, Matunga, Bandra east, Goregaon and Vile Parle) Mr Panshikar told me that each of them was run independently by members of the Panshikar family, including some by the descendants of the late Bhalachandra Narayan Panshikar. Each shop has its set of loyalists and the owner of each has left their own mark on what's sold at their stores. For instance, Prakhashji often asks his team to experiment with flavours he has tried elsewhere, so that his shop can come up with new and exciting sweets.

He, however, doesn't cook himself. 'I've not made a cup of tea in my life,' he told me with a twinkle in his eyes. However, he does taste the sweets and gives his team his personal take on them.

The Panshikars are originally from Sawantwadi, Sindhudurg district in coastal Maharashtra. Their surname was originally Khandekar. They then took on the name Panshikar after the name of the village Panshi in Goa around four generations back.

Most of the staff at Prakashji's shop are from Ratnagiri in coastal Maharashtra, which borders Sindhudurg, and have been with him ever since it opened a quarter of a century ago. The sweets and savoury snacks on sale here are made fresh every day.

It was all hands on deck the morning I went there. After all, it was Diwali. Even Prakashji's driver was helping out with churning the mithai mixes in the hot kadais.

Customers streamed in endlessly. I spotted a middle-aged lady who had come in with a box of torans and diyas, which she gave to Prakashji.

'Her family has been our customer for years. This is a Diwali gift from them,' explained Prakashji, seeing my curious expression.

Two of the most traditional Maharashtrian sweets at the shop are the peda and the barfi. Both are made with mawa (thickened milk). The mawa at Panshikar is freshly made in the shop. Milk is gently stirred and reduced over a hot flame for over 3 to 4 hours till it produces the semi-solid mawa. A litre of milk produces only about 250 gm of mawa. The advantage of using mawa is that it makes the sweets last longer, at least three to four days, without refrigeration versus the milk-based Bengali sweets, which have a much shorter shelf life.

Various additions are then made to the mawa to make a variety of barfis and pedas. There are various types of barfi, mawa, anjeer, mango (made with mango pulp from Ratnagiri) to name a few.

Having tasted the fresh mawa first, and then the barfis, I was amazed to see the transformation of the simple raw ingredient into a delicately flavoured sweet.

They also make their own shrikhand at Panshikar. This is made by straining curd through a cotton cloth called the *chakka*. This process helps break down the acidity of curd, as Prakashji tells me. Sugar and spices such as cardamom and saffron are added to this hung curd to make the different varieties of shrikhand. Mango pulp is added to this to make amrakhand.

The mark of a good shrikhand is that when you upturn the bowl, it doesn't fall out, Prakashji told me and then went ahead with a demonstration. I tried a bit of the hung curd and found it to be moist but extremely sour. Once again, it was amazing to see the magical transformation. Shrikhand is actually quite sweet; in fact, if you are not used to its extreme sweetness, the taste can take some getting used to.

The ladus (Maharashtrian laddoos) at Panshikar are also hot favourites. Traditional versions are besan (gramflour) ladus and rava (semolina) ladus. I was fortunate to see some fresh motichur ladus being made at the shop. This sweet has Rajasthani origins, but is a part of the traditional Maharshtrian repertoire too, according to Prakashji. I felt like a kid in a candy shop as I watched the sweet makers of Panshikar strain out the wet besan mix into a kadai full of hot ghee and transform this into tiny boondis and then shift the freshly formed granules into another kadai in which cashews and raisins had been fried in ghee. The two were integrated together and, once cooled, hand rolled into motichur ladus.

Puran poli is another festive Maharashtrian dish which, according to Prakashji, dates back to the time of Chhatrapati Shivaji. It is more popular during festivals such as dussehra and holi, he told me, though you get them throughout the year in shops such as his. They roll out maida rotis at Panshikar and stuff these in the middle with a paste of mashed channa dal cooked with jaggery. This roti is then toasted on a tava to make the puran poli. (The Parsis have a thicker version of this which they call dal ni pori.)

At sweet shops such as Panshikar, Prakash and Aaswad, you also get faral. It's a mix of savoury snacks which are especially popular during Diwali and are also called Diwali faral. Many Maharashtrians make this at home and serve it to guests.

One of these is the pohe chivda made with flattened rice flakes, fried in a fresh green-chilli-paste base. The end result is a mix of tastes though – sweet, sour with just enough heat. A rich aroma of curry leaves enveloped me as they opened a barrel in which the chivda was kept at Panshikar. This was then measured out and sealed in plastic bags for sale.

The crunchy chakli is another faral, similar to the murukku of the south. It is made with a batter of rice, udad and channa dal and a spice mix that varies from house to house. Another interesting faral is the kad boli which has similar components as the chakli mix, but a higher proportion of udad dal, and is denser in texture than the chakli. The airy and light chirote, which is made with rice flour, is also very uniquely Maharashtrian.

Another festival favourite is karanji. These are half-moon shaped stuffed maida dumplings, stuffed with sweetened grated coconut and deep fried. At Aaswad they serve karanjis along with varan bhaat toop (dal rice with ghee).

 Tip: Once you've had your fill of mithai at Panshikar, end your meal with piyush, a sort of Maharashtrian lassi made with a bit of cardamom and saffron. It tastes somewhat like shrikhand, although the recipe varies in every Maharashtrian household. The piyush at Panshikar is delightfully light and frothy.

THE COASTAL HEART OF MAHARASHTRA

There are a number of restaurants that came up in central Mumbai to feed the people from Malvan, in coastal Maharashtra, who had come to Mumbai to work in the cloth mills. Most of these people had left their families behind and craved home food, so a number of tiny restaurants popped up, offering inexpensive Malvani food, which is seafood based and heavy on coconut. Most of these eateries and their menu have not changed over time.

LALBAUG'S MALVANI PRIDE

Nowhere is the civic dichotomy of Mumbai captured as poignantly as it is in Lalbaug in Central Mumbai. Lalbaug was once the heartland of Mumbai's textile mills, the manufacturing core of the country's commercial capital. It was a commercial area surrounded by the homes of the numerous mill workers who lived there. It is also the home of Lalbaugcha Raja, Mumbai's favourite god.

With the tide of time, the cloth mills of Mumbai lost their place in the sun. The mills were shut down one after the other. Mumbai was no longer a textile manufacturing city. The mill lands were given a new life in the 21st century in keeping with Mumbai's aspiration to be a modern city. The mills were sold to developers who began to create malls and then swanky residential and corporate complexes – Parel, Lalbaug, Lower Parel or Upper Worli – all home to rather incongruous islands of plush modernity springing up in place of a lost land. The past and the future stand separate from each other in Lalbaug. You have plush highrises and malls here. You also have the chawls where the families of mill workers, who lost their means of livelihood, continue to stay.

They are almost like two cities residing in one.

If you stroll down the lanes of Parel you will come across the modern ITC Grand Central Hotel, the offices of MTV and ad agencies, the newly set up Global Hospital, the oldest Parsi colony in Mumbai, Navroze Baug, and then, tucked away in one corner, the Kshirsagar Hotel (also spelt as Shir Sagar). It is not a hotel though, but a simple Malvani restaurant which is always packed during lunch time.

I found Hotel Kshirsagar one afternoon after a meeting at an ad agency in Lalbaug. I was looking for a place to eat and tweeted asking for suggestions. Food journalist Antoine Lewis's reply set me off in search of Hotel Kshirsagar.

It is located at the corner of Dr S.S. Rao Road. Hotel Kshirsagar is one of those nondescript places which you would not give a second glance to unless someone pointed it out to you. Yet the place was packed when I went there for the first time and on subsequent visits too. You have to wait in a queue to get in.

Hotel Kshirsagar serves Malvani food from coastal Maharashtra. However the clientele does not consist of only Maharashtrians. Lunching around me that afternoon was a Sikh gentleman in a turban and a mithaiwala from Uttar Pradesh. The love for the food at Hotel Kshirsagar cuts across communal and regional boundaries. Despite its evident popularity, I had not heard of the restaurant till that afternoon. I was ready to make amends.

I ordered a mutton masala for lunch, as suggested by Antoine on Twitter. I also asked for a surmai fry which was strongly recommended by the strangers I was sharing my table with.

I find it amusing when promoters of modern restaurants claim that they have introduced Mumbai to the concept of community table-sharing. Sharing tables has been a prevalent practice in smaller eateries across India. It is a big part of our restaurant culture. I love chatting with fellow table-mates while eating alone in restaurants. I often ask them for recommendations on what to eat and have discovered many gems thanks to this.

The surmai fry, for example, at Hotel Kshirsagar was brilliant. The fish was fresh, the spicing simple and it was bursting with the flavours of the sea. One often hears chefs from the West talking about the virtues of 'respecting the produce' in a kitchen. The cooks at Hotel Kshirsagar had done that with the surmai fry and the fish was the hero of the dish. I was also served a sharp and full-flavoured coriander and green chilli chutney that complemented the fish really well.

The mutton masala was quite memorable too. The masala was fiery, but once I recovered from the spice hit, I was amazed by the soft and pliant goat meat, which spoke of the great quality produce being used. Malvani cooking uses a fair bit of coconut and the mutton masala had grated coconut in it, which I enjoyed. I had my mutton with vade. Vade is a Maharashtrian 'multigrain' puri made from a dough of rice, corn, urad dal, channa dal, black pepper, coriander and methi seeds. I've had vades in local restaurants before and they were pretty oily. The ones at Hotel Kshirsagar were fried just right and the grainy texture of the puris combined very well with the mutton masala.

 Tip: While they serve rice in a mutton thali too, I feel that it pairs better with vade.

There was a certain rustic innocence to the food at Hotel Kshirsagar that spoke directly to my heart and I was floored by the experience.

Lunch done, I walked up to the elderly gentleman at the counter to compliment him on the food that I had eaten. It turned out that he was the owner, Mr Gopal Totaram Gore. Mr Gore set up his restaurant 50 years ago. His aim was to provide native Malvani food to those who had come in from coastal Maharashtra to work in the mills. The mutton thali that cost me ₹130 on my first visit to Kshirsagar in 2012 was priced at 80 paisa or ₹0.8 when he first opened his restaurant. Mr Gore gave me a single-toothed smile when I said that he must have seen a lot of changes since then.

While Parel has changed quite a bit these days, the one thing that has been constant is Mr Gore's coming to the restaurant every morning and every evening, to take out the spices to be used for the day's cooking. He told me that he always tastes the end product for consistency before it is served.

Is it any wonder that the food served at Hotel Kshirsagar is so magical?

 Tip: Some of the other popular restaurants in Parel are Shree Datta Boarding House and Ladu Samrat.

BEHIND-THE-SCENES AT SINDHUDURG

Prabhakar Desai's Sindhudurg, opened in 1982, was possibly one of the first Malvani restaurants in the Shivaji Park area. It was also one of the first air-conditioned restaurants to open there, having been so right from the start.

The owner Mr Desai's story is straight out of a Bollywood flick, except that it is real.

Mr Desai started off as a coolie in a Jhankar Radio in Boisar in the mid 1950s. He then quit the job and got a small restaurant or *khanawal* called Samadhan Bhojanalay in Goregaon where he worked as a manager. Desai used to cook there too, remembering the lessons in the kitchen that he had learned from his elder sister and mother. He gave up the restaurant after a couple of years as it was not making money. But the seeds of a future restaurateur were sown. He headed to Dombivli in the 1960s and worked as a plumber. The ever-enterprising young man then expanded his work and got into the construction business. As his business grew in the 1960s, he began to get involved in politics. In the 1970s, he gave up politics to focus on construction and moved towards Mumbai from far-off Dombivli. He was encouraged by the late Shiv Sena leader, Bal Thackeray, to try his hand at setting up a business. His friends in the construction business gave him an opportunity to develop the property on which Sindhudurg stands today. In 1982 Desai opened Sindhudurg as an air-conditioned Malvani restaurant at a time when there were very few around, barring the odd eating house. The restaurant was a hit and within a year, Desai paid off the loan he had taken.

There was a shift in the clientele in the later years. While it started as a working man's eating place, its patrons became more well-heeled over time. Noting this change, Desai made his food less oily and spicy to cater to the 'health-conscious' middle class.

Its 25th year was celebrated with great fanfare with the late Bal Thackeray (you can't write about Shivaji Park restaurants without evoking his name) giving them a congratulatory plaque to commemorate the occasion.

Sindhudurg is a local legend. Its patrons include the Parsi and Punjabi head honchos of two of India's biggest corporate giants, Maharashtrian movie stars, prominent politicians, playback singers and so on. The menu here offers Malvani food from coastal Maharashtra and not the Mangalorean fare that you get in the more famous Trishna, Mahesh Lunch Home or even Apoorva and The Excellenssea restaurants.

I fell in love with Sindhudurg on my first visit. I got to meet Mr Desai and hung on to every word of his life story, which he told me in slow and measured English. I even had the privilege of going into the kitchen and was amazed by how clean it was. There was no smell of fish or heavy masalas at all. I met the cooks too, all of whom have been working here since the start in 1982 and are extremely proud of it. The methodical way they went about their work, churning curries, making puris and rotis and frying fish, would be the envy of any five-star kitchen, I am sure.

The highest-selling item on the menu is the surmai thali. I tried it and was enchanted by the perfection of the highly nuanced curry and the freshness of the fish. I tried some of the surmai and Bombay duck fries and was pleased with the thin semolina and rice batter coating, which allowed the fish to be showcased in their full glory. I loved the vade, which had a wonderful texture and was not oily at all, and was great to mop up the grainy and fantastically flavoured chicken masala. The prawn fry, with the tail attached, was utter crunchy goodness. My brother is particularly fond of the crab masala here.

There is a secret to the freshness of the food at Sindhudurg. Till recently, Mr Desai used to go to the Sassoon Dock market to get fish for the restaurant. Old age has come in his way and he can't handle the crowds and slippery floors of the markets now but he still keeps an eye on the produce coming into the restaurant. He has also set up a huge farm in his native place. Fresh coconuts, bananas, raw mangoes, when in season, and cashews come from the farm to the restaurant in Mumbai every day. The freshness of this shows in the zest of the in-house mango pickle, for example. The masalas used in the curry are ground at his farm using fresh chillies, which gives the curries their distinctive flavour. Desai is a big believer in agriculture and laments the fact that folks from the villages are coming to the city to seek their fortune. Back at his farm, he uses modern machinery wherever possible, including in the plucking of coconuts, to make his operations more efficient.

So what's next in the eventful story of Prabhakar Desai?

Well this coolie turned plumber turned building contractor turned politician turned restaurateur turned agriculturist is an educationist too. Decrying the lack of higher educational facilities in Dombivli, he set up the Dombivli Shikshan Prasarak Mandal which has since set up an English-medium school and a college too.

The restaurant remains his passion, though, and he says with a smile that he will retire only when he is 'gone'. The problem with such family-run businesses is that they run entirely on the involvement of the owner. So the biggest challenge for Sindhudurg is to maintain the quality and standards it is known for now that Mr Desai can't sit at the restaurant every day.

My picks at Sindhudurg are the surmai thali, the fish fries, the vade with chicken masala, the prawn fry – all of it washed down with the solkadhi (made with coconut milk and kokum). The clams are pretty popular too, I am told.

 Tip: Malvan Katta nearby is favoured by many local Maharashtrians for its seafood.

SEAFOOD IN ALL ITS GLORY

Malwani Aswad is a humble Marathi eatery (is there any other kind?) at Vile Parle East, far away from the Marathi heartlands of Dadar and Parel.

This is where I first fell in love with Malvani curries. I discovered Malwani Aswad through some colleagues when I was working out of an office in a godforsaken stretch of Andheri East.

Malwani Aswad is a tiny non-air-conditioned place, which packs in about 16 to 20 people through some pretty cramped seating. The food is so good though that no one cares that the elbow of their neighbour, often a stranger, could be shoved into one's face while one eats.

The restaurant is 15 years old and is run by the industrious Mr Krishna. You will see this small framed gentleman running from table to table during lunch time, frantically taking orders and then running upstairs to the kitchen to relay them to the cooks.

I love the pomfret fry thali here. It is the most expensive dish on what is otherwise a moderately priced menu but there is something about the freshness and juiciness of this fish fry which I am just addicted to. There is hardly any batter on the pomfret so all you get is the undiluted taste of some pretty great fish.

The typically Malvani fishbone-flavoured curry that they serve with the thali is one of the most flavour-packed Malvani curries that I have come across. It combines very well with the short grained rice that it is served with. They also make a great prawn fry masala with a very zesty, thick curry base, with fresh and juicy prawns in them. I once got these for my brother when he was visiting from Delhi and wanted seafood. He absolutely loved it.

My picks at Malwani Aswad would be the pomfret fry thali, the prawn masala thali and an extra serving of solkadhi.

 Tip: Try to get a table by the door with the open road in front of you to feel less cramped.

If you come to Mumbai and are looking for seafood, then do make the effort to seek out its Malvani eateries to get a flavour of Maharashtra. The beauty of eating at such place is that the dedication of their owners makes the food here really special.

I have a confession to make. It took me more than 15 years in Mumbai before I began to discover the local Maharashtrian restaurants here. That's possibly because most of them are restricted to areas such as Dadar and Girgaon where I didn't eat as often as South Mumbai and Bandra.

It was when I began food blogging that I came across friends who took me to these restaurants – which I have learned to love since. I have made it my mission to help share my discoveries in this genre with those who come to Mumbai. I have mentioned a few restaurants in this chapter but there are many more. For Malvani food there is Chaitanya in Prabhadevi. Do try the Malvani dishes at Sadichha Restaurant in Bandra East, which is very popular with the locals and where the service is very warm. Then there are Pune-based chains such as Potoba, which offers Puneri vegetarian fare and Purepur Kolhapur which offers Kolhapuri fare (high on mutton, low on coconut and served with broths such as pandhra rassa and tambara rassa).

 Tip: There are a number of seafood festivals held in winter, in places such as Versova and Mahim, which offer seafood based dishes typical of the Kolis, the fisherfolk of Mumbai.

If you want to get to the pulse of Mumbai then you should definitely explore the food in its Maharashtrian restaurants.

Mumbai and I have a very special relationship. This city has given me the courage to go beyond the well-trodden path and chase my dreams, like it has to so many others who've come to the city. It has given me a family, and great new friends – folks across communities and countries – with whom I've shared many laughs over shared meals. But most importantly, Mumbai has given me its food, in all its glory. Kolkata might have been the place that kindled my love for food, but Mumbai is where that love has been nurtured into what can now be called my profession. Mumbai is where I started my food blog, and my food walks, which has led to many a food adventure since then. And the city continues to inspire me, with its warmth, its people, its curious blend of cuisines from across the world.

Which is why I can say, quite simply: Mumbai, I love you.

FOOD WALK

👣 The Bandra walk

Start with wild berry ice tea or cappuccinos and sandwiches and chops at Candies. Walk down Pali Market and check out Vijay Provision Stores to buy an array of packaged masalas. You can stop at Ashmick's Snack Shack for some Parsi fare, like the chicken cutlace and salli per eedu. Then go to Punjab Sweets for chaat made with filtered water and freshly fried samosas and jalebis. Head to Khane Khaas and have tandoori chicken, kali dal and assorted rotis. If this is a lunch walk, you can go to Sweet Bengal for Bengali sweets for dessert. It shuts around 9 p.m., though.

👣 The Bandra East brunch walk

Start with polie and chhaas at the Aai Tuljabhawanni Prasann Stall beside the Guru Nanak Hospital. Cross over and have fresh medu vadas and idlis at the Sai Balaji stall. Walk down to have hot batata vadas at Sri Krishna Fast Food. For the finale, go to Sadichha for bombil fry, prawn masala, mutton fry and vade thali.

👣 The Irani Café walk

Start with tea and bun maska at Yazdani Bakery. Then head to Ideal Corner and have some akoori and salli boti. Then go to Military Café for keema ghotala and caramel custard. End your walk with the *lagan nu bhonu* at Jimmy Boy and don't forget to have a raspberry drink with it.

👣 The Fort walk

Start with puri and bhaji at Pancham Puriwala. Go to Moti Halwai for some lassi to wash it down. Then go

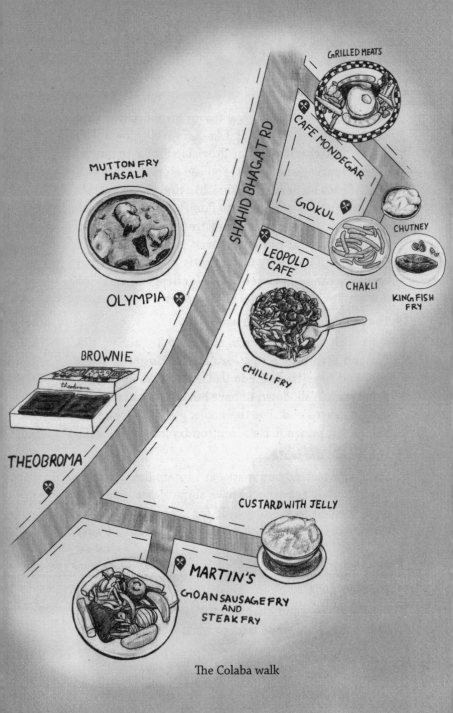

GRILLED MEATS

CAFE MONDEGAR

MUTTON FRY MASALA

SHAHID BHAGAT RD

GOKUL

CHUTNEY

LEOPOLD CAFE

CHAKLI

KING FISH FRY

OLYMPIA

BROWNIE

CHILLI FRY

theobroma

THEOBROMA

CUSTARD WITH JELLY

MARTIN'S

GOAN SAUSAGE FRY
AND
STEAK FRY

The Colaba walk

to Apoorva for prawn gassi and neer dosa. Pop in at Hotel Deluxe for a banana-leaf sadya. Head to Pradeep Gomantak Bhojanalaya for some bombil fry. End your meal with freshly fried jalebis at Vidya Dairy Farm. This walk is best done on weekdays at lunchtime.

👣 *The Bohri Mohalla walk*

Start with gurda kapuda at India Hotel. Cross over to Haji Tikka and have the khiri kebab, kofta kebab and paratha. Try out bara handi dishes at Surti after that. Head to Taj Ice Cream for ice cream to cool you down after all the meat.

👣 *The Colaba walk (best done in the evening)*

Start your walk at Gokul with some kingfish fry, chakli and chutney and beer. Walk into Café Mondegar for some grilled meats and more beer. Your third beer could be at Leopold Café with chilli fry. Cross over to Olympia and have the mutton fry masala. Then walk down to Martin's and have the Goan sausage fry and steak fry with onions and custard with jelly. Then go to Theobroma and end your night with dark-chocolate brownies.

👣 *The Dadar Maharashtrian food walk*

Start with puri bhaji at Prakash Restaurant and wash it down with piyush. Next head to Aaswad for misal, sabudana vada and thalipeeth. Then cross the lane and have freshly fried vada with pav at the Shri Samarth vada pav stall. End your dinner with your fill of seafood at Sindhudurg or the other local favourites, Hotel Sachin and Malvani Katta.

ACKNOWLEDGEMENTS

There are lots of people whom I need to thank for this book so let me try to do this chronologically.

I will start with my father, the late Dr Mukul Karmakar, who indulged my every whim. This book is a tribute to his spirit of embracing people from all cultures, helping them understand our country better. My mother, Rekha Karmakar, who brought me up as a single parent after my dad passed away, who encouraged me to write even when I was very young and is my most loyal reader today.

I can't thank Anurupa Roy and the late Narendranath Roy, my maternal grandparents, and my aunts and uncles enough for supporting my mother while she brought up me and my brother.

My brother and my sister-in-law, Siddhartha and Soyel, especially for bringing into this world the little princess Kimaya who is a source of such joy for us all. A special thanks to my Aunt Rita: My writing skills were built over the letters I wrote to her as a child.

My wife, Kainaz, whose support and encouragement helped me switch tracks from a career in market research to chase my dream of becoming a food writer. She started my blog nine years back and named it *Finely Chopped*. Just as she later came up with the name for this book.

My father-in-law, the late Marzban Bilimoria, and my mother-in-law, Pervin Bilimoria, for taking care of me in Mumbai and for making it feel like home. My wife's mama and masi and our dear family friend, Jamshed Adrianvala, for being people we can always count on.

Our cook, the legendary Banu, famous among our friends for the kebabs she makes, and who keeps the house running so that we can focus on our work.

The market research and advertising agencies that I worked at for the opportunities to travel, which form the foundation of this book. Shubhranshu Das, Kashinath Samanth and Chinmay Prabhune from my agency years, who have been loyal supporters of my blog, and two of my earliest bosses, Jasojit Mookerjea and Shashi Sinha for all the life lessons imparted over some great meals.

The publications that gave me an opportunity to write and my editors there, especially Rajyasree Sen and Harnoor Channi Tiwary. The brands and social media agencies that have given me opportunities to work on some interesting projects.

I must also acknowledge my many mentors in the world of food who've helped me along over the years.

Anthony Bourdain, whom I have not met yet, but whose TV series, *No Reservations*, and book, *A Cook's Tour*, motivated me to begin food blogging all those years ago. Chitrita Banerji, whose writing has been a big source of inspiration for me, and whom I had the good fortune of meeting once. Simon Majumdar, whose book, *Eat My Globe*, I read on a flight from Mumbai to Kolkata, and to whom I reached out to the moment I landed. Over the years, he has guided me, and has remained my sounding board despite his busy schedule. Vir Sanghvi, whom I've had the opportunity to work with, and whose book, *Rude Food* is the one I keep returning to for inspiration. Rashmi Uday Singh and Marryam H. Reshii, who have taken it upon themselves to be my godmothers in the world of food writing. Kunal Vijayakar, Vikram Doctor, Ranveer Brar, Mayur Sharma and Rocky Singh, Antoine Lewis, Sanjeev Kapoor and Aneesha Baig, who are among the Indian food media stalwarts who have been such big sources of encouragement for me.

Then there are food bloggers across the globe, who have been a source of inspiration and support and have become friends over the years: Pamela Timms, Robyn Eckhardt, Meera Sodha, Asma Khan, Niamh Shield, Zoe Perett, Mallika Basu and Maunika Gowardhan. In India, Saee Koranne Khandekar, Rhea Mitra Dalal, Nandita Iyer, Anjali Koli, Alka Keswani, Monika Manchanda and Nikhil Merchant are among the many wonderful food blogger friends I have made. Special thanks to Dr Kurush Dalal who has given me so many stories to write about and who always takes my call when I am stuck while writing. A big shout-out to the lovely folks whom I have met through food blogging and who have become family friends: Manisha Talim, Gia Fernandes, Kaniska and Manishita Chakraborty, Sue and Nathan Cope, Jean and Brian Spraker. Plus, there are the people with whom I have had many exciting meals. Their stories form the backbone of this book: Soumik Sen, Vipul Yadav, Mohit Balachandran, Amit Patnaik, Julia Edwards, Suprio Bose, Sankarsan Banerjee, Nilaakshi Sengupta, Jaideep Riar, Anurag Mehrotra and Yajnaseni Chakraborty with whom I hang out when I visit their cities. Vishal Vij for being such a source of advice and encouragement through my years in Mumbai. And all the people whom I've mentioned directly and indirectly in the book, who've shared with me their invaluable expertise, either in person or on social media.

I must make special mention of my friend, Rushina Munshaw Ghildayal, one of the earliest food bloggers in the country, who has often been a sounding board for me and who connected me with Poulomi Chatterjee of Hachette. Which brings me to the team at Hachette India, who believed in us bloggers and gave us a voice. I'd always wanted to write a book but Poulomi was the one who helped me crack the idea on what it should be about. I would also like to thank Sohini Pal at Hachette for working with me, being on call whenever I needed her, patiently editing and giving the book shape. I have to thank Mistunee Chowdhuree, for the illustrations which bring the book alive.

A big vote of thanks to my wife's partner at work, and dear friend, Harshad Rajadhyaksha, for taking the time out from his buy schedule to shoot and design the wonderful cover. And to Gomti and Pandiyan Konar of Sai Balaji Snacks for allowing us to use their stall for the cover.

I can't thank Allan Pereira and the entire team at Candies enough for the hours I have spent writing this book at their café and a special mention to Sylvia at the counter. And Zeno at Smoke House Deli Bandra for making sure I felt at home when I went there to write on Mondays when Candies was shut.

There have been many wonderful chefs, hoteliers and restaurateurs whom I have had the fortune of meeting thanks to food blogging. Many of my conversations with them have found their way into the book. Some chefs I would like to thank are Vineet Bhatia, Ashish Bhasin, Anirudhya Roy, Manjit Gill, Deepti Jadhav, Matteo Arvonio and Vikramjit Roy for our conversations on food. There are a few restaurant owners in Mumbai that I want to especially thank for the love and affection that they have showered on me. Baba and Nini Ling of Ling's Pavilion, Hardeep Chaddha and Atul Sahni of Khane Khas, Suryakant Shrikrishna Sarjoshi of Aaswad, Amit Roy of Peetuk, Siddhartha Bose and Rajeev Neogi of Bhojohori Manna, Pinky Chandan Dixit of Soam, Mohsen Hussaini of Lucky, Tirandaz Irani of Yazdani, Parvez Patel of Ideal Corner,

Pooja Dhingra of Le 15 Patisserrie, Irfan Pabaney of Sassy Spoon, Arpana Gvalani and Lenny of Gostana and Anil Kably of The Bagel Shop.

Forgive me if I'm forgetting someone. There have been so many wonderful people in my life and I am grateful to each and every one of them.

I would also like to thank Bindu Panicker and the ITC Hotel group for their hospitality support which was crucial when I travelled for the final research. I also want to thank the teachers of The Yoga Institute at Santa Cruz. Going there in the evenings helped me keep my calm and recharge myself while I made my transition from the corporate world to that of a freelance food writer. I would like to express a debt of supreme gratitude to Dr Daisaku Ikeda, the president of the Soka Gakkai International for being such a great source of strength and motivation and my fellow SGI members, especially Vishal Vij, who has been a source of advice and encouragement through my many years in Mumbai.

Finally, I would like to thank you, the readers of my blog, whose support has kept me going over the years, and those who came to my food walks. I owe all the wonderful things that has happened to me in recent years to my blog, and to you.